MW01119490

Charismatic Leadership and Social Movements

International Studies in Social History
General Editor: Marcel van der Linden,
International Institute of Social History, Amsterdam

CHARISMATIC LEADERSHIP AND SOCIAL MOVEMENTS

The Revolutionary Power of Ordinary Men and Women

Edited by

Jan Willem Stutje

Berghahn Books
New York • Oxford

Published in 2012 by
Berghahn Books
www.berghahnbooks.com

Library of Congress Cataloging-in-Publication Data

Charismatic leadership and social movements: the revolutionary power of ordinary
men and women / edited by Jan Willem Stutje.
    p. cm. – (International studies in social history ; v. 19)
Includes bibliographical references and index.
ISBN 978-0-85745-329-7 (hbk. : alk. paper) – ISBN 978-0-85745-330-3 (ebook)
1. Political leadership–Psychological aspects. 2. Charisma (Personality trait)–
Political aspects. 3. Political psychology. 4. Personality and politics. 5. Social
movements–Psychological aspects. I. Stutje, Jan Willem.
JC330.3.R43 2012
303.3'4–dc23
                                                                    2011046326

British Library Cataloguing in Publication Data
A catalogue record for this book is available from the British Library

Printed in the United States on acid-free paper

ISBN: 978-0-85745-329-7 (hardback)
ISBN: 978-0-85745-330-3 (ebook)

CONTENTS

II. Charismatic Observations

LIST OF ABBREVIATIONS

AHPCE	Archivo Histórico del Partido Comunista de España (Archive of the Communist Party of Spain)
ATV	Afrikaanse Taal Vereniging (Afrikaans Language Association)
Comintern	Communist International
CWMG	Collected Works of Mahatma Gandhi
GDR	German Democratic Republic
IISG	Internationaal Instituut voor Sociale Geschiedenis (International Institute of Social History)
IISH	International Institute of Social History
INCH	Institute for Contemporary History (University of the Free State)
KAB	Kaapse Argief Bewaarplek (Cape Town Archives Repository)
NWFP	North West Frontier Province
PCE	Partido Comunista de España (Spanish Communist Party)
PRC	People's Republic of China
PSI	Partito Socialista Italiano (Italian Socialist Party)

SAB   Sentrale Argief Bewaarplek (Central Archives Depot,
              South Africa)

SDAP   Sociaal Democratische Arbeiders Partij (Social
              Democratic Workers' Party)

SDB   Sociaal Democratische Bond (Social Democratic League)

SDP   Sociaal Democratische Partij (Social Democratic Party)

SGPC   Shiromani Gurudwara Parbandhak Committee

SPD   Sozialdemokratische Partei Deutschlands
              (Social Democratic Party of Germany)

UN   United Nations

Acknowledgements

One of this volume's origins was an international conference on 'Charisma and emergent social movements' held at the University of Groningen in November 2008. The conference was organized by The Institute of Biography of the University of Groningen and the International Institute of Social History, Amsterdam. I should like to thank Hans Renders and Marcel van der Linden for their support in organizing this event. I would also like to thank SNS-Reaal, The Royal Netherlands Academy of Arts and Sciences (KNAW) and the University of Groningen Faculty of Arts for their financial support.

An extra warm vote of thanks goes to all those friends and colleagues who participated in the discussions. The publication of these essays was only possible because of their help and criticism. My thanks are especially due to Touraj Atabaki, Juan Avilés, Doeko Bosscher, Arif Dirlik, Lindie Koorts, Carl Levy, Roel Meijer, Leonard Ornstein, Marc Reynebeau, Kees Rodenburg, Dilip Simeon, Christoph Twickel, Henk te Velde, Gerrit Voerman and Dirk Jan Wolffram.

Kate Eaton did the revision of most of the essays. Her assistance was invaluable.

Jan Willem Stutje

INTRODUCTION

Historiographical and Theoretical Aspects of Weber's Concept of Charismatic Leadership

Jan Willem Stutje

In the 1920s Karl Löwith called Max Weber the 'bürgerlichen Marx'.[1] While Weber disagreed widely with Marx, he was, as Eric J. Hobsbawm noticed, always in dialogue with Marx and Marxism.[2] As thinkers, Hobsbawm said, they shared more ideas than one would expect considering their differing political outlooks (socialism versus liberalism).[3] They converged even in their understanding of modern capitalism: they both perceive it as a system where 'the individuals are ruled by abstractions (Marx), where the impersonal and "thing-like" (*Versachtlicht*) relations replace the personal relations of dependence, and where the accumulation of capital becomes an end in itself, largely irrational'.[4]

Apart from their shared interest in economic history, Marxists and Weberians agree on the significant role certain individuals play in history, or to use an expression of the German historian Wolfgang J. Mommsen, on their 'außeralltägliche Werthaltungen und charismatisches Handeln' [extraordinary moral conduct and charismatic action].[5]

Both Marx and Weber insisted that in times of transition some figures can influence the course of history, even decisively, and this not only in religion, the arts or sciences, but also in politics. And here charisma comes up.[6] As Arif Dirlik writes in his contribution to this volume: 'it seems fairly safe to observe that while not all charismatic leaders are radicals or revolutionaries, all successful revolutionary leaders are charismatic'.[7]

However, while the term 'charisma' is in the scholarly vocabulary of every social movement theorist, few have sought to delineate a precise conceptualization or theory of charisma. More particularly, the concept's relevance to the study of social movements is never made clear. Why has

---

Notes for this chapter begin on page 16.

there been this relative inattention to what leaders, and charismatic leaders in particular, do? Several reasons might be given.

First there is the understandable desire to avoid 'great man' theories of history and to give due weight to the relationships and conflicts between social forces in determining the course of history. The attention is primarily directed to the circumstances in which movements develop and to the collective experience, the needs, the grievances and the hopes motivating their participants. The tendency to propose the individual as the decisive factor in the historical process is considered as the hallmark of the primitive phase of historical consciousness. This feeling is even stronger in the labour movement, in which the primacy of collective action over individual aspirations is proverbial. Yet there is a risk in this view, of babies following bathwater down plug-holes.

Second, academic theory is itself affected by ideology. Meyer and Tarrow suggest that thinking about movement leadership was for a long time dominated by movement forms like the 'traditional mass organizations of the European Left', with their permanent presences, bureaucratic structures and centralized leadership, whose core participants 'are highly professional, even as they put forward ideologies of spontaneity'.[8] Charisma was primarily associated with the irrationality of right-wing movements, regarded as a diabolical quality that bewitched people and made them do horrible things. However, even when these formal, traditional mass organizations have been supplanted by more decentralized networks without strong central leadership, the attention to leadership has not increased. This is even more true for charismatic leadership, whose promise of redemption seems to block the development of self-reliance, so strongly associated with the notion of self-emancipation. In this more libertarian sphere a suspicion of leadership still hinders academic theorizing.

Third, Barker, Johnson and Lavalette stress that in the social sciences underlying patterns of social movement theorizing have tended to divert attention from issues to do with leadership. The 'collective behaviour' tradition, stressing movement irrationalism, could never explore leadership questions satisfactorily. Alternative approaches reveal a strong structuralist bias in explanation, paying even less attention to actors' purposive agency and thus to questions about leadership.[9]

Yet the need to study leadership in social movements in general and charismatic leadership in particular has been reiterated constantly. In the 1990s Klandermans, for example, pointed out the lack of progress in this field, arguing that despite their obvious importance, 'leadership and decision-making aspects of social movements ... are more often debated than studied empirically'.[10] And this is even more true for charismatic leadership. It is hard not to agree with those who argue that, whilst there have been many generalizations, the theory of charisma has hardly moved since Weber's initial formulations. According to two American specialists 'there seems to be little cumulative advance in our understanding: the empirical regularities are neither robust nor compelling; the theoretical formulations are neither precise nor reliable'.[11] Since the 1990s social movement theorists fortunately have made some progress in the study of leadership – though charismatic leadership still remains undertheorized.[12] Historians, however, have hardly participated in this debate, and if they have, then they have done so mostly in relation to so-called political religions, not in the field of social movements.[13]

At the same time, however, most authors refer to the historical context which influenced Weber's work, arguing that Weber exemplified his theory of charismatic leadership with concrete personalities in mind, such as the first major leader of the Socialist Party, August Bebel (1840–1913), and the early socialist leader Ferdinand Lassalle (1825–64) in Germany, Ferdinand Domela Nieuwenhuis (1846–1919) in the Netherlands and in particular, the popular liberal leader William Gladstone (1809–98) in Britain.[14] In his classic *Max Weber und die Deutsche Politik* Wolfgang Mommsen pointed out how Weber, out of concern with the bureaucratization of German politics, insisted on electoral competition for the President of the Weimar Republic as a means of bringing charismatic personalities to political leadership.[15] Against this background historians are the obvious ones to rediscover the historical reality behind Weber's theory and to fill the concept of charismatic leadership with a more specific, pregnant historical content.

The contributors to this volume seek in various ways to re-open the debate on charismatic leadership from this historical perspective. They do this with a special focus on Max Weber, the German sociologist whose concept of charisma acquired an almost universal reputation. Weber's focus was on the emergence of exceptional, radical leaders in times of crisis. The important thing was that the public attributed to the charismatic leader the supernatural powers necessary for the fundamental social changes they wanted.[16] Charisma was, then, not something a politician possessed irrespective of circumstances, but rather an almost religious relationship between a leader and his adherents in a specific situation. Even the type of political leadership that seems to concentrate on the extraordinary qualities of an individual appears in reality to have quite strong social aspects. This charismatic bond makes Weber's concept a fruitful instrument that redefines the characteristics by which individuals are judged.

In this respect it is meaningful to question in which type of movements and in which social and political circumstances charismatic leadership developed. How were these leaders perceived and how might we understand the symbiotic relationship between the leader and his or her adherents? Though Weber briefly discussed possibilities for continuity, including forms of 'institutional charisma',[17] it is interesting to explore whether such personalized rule could be stabilized or not. Having argued that charisma is not a personal quality, one should also point out that not every politician could become a charismatic leader. This urges us to examine whether charismatic leaders possess certain traits in common or behave in certain ways. Whilst this dimension has not been a major focus of Weber's thinking, it is also useful to analyse the process of charismatization, that is the managing of charisma, for example the deliberate attempt to create a sense of almost religious aura around a leader.[18]

This introduction does not provide a clear-cut definition of charisma as concept. It only highlights some perspectives, convinced that conceptualizing charisma as a time- and spaceless thing, rather than as a relation which may differ from context to context, brings the concept into a mire of confusion and impedes empirical research.[19] If we explain a leader's success in terms of his or her charisma, what have we explained? Oratorical superiority or charm may be the trait we have in mind in calling a leader charismatic, but then all we have done is to label the ability to speak well 'charisma'. Charisma thus becomes a way of avoiding naming the individual attribute in a more precise way. Moreover, inability to specify precisely the traits that constitute charisma leads to establishing, as Richard J. Ellis aptly argued, 'the charismatic credentials of a leader by reference to the effect a leader has upon followers. At this point the "explanation" lapses into tautology: the leader's success is explained by his success'.[20]

The Reductionist Trap

Weber's writings on charisma are suggestive, elusive, brilliant and fragmentary. Although Weber hints at the possibilities of a multidimensional understanding of charisma, many of his successors have elected to read him in a reductionist way. They have interpreted leadership either in the frame of a psychologically defined charisma – reducing the study of charisma to personal traits on the one hand or emotional needs and group dynamics on the other – or in a frame with an emphasis on social structures, which converts charisma into a seemingly automatic appendage of hierarchical systems and instrumental manipulations associated with power and money. Even the pioneer mass-society theorist, Hannah Arendt, did not escape a reductionist reading. She held that Adolf Hitler was charismatic but saw this largely as the fruit of his immense self-confidence.

> The problem of Hitler's charisma is relatively easy to solve ...[. I]t rested on the well-known experiential fact that Hitler must have realised early in his life, namely, that modern society in its desperate inability to form judgements will

take every individual for what he considers himself and professes himself to be
.... Extraordinary self-confidence and displays of self-confidence therefore inspire confidence in others; pretensions to genius waken the conviction in others that they are indeed dealing with a genius .... Hitler's real superiority consisted in the fact that under any and all circumstances he had an opinion.[21]

These comments are typical of much of the writing on charisma, which
focuses on specific traits associated with exceptional leaders – facets which
are often related to psychological explanations. In this context almost
every political leader with marked popular appeal, and this is even the
case for media and sport stars, is indiscriminately tagged as charismatic.[22]
This practice has broadened the concept of charisma to such an extent
that it loses its distinctiveness – and therefore its utility.[23] It seems as if
the concept has developed its own charisma, its own promise of salvation
and universal remedy for all scholarly dilemmas. With such an inflationary
meaning it is not surprising that scholars have questioned the meaning
and utility of the concept of charismatic leadership.[24]

The somewhat misleading search for the source of charisma in the personalities of leaders may have resulted in misreading Weber's frequently cited definition of charisma as a certain quality of an individual personality by
which *he is set apart* from ordinary men and *treated as endowed* with supernatural, superhuman or at least specifically exceptional powers or qualities.
For, as the words deliberately italicized here suggest and Weber repeatedly
emphasized, it is not so much what the leader is but how he is regarded by
those subject to his authority that is decisive for the validity of charisma. His
charisma resides in the perceptions of the people he leads.[25]

More recently research has been concentrating (and, as we already
have said, this volume joins this tendency) on the nature and causes of
what can be called the 'charismatic bond', which is often seen in quasireligious terms.[26] And for good reasons, the British socialist leader James
Keir Hardie (1856–1915), for example, was usually called 'the prophet,
priest, and patron saint of his class'.[27] But even where the quasireligious
side is stressed less strongly, the focus remains heavily upon charisma as
an affective relationship.[28] Sometimes the interaction has been so strong
that leader and following simply seem to fuse into one, as was shown by
the Dutch socialist Pieter Jelles Troelstra (1860–1930), who once wrote:
'At some point during my speeches there often came a moment when I
wondered who is speaking now, they or myself?'[29]

Conceptualizing charisma as a relation rather than as a thing helps to overcome some of the difficulties that have plagued the concept of charisma. A
relational definition has the virtue of leaving more scope for empirical research. But to say that charisma is a relation leaves unanswered the question

of what type of leader is to be counted as charismatic. Not just anybody is ascribed extraordinary or even supernatural capacities, and so it makes sense to find out which type of leader one was looking for in specific periods and with which kind of techniques these leaders inspired the charismatic bond. This field of research is at least as important as an examination of the other – social, political and cultural – factors which have allegedly helped to create and sustain this bond between the leader and his or her adherents.

Moreover, the focus should not be directed exclusively to the societal or individual level. The process is more complicated. Local and group perspectives are also crucial to understanding support. These perspectives point to the possibility that charisma may act mainly upon a small minority, an initial elite, whom the leader first inspires or who throw up from among themselves one who can inspire others and who then recruits – often by using other forms of appeal – a wider constituency. It is also important to note that within these locally based inner circles, dozens of activists may have a similar charismatic appeal. Most of these disciples must make a living out of their calling. They often tend to develop their own sometimes heretical views, trying to protect their power and economic chances in the long run. It will be clear that this behaviour carries the risk of undermining the leader's charisma.

And finally, a more elaborate answer to the question of the charismatic personality would need to consider both diachronic and synchronic approaches: a leader's image can indeed be multifaceted, and techniques and themes can change through time. The British political scientist Roger Eatwell noticed, for example, that in 1919 Mussolini's image was heavily based on his wartime experiences, on being part of a young male 'trenchocracy'; by the 1930s Mussolini had new dimensions to his appeal, including a father-like image targeted at young women.[30]

The Nature of Charismatic Leadership

In this volume the main case studies concentrate on examining the role of leaders in emerging social movements – not least because these types of leaders belonged to the major examples Weber himself referred to in theorizing charisma as an explanation for the major support these movements received. In these movements charismatic leaders sustained a strong symbiotic relationship with their followers, a symbiosis which stimulated devotion to the leader and which created a real group identity. Here, the charismatic leader was not just a professional politician or administrator, but became a people's or working-class hero, capable of arousing the masses.

Here, the charismatic leader also manifests his revolutionary power. Charisma does not mean mere behavioural change. It involves a transformation of followers' values and beliefs. This distinguishes the charismatic person from a merely populist leader who may affect attitudes towards specific objects, but who is not prepared or capable, as the charismatic leader is, to transform the underlying normative orientation that structures particular attitudes.[31] Populists may be involved in antielitist mobilizations, but they leave the social system unchallenged. To put it in another way, populists claim that they speak *for* 'the people'.[32] But in substituting the will of the people for their own, they are not really interested in adjusting their own activity to overcome social or political conservatism. At the most they only bother to adjust their ideas and convictions to the shifting moods and perceptions of the public.

If we study the main leaders of social movements in the late nineteenth century and the beginning of the twentieth century, when Weber introduced the concept of charisma, what common features can we find? Examining the existing literature, it seems justified to isolate four main leadership traits.

First, leaders like Lassalle and Gladstone, but also James Keir Hardie (1856–1915) and Ferdinand Domela Nieuwenhuis (1846–1919), the first Dutch socialist leader who had been a Lutheran priest and later turned anarchist, were driven by some form of mission. Domela Nieuwenhuis, for example, was relatively apolitical while young. In Domela's case the epiphany seems to have come after the successive deaths of three of his wives. After these experiences he felt destined to help the working class in the struggle for emancipation. To Multatuli, the author of *Max Havelaar*, the famous indictment of Dutch colonialism, he wrote: 'I may not leave my poor suffering brothers to their own devices .... Is not the suffering of oneself the reason for compassion with others?'[33] 'Rebirth' and a variety of other terms derived from Christianity, such as 'redemption' and 'salvation', mostly seen in the context of 'struggling and suffering', were subsequently central to the language of these leaders.

Since charisma constitutes a calling, a charismatic leader ignores economic considerations. He may need the material means of power and prestige. But all leaders repudiate the entanglement in the everyday world that inevitably accompanies the routine pursuit of economic gain. Domela Nieuwenhuis, who lived from property as a rentier, supported his party financially in a generous way. He refused any regular benefit.[34] A faithful socialist, Domela said, wants to be compensated only by the pleasure of having done the right things.[35]

Second, these charismatic leaders presented themselves as ordinary men, merely obeying the wishes of the people; an extraordinary effort because they often had their roots in the middle or upper middle classes, as did Gladstone, Lassalle and Domela Nieuwenhuis, and fraternizing with the workers did not come naturally to them. Lassalle, a dandy, an aristocrat and adventurer, in particular abhorred shaking the sweaty hands of workers. Domela Nieuwenhuis, 'das Holländische Pfäfflein' [that little Dutch vicar] as Karl Marx typified him, used to come to meetings by carriage.[36]

They were, however, idolized because they showed solidarity the workers did not expect in the class-ridden nineteenth century. 'I am one of yourselves', Gladstone shouted to a mass audience, and then continued using the word 'we'.[37] Other charismatic leaders used similar expressions. Workers joining Bebel's party often thought that for the first time politics really mattered and saw their self-esteem highly raised.

On a deeper level, the charisma of this type of leaders may even depend upon their becoming assimilated, in the thought and feelings of a populace, with its sacred figures or heroes. Their actions, recounted in myth, express the fundamental values of a culture. Insofar as myths can be regarded as charters for action, validating ritual and moral acts, the assimilation of a given individual with a mythic figure or a legendary historical event, such as the French Revolution or the Paris Commune, endows the individual with the aura or sanction of the myth itself. The capacity to communicate to his followers a sense of continuity between himself and his mission and their legendary heroes and their missions strengthens the interplay or even symbiosis between leader and audience, and is an element of charismatic leadership.[38]

However, is there not a discrepancy between wanting to be seen as an ordinary person, as pointed out above, and being given a mythic status? Perhaps this is not as surprising if we consider that the development of personal identity is so influenced by legendary figures as social ideals that one sees the ideal part of oneself in such mythic terms and is delighted to find someone who incarnates that ideal, 'mythic' element of personal identity.

Third, charismatic leaders have an impressive personal presence, a strong 'magnetism'. In some cases this involves even physical traits, in all cases at least a convincing power of oratory including the capacity to present their mission in written form. As Weber casually remarked on the importance of rhetoric in allocating charisma: 'rhetoric has the same meaning as ... street parades and festivals: to imbue the masses with the notion of the party's power and confidence in victory and, above all, to convince them of the leader's charismatic qualification'.[39] Charismatic politics is not ordinary, routine politics. It has the revivalist flavour of a movement, powered by the enthusiasm that draws normally a non-political people into the political arena.

It should be stressed that the elements of this behaviour vary from culture to culture, from time to time. This of course is true for the behaviour of any leader, charismatic or not, who seeks to mobilize popular support. Specific to the charismatic leader is probably the role of myth in validating his authority.[40] His appeal, therefore, can best be understood by reference to the body of myth in a given culture, and the actions and values associated with and sanctioned by these myths.

And finally, because charisma hangs upon salvation narratives, images of 'evil' must be present in the forest of symbols surrounding each charismatic leader. There must be something for them to fight against, something from which their followers can be saved. In many cases this evil is an abstraction such as poverty, injustice, capitalism or imperialism. In yet other cases, this evil finds its embodiment in another individual actor, a threatening person who can be taken as embodying a powerful negative charisma. Love of the charismatic leader often seems to be based on hatred of the evil against which they fight, and indeed will be magnified as this perceived evil intensifies and is incarnated in a specific contending 'renegade', who is seen as traitor to the projected ideal.

But this style and these themes are not enough to explain why charismatic personalities might appeal. One should not treat leadership as an independent variable. A prior question needs to be addressed, of what the organizational and social conditions that gave rise to charismatic leaders might be. In this respect three elements seem crucial.

First: social crisis. Although Weber paid little attention to the conditions under which charismatic leadership can emerge – merely mentioning times of physical, psychic, economic, ethical, religious or political distress – most studies see some form of structural crisis as the necessary starting point. For example the working people's loss of autonomy, and the crushing of social certainty and traditional rights as the result of deep social disruptions in the wake of an expanding industrial capitalism in the late nineteenth century. The attraction exercised by the charismatic leader can, in part, be attributed to his ability to focus and channel various grievances and interests in a common appeal, unifying a segmented and distressed population in pursuit of a common goal. According to Weber these masses attributed to the charismatic leader the supernatural powers necessary for the fundamental social changes they wanted.[41]

Second: political space. Charismatic authority is not a permanent state of allegiance; it is inherently short-lived. It is constructed in time; it is never totally unqualified; it is inherently unstable and can be subverted or demolished through a combination of personal decisions of the leader that are perceived as wrong and situational factors that are beyond his control. A charismatic leader has to prove his qualification for leadership anew every day, and a good deal of success is therefore essential for maintaining his position.[42]

It would probably be correct to argue that charismatic leaders are most likely to emerge and flourish when political parties are weak or held in contempt. Recent examples of charismatic far-Right figures like Le Pen in France, Haider in Austria and Fortuyn and Wilders in the Netherlands who thrived on the contempt for traditional political parties seem to confirm this condition.

In the late nineteenth century popular leaders mobilized the people in circumstances in which mass politics and mass political parties outside parliaments were still in their infancy. Gladstone, Lassalle and Domela Nieuwenhuis did not have many ties to party or bureaucracy. Their success depended on the dynamics of the open and pluralistic, more or less spontaneous movements they were leading. As these mostly egalitarian movements transformed into well organized, hierarchical parties, charisma and organizational and political discipline proved to be uneasy partners.[43] Strictly speaking a type of charismatic domination is an impossibility, for pure charisma loathes any form of institutionalization.[44] Charisma represents a strong anti-institutional impulse: the romantic impulse to directness, spontaneity and the overcoming of alienation.

It is important to note that this revolutionary voluntarism was far from compatible with the specific Marxist current which became dominant at the end of the nineteenth century. The fatalist Kautskyanism, strongly embedded in the huge, disciplined German Social Democratic Party, showed an open hostility to the revolutionary natural law which so often proved to be the mirror for charismatic politics. Above all this law pointed to a rehabilitation of human dignity, to what the German Marxist philosopher Ernst Bloch called 'der aufrechte Gang', that urges one to stand tall and not to bow.[45] More than anything else, it was just the infringement of this dignity that provoked the protests in the 1880s and 1890s and that made workers sensitive to charismatic leadership. These were protests of romantic inspiration, aimed against the industrial, capitalist civilization – i.e., a critique of modernity based on precapitalist social and cultural values: essentially a critique of the abstract and calculating reason that reduces all qualitative values to figures.[46] The Marxism of the Second (Socialist) International – either orthodox or revisionist – completely ignored these motives, being captured in its evolutionistic and deterministic ideology. With a strong belief in progress they tried to formulate rational, scientific solutions to explosive social problems and gave priority to organization and discipline over movement and spontaneity. In these bureaucratically organized mass organizations charisma lost its effectiveness.[47]

Charisma is based on persuasion and voluntary subscription to a mobilizing myth. In this respect, it is not surprising that its appeal ran aground when it came into competition with alternative (organizational, bureaucratic) forms of loyalty, not to mention the tendency inherent in modern societies to breed moral and political apathy that counteracts the trend towards charismatic domination.

Third: religious attraction. The end of the nineteenth century saw the emergence of movements in many European countries in which, to use an expression of Emilio Gentile, some kind of 'religionization' of politics took place.[48] Politics was not exclusively a matter of parliamentary debate any more. It acquired what you could call a 'religious' function in the life of the political activist.[49] Socialist parties, for example, introduced new elements that made politics a matter of identity and belonging. They were not only organizations meant to struggle for socialism. They were also quasireligious communities with a unique atmosphere and lifestyle, and with rites and symbols of quasicollective liturgies, longing for martyrs, apostles and prophet-like leaders. These parties acquired a role similar to that of religion: they provided a sense of shared fate.[50] Whoever wanted to attract a new following among nonpolitical people automatically used a vocabulary with a strong religious bias. Sympathy could more easily be won: a young worker in Berlin believed he was attending a religious service and was impressed by the pastor who spoke much better than his own '*Pfarrer*'. When he told his neighbour about this experience, the man informed him he had attended a meeting of freethinkers and not a religious service.[51]

The religious style was not just a residue of traditional religiosity, but a consequence of modernity and of secularization. It was connected to mass society, to the decline of traditional religions and to the spreading of irrationalism. The revival of a religious style in politics shocked the liberal circles Weber was frequenting. Here the belief in progress, in rationality and science and thus in the progressive disenchantment of the world became discredited. It stimulated Weber to seek explanations for this phenomenon. At the beginning of the twentieth century, he transferred the term 'charisma' from religious studies into political science; the word means a gift of grace, a gift of God.[52] It may have become clear that this religious link was not in the least a coincidence.

It is not the intention of the contributors to restrict themselves to Weber's findings. Discussing Weber is, however, the right way to address the crucial themes of the charisma concept without losing the ground of historical empiricism. The case studies primarily highlight original historical sources. This has resulted in a convergence among most authors on some crucial elements of the concept of charisma, for example, the interaction between the charismatic leader and his following and their symbiotic relationship, the role of religion and emotions, the crucial role of historical contingency and context in making and unmaking charismatic leaders, or the risky stability of charismatic leadership and its relation to well organized and disciplined organizations.

This volume brings together essays discussing the role of charisma in the rise of the so-called key figures in emergent social movements – leaders from the nineteenth century but also from the twentieth century, not only from Europe but from other continents as well. What insights does the comparison of these social movements and their leaders have to offer? Why was there a rapid *Veralltäglichung* (routinization) with respect to Dolores Ibárruri (La Pasionaria), D.F. Malan and the Dutch social democratic leader Pieter Jelles Troestra, while this was apparently not the case or only occurred more slowly as far as Mao Zedong, Mahatma Gandhi, Errico Malatesta and Ferdinand Domela Nieuwenhuis are concerned? These are some of the themes that will be discussed in order to put Weber's theory of charisma to the test historically and transculturally.

In Part I the reader will find case studies on Gandhi and Daniel F. Malan, on Domela Nieuwenhuis and Malatesta, on La Pasionaria and Mao Zedong. The first two represent charismatic leadership of anticolonial national movements of the Left and the Right, the second two, socialist-anarchist leaders of the era preceding the Great War, and the last two communist leaders of the Stalinist era. In Part II the reader will find three essays, discussing more conceptual questions and theoretical aspects.

A Short Preview

In August 1947, the month of India's partition, the British officer Viceroy Mountbatten paid tribute to Gandhi (1869–1948) for being 'the One Man Boundary Force'. At the same time, the Muslim League office in Delhi expressed its 'deep sense of appreciation' for restoring the peace in Calcutta. These instances, Dilip Simeon argues, render Gandhi's charisma unique. They fuse magical, religious and prophetic dimensions in a new kind of politics. Simeon is fascinated by the man that could articulate virtues that many of his countrymen believed to be effeminate and yet command tremendous stature among the most 'virile' of communities, such as the Pathans and Sikhs. After positioning Gandhi's politics and moral philosophy opposite the ethical nihilism and pessimism rampant in the first half of the twentieth century, Simeon discusses Gandhi's charisma, showing how Gandhi managed to play upon the popular significance of the ideas of courage and manliness by giving them a fresh meaning. It appealed to large numbers of helpless people and drew the most humble into mainstream politics. In this sense, Simeon argues, Gandhi's charisma was profoundly democratic.

Lindie Koorts pays attention in her chapter to the ambiguous attitude of charismatic leadership towards democracy and organization, discussing the unlikely charismatic leader D.F. Malan (1874–1959). Preparing the biography of the architect of Apartheid, she tries to grasp how, in a post-Second World War context, the South African population could support a policy that assigned them to effective pariah-status. The figure of the prophet is the key to understanding Malan's leadership style in general and is, as Koorts puts it, the link that binds him to Weber's charismatic leader. Malan entered the political arena in a time of crisis and the concepts of 'calling' and 'mission' became the driving forces behind the career of the man who with a deep, vibrant voice could keep his Afrikaner audiences spellbound for up to hours at a time.

In general the revolutionary passion cools down after some time. It is a matter of 'Veralltäglichung des Charisma', a phase Weber defined as the process of trivializing due to the impact of a rational, bureaucratic framework. Jan Willem Stutje examines how Ferdinand Domela Nieuwenhuis embraced discipline, hierarchy and organization, which decisively contributed to trivializing his charisma and which finally provoked his downfall. This was occurring while he was in conflict with his rival, Pieter Jelles Troelstra, who in 1894 became the prominent leader of the Dutch reformist Social Democratic Workers Party (SDAP). Using the Weberian terminology Stutje characterizes each of them as representing and emphasizing another side of the entanglement of charisma and reason: Domela the example of a more or less spontaneous charisma and Troelstra the example of a vulgarization into a pseudocharisma. Stutje links their different roles to the specific motives that inspired them: Domela, the leader of a romantic revolt against modernity, conditioned by precapitalistic values, and Troelstra, the representative of an anticapitalism, criticizing the dominant social order in terms of modern rational values.

Carl Levy examines the role of charismatic leadership in the Italian anarchist and socialist movements in the period up to the *biennio rosso* (1919–20), focusing on the figure of Errico Malatesta (1853–1932). Even if Italian anarchism was a minority movement within the Italian Left by 1914, its symbols, repertoire of actions and geographically specific political cultures allowed it to have a notable effect during the social mobilizations in these years. Malatesta was the embodiment of these forces. Having discussed Weber's conception of charisma and Robert Michels' relationship to Weber, Levy analyses the leadership of Malatesta, who showed distaste to many of the attributes of charisma: his oratorical style was rather conversational and he shunned the adulation of his followers or the press. Though one of the heroes in the Red Week of June 1914 and of the huge social mobilizations of 1919–20, Malatesta did not relish the charismatic situations in which he found himself. As Levy shows, he strongly disapproved of the idolatry of his person by the crowds or the anarchist movements and criticized anyone who acclaimed him the Spartacus or Lenin of Italy. The paradox of Malatesta's persona with the legend created by the Left and the press was striking. If he possessed a charisma, Levy concludes, it was the charisma of a countercultural leader, believing in making anarchists one by one, not swaying oceanic crowds.

In his contribution on Dolores Ibárruri (1895–1989), Juan Avilés emphasizes the crisis-like, anomic circumstances in which the charismatic leadership of Ibárruri emerged, namely the revolutionary situation of Spain and the specific circumstances of the Spanish Civil War in the 1930s. In his analysis Avilés argues that the communist movement, with its revolutionary vocation, was particularly suitable to charismatic leadership. Following Liah Greenfeld he distinguishes between personal and institutional charisma, a type of authority characterized by embodying the fundamental values and principles of the group. Ibárruri, as Avilés puts it, may be considered as an example of this last type of charisma, while she simply followed in the footsteps of her predecessors. She practised charisma through representation, i.e., she symbolized the communist values without creating new ones.

In his essay on Mao Zedong Arif Dirlik not only considers Mao (1893–1976) as a charismatic leader but also questions what Mao's career may reveal about the issue of charisma. Dirlik's inquiry has three dimensions. The first is theoretical: what is the relationship between charisma (understood as having both rational and affective dimensions) and the persuasiveness of a revolutionary leader? What are the public and the private dimensions of charisma, since a leader does not need to be equally persuasive at both levels? And what is the relationship between the leader and the led, since charisma may depend as much on the receiver as on the transmitter. This also introduces a historical dimension, of the contingency of charisma on historical circumstances.

Dirlik suggests that in the context of socialist revolutions such as in China the question of charisma may not be disassociated from the question of rationality, because the two were equally important in empowering revolutionary leadership. However, Dirlik argues, both were also at the source of fundamental contradictions of a divisive nature. When the two clashed, and the charisma took over at the expense of the rationality, the consequences could be disastrous, as they were during the Cultural Revolution. That event could be viewed as an effort to overcome the contradictions between charisma and its routinization.

Part II starts with Henk te Velde discussing the involvement of religion in charismatic leadership and politics, a theme that recurs in almost all the other contributions. 'Political religion' has often been associated with totalitarianism, the opposite of democracy. On the other hand, the period of the democratization of European politics of the late nineteenth century was full of charismatic leaders who were also great emancipators. At the same time the charismatic figures often inspired new organizations themselves. Te Velde analyses the ambiguous attitude of nineteenth century charismatic leadership towards democracy and organization and its discomforting message for the relationship between democracy and 'normal' politics.

In his thoughtful exposition Marc Reynebeau argues that Weber's ideas on charisma, dating from the early twentieth century, are still the main reference for most studies on the subject. No new major theoretical framework on the issue has been developed, and this, Reynebeau maintains, is odd considering that even in long-established democracies the practice of political power is increasingly becoming more personalized. Taking the main threads of different case-studies together Reynebeau observes problems on three different levels. First, a conceptual problem, due to the nature of the phenomenon; it often seems fuzzy, difficult to grasp. Second, a metaphorical problem, originating in the word *charisma* itself ('gift of grace'), which implies a tendency to describe the phenomenon in a religious terminology. And third, a methodological problem. One should avoid an essentialist approach and treat the occurrence as what it is: as a historical and hence contingent phenomenon. Concluding his essay Reynebeau makes a modest proposal to choose for a pragmatic approach highlighting charisma's contingency and making its function within a specific historical or political context the focal point of the research. The emphasis in the study of charisma should shift to the interaction with the followers, away from the sometimes speculative description or tautological contemplation of a leader's presumed extraordinary qualities. Indeed, charisma only becomes relevant when it is acknowledged and 'activated' in the interaction between a leader and the led.

The volume is completed with an essay by Thomas Welskopp. This insightful essay brings the other contributions into its discussion and offers some new, stimulating ideas as well. According to Welskopp it is almost impossible to observe charismatic interaction *in actu*. It implies an emotion like 'love', and although nearly everybody has experienced this intensive sentiment, nobody would be able to exhaustively communicate this intensity by giving reasons or constructing phenomenological taxonomies. For this reason, Welskopp argues, we find charisma frequently described in religious and/or metaphorical terms. Saying this should make clear that Welskopp's point of departure to come to terms with the inflationary use of the term would be to treat 'charisma' as a phenomenon first of all rooted in the micro-level of social interaction.

The narrow definition of charisma as a phenomenon of face-to-face interaction redirects the focus onto the question of what outstanding personal qualities constitute charismatic authority. Especially provoking is Welskopp's hypothesis that charismatic personalities, leaving the impression that they operate in another key, more highly tuned to the collective moment, show the kind of features recent medical research attributes to symptoms that people with attention deficit disorder display. While they have problems concentrating themselves, they are able to mobilize unusual amounts of energy in specific moments that observers might then experience as charismatic. Equally appealing is the idea that charismatic authority has a strong aesthetic component. It is this aesthetic component – beauty and strength of voice, suppleness of mind, badinage – that makes charismatic oratory stand out among the bulk of dull and boring addresses.

Welskopp's anthropological orientation, his emphasis on face-to-face interaction and on the relations of mutual dependency, the presentation of 'social appropriation' through charismatic leadership and his position that charisma in social movements is essentially a bottom-up phenomenon all make the essay particularly thoughtful and of much value.

Notes

1. K. Löwith. 1923. 'Max Weber und Karl Marx', *Archiv für Sozialwissenschaft und Sozialpolitik* 67. Band, Tübingen. Recent summaries of Weber's thought are found in K. Allen. 2004. *Max Weber, a Critical Introduction*, London: Pluto Press; F.K. Ringer. 2004. *Max Weber, an Intellectual Biography*, Chicago: Chicago University Press; S. Whimster. 2007. *Understanding Weber*, London: Routledge; J. Radkau. 2009. *Max Weber*, Cambridge: Polity; and P.R. Baehr. 2008. *Caesarism, Charisma and Fate: Historical Sources and Modern Resonances in the Work of Max Weber*, New Brunswick: Transaction Publishers.

2. E.J. Hobsbawm. 1986. 'Weber und Marx. Ein Kommentar', in J. Kocka (ed.), *Max Weber, der Historiker*, Göttingen: Vandenhoeck & Ruprecht, 84. Cf. W.J. Mommsen. 1987. 'Max Weber and German Social Democracy', in C. Levy (ed.), *Socialism and the Intelligentsia 1880–1914*, London and New York: Routledge & Kegan Paul, 91–92; J. Kocka. 1966. 'Karl Marx und Max Weber. Ein methodologischer Vergleich', *Zeitschrift für die gesamten Staatswissenschaften* 122(April), 328–57; and J. Janoska-Bendl. 1965. *Methodologische Aspekte des Idealtypus. Max Weber und die Soziologie der Geschichte*, Berlin: Duncker und Humblot, 89–114.

3. For many years the dominant viewpoint in the Academy has been that Weber and Marx represent two contradictory and mutually exclusive systems of thought. Talcott Parsons' works, by proposing a neopositivist reading of Weber, have surely contributed to this image. As early as 1929 he declared that *The Protestant Ethic and the Spirit of Capitalism* was 'intended to be a refutation of the Marxian thesis in a particular historical case'. T. Parsons. 1929. 'Capitalism in Recent German Literature', *Journal of Political Economy* 37, 40. The French sociologist Michael Löwy on the other hand argues that only a tenacious misunderstanding has made *The Protestant Ethic and the Spirit of Capitalism* a work of 'spiritualist' polemic against historical materialism – while its true aim was quite different: to reveal the elective affinity between Calvinism and capitalism. M. Löwy. 1996. 'Figures of Weberian Marxism', *Theory and Society* 25(3), 431. Idem. 1993. 'Weber against Marx? The Polemic

with Historical Materialism in *The Protestant Ethic*', in *On Changing the World: Essays in Political Philosophy, from Karl Marx to Walter Benjamin*, Atlantic Highlands: Humanities Press, 43–54. Since the end of the twentieth century we notice a strengthening of this approach, focusing on the numerous convergences between the two thinkers. Scepticism on these convergences, however, holds on. See for example G. Roth. 1971. 'The Historical Relationship to Marxism', in R. Bendix and G. Roth (eds), *Scholarship and Partisanship: Essays on Max Weber*, Berkeley: University of California Press, 227–52.

4. M. Löwy. 2007. 'Marx and Weber: Critics of Capitalism', *New Politics* 11(2). The sociologist Derek Sayer even argues that 'to a certain extent his [Weber's] critique of capitalism, as a life negating force, is sharper than Marx's'. D. Sayer. 1991. *Capitalism and Modernism: An Excursus on Marx and Weber*, London: Routledge, 4. This is an exaggerated assessment, but it is true that some of Weber's arguments touch at the foundations of the modern industrial capitalist civilization.

5. Weber did not present an idealistic concept of social change, although his empathic polemics with historical materialism sometimes seems to suggest it. On the one hand Weber emphasizes the role of great men, on the other he emphasizes the determination of social processes by ideal and economic structures, in which the individual is bound. W.J. Mommsen. 1986. 'Max Webers Begriff der Universalgeschichte', in Kocka, *Max Weber, der Historiker*, 56. Wolfgang Mommsen explains Weber's concern with charisma in the context of his fears for the bureaucratization of German politics during the transition to the Weimar Republic. W.J. Mommsen. 1974. *Max Weber und die Deutsche Politik 1890–1920*, Tübingen: Mohr, 431–36.

6. As Roman Rosdolsky argued, Marx and Engels considered the role of the individual in history as part of the broader philosophical problem of the relation of chance and necessity in history. Cf. K. Marx and F. Engels. 1953. 'Die Deutsche Ideologie', in *Marx-Engles-Werke*, Berlin, vol. 3, 3–67; R. Rosdolsky. 1977. 'Die Rolle des Zufalls und der Groszen Männer in der Geschichte', *Kritik*, Vol. 5(14), 67–96; E. Mandel. 1986. 'The Role of the Individual in History: the Case of World War Two', *New Left Review* 157, 61–77. Only at the end of his life did Weber study the notion of charisma intensively. Weber's theory of the 'three pure types of legitimate domination' was published in three different versions. The most mature and, in Weber's view, definite version is 'The Types of Domination', printed in Part I of *Wirtschaft und Gesellschaft* (pp. 122–76). The extensive chapter IX (pp. 541–868) has been selected by the publisher from published and unpublished materials. The essay 'Die drei reinen Typen der legitimen Herrschaft' was posthumously published by Marianne Weber in 1922 in the *Preußischen Jahrbüchern* 187 (pp. 1–12) and is included in the fourth edition of *Wirtschaft und Gesellschaft*. M. Weber. 1956. *Wirtschaft und Gesellschaft, Grundriss der Verstehende Soziologie*, 4th ed., 2 vols, Tübingen: J.C.B. Mohr (Paul Siebeck). It was removed again from later editions. W.J. Mommsen. 1974. *The Age of Bureaucracy: Perspectives on the Political Sociology of Max Weber*, Oxford: Basil Blackwell, 15–17. For those seeking a fuller picture of Weber's life see: M. Weber. 1975. *Max Weber: a Biography*, New York: Wiley-Interscience. And especially Joachim Radkau's 2005 biography *Max Weber: die Leidenschaft des Denkens*, Munich: Carl Hanser, translated as J. Radkau. 2009. *Max Weber: a Biography*, Cambridge: Polity.

7. Arif Dirlik, 'Mao Zedong: Charismatic Leadership and the Contradictions of Socialist Revolution', this volume, p.117.

8. D.S. Meyer and S. Tarrow. 1998. 'A Movement Society: Contentious Politics for a New Century', in D.S. Meyer and S. Tarrow (eds), *The Social Movement Society: Contentious Politics for a New Century*, Lanham: Rowman and Littlefield, 1–28, 16–17.

9. C. Barker, A. Johnson and M. Lavalette (eds). 2001. *Leadership and Social Movements*, Manchester and New York: Manchester University Press, 2.

10. B. Klandermans. 1997. *The Social Psychology of Protest*, Oxford: Blackwell, 333.

11. M.P. Fiorina and K.A. Shepsle. 1989. 'Formal Theories of Leadership: Agents, Agenda Setters and Entrepreneur', in B.D. Jones (ed.), *Leadership and Politics*, Kansas: University of

Kansas Press, 17–40. See also R. Eatwell. 2006. 'The Concept and Theory of Charismatic Leadership', *Totalitarian Movements and Political Religions* 7(2), 153.

12. This charismatic aspect is still a black box in leadership studies. The index in Barker, Johnson and Lavalette, *Leadership and Social Movements* gives only three references.

13. See for example the volumes of *Totalitarian Movements and Political Religions*, a journal that was first published in 2000. J. Potts. 2009. *A History of Charisma*, Basingstoke and New York: Palgrave Macmillan provides the most recent conceptual history of the term.

14. H. te Velde. 1996. 'Ervaring en zingeving in de politiek. Het politieke charisma in de tijd van Abraham Kuyper', *Theoretische Geschiedenis* 23(4), 520. H. te Velde. 2005. 'Charismatic Leadership, c. 1870–1914: a Comparative European Perspective', in R. Toye and J. Gottlieb (eds), *Making Reputations: Power, Persuasion and the Individual in Modern British Politics*, London and New York: I.B. Tauris, 42–55.

15. Mommsen, *Max Weber und die Deutsche Politik*, 431–36.

16. The term *charisma* is of Greek origin, meaning 'gift', and was originally identified as a 'gift of grace' or a divinely inspired calling to service, office or leadership. The term derives from a reference in the New Testament's *Corinthians* II, which describes the forms in which the gifts of divine grace appear. The term was secularized by Max Weber in the early twentieth century. See especially M. Weber. 1968. *Max Weber on Charisma and Institution Building*, ed. S.N. Eisenstadt, Chicago: University of Chicago Press.

17. Weber, *Wirtschaft und Gesellschaft* . L. Greenfeld. 1983. 'Reflections on Two Charismas', *The British Journal of Sociology* 36(1), 117–32.

18. Eatwell, 'The Concept and Theory of Charismatic Leadership', 143.

19. Liah Greenfeld offers such a definition. According to her, 'charisma' means 'the ability to internally generate and externally express extreme excitement, an ability which makes one the object of intense attention and unreflective imitation by others. It is this quality which makes it possible for a charismatic person to become a leader'. Greenfeld, 'Reflections on Two Charismas', 122.

20. R.J. Ellis. 1991. 'Explaining the Occurrence of Charismatic Leadership in Organizations', *Journal of Theoretical Politics* 3(3), 307.

21. See M. Canovan. 2004. 'Hannah Arendt on Totalitarianism and Dictatorship', in P. Baehr and M. Richter (eds), *Dictatorship in History and Theory*, Cambridge: Cambridge University Press, 246. H. Arendt. 1994. 'At Table with Hitler', in H. Arendt, *Essays in Understanding 1930–1954*, ed. J. Kohn, New York: Harcourt, Brace, 291.

22. Obama, Chavez, Khomeini and Berlusconi, but also Michael Jackson, Pope Benedictus and Osama Bin Laden are just a few of the personalities who have been called charismatic in recent years.

23. G. Roth. 1979. 'Charisma and Counterculture', in G. Roth and W. Schluchter (eds), *Max Weber's Vision of History*, Berkeley: University of California Press, 128.

24. This scepticism was already noted in 1964 by: K.J. Ratnam. 1964. 'Charisma and Political Leadership', *Political Studies* 12(3), 341–54. See also: A.R. Willner and D. Willner. 1965. 'The Rise and Role of Charismatic Leaders', *The Annals of the American Academy of Political and Social Science* 358(1), 78; W. Spinrad. 1991. 'Charisma: A Blighted Concept and an Alternative Formula', *Political Science Quarterly* 106(2); Bendix and Roth, *Scholarship and Partisanship*, 170; and Eatwell, 'The Concept and Theory of Charismatic Leadership', 142.

25. H.H. Gerth and C. Wright Mills (eds and trans). 1947. *From Max Weber: Essays in Sociology*, London: Kegan Paul, 245–52. In his posthumously published essay 'Die drei reinen Typen der legitimen Herrschaft' Weber expresses the concept of charisma in very strong phrasing: 'Der manische Wutanfall des nordischen "Berserkers", die Mirakel und Offenbarungen irgendeiner Winkelprophetie, die demagogischen Gaben des Kleon sind der Soziologie genau so gut "Charisma" wie die Qualitäten eines Napoleon, Jezus, Perikles. Denn für uns entscheidend ist nur, ob sie als Charisma galten und wirkten, d.h. Anerkennung fanden.'

M. Weber. 1982 (1968). *Gesammelte Aufsätze zur Wissenschaftslehre*, ed. J. Winckelmann. Tübingen: J.C.B. Mohr, 483.

26. R.A. Willner. 1984. *The Spellbinders: Charismatic Political Leadership*, New Haven: Yale University Press. See also the essay in this volume by Henk te Velde, 'Charismatic Leaders, Political Religion and Social Movements in Western Europe at the End of the Nineteenth Century'.

27. T. Johnston, 1925. 'James Keir Hardie: The Founder of the Labour Party', in H. Tracey (ed.), *The Book of the Labour Party: Its History, Growth, Policy, and Leaders III*, London: Caxton, 105. See Velde, 'Charismatic Leadership', 47.

28. One of the few books which recently has appeared specifically on political charisma defines it as a 'compulsive, inexplicable emotional tie linking a group of followers together in adulation of their leader'. C. Lindholm. 1990. *Charisma*, Cambridge: Basil Blackwell, 6.

29. P.J. Troelstra. 1931. *Gedenkschriften IV, Storm*, Amsterdam: Querido, 300.

30. Eatwell, 'The Concept and Theory of Charismatic Leadership', 152.

31. See Ellis, 'Explaining the Occurrence of Charismatic Leadership in Organizations', 305–308; and M. Weber. 1978. *Economy and Society, an Outline of Interpretive Sociology*, 4 vols, ed. G. Roth and C. Wittich, Berkeley: University of California Press, vol. 2, 1117. As 'charisma populism' is a notoriously vague term, attempts at a general theory have been problematic. For a recent attempt, see D. Westlind. 1996. *The Politics of Popular Identity: Understanding Recent Populist Movements in Sweden and the United States*, Lund: Lund University Press. For a phenomenological approach that sorts the cases into types rather than attempting a general theory, see M. Canovan. 1981. *Populism*, New York: Harcourt Brace Jovanovich. On the relation between populism and democracy, see M. Canovan. 1999. 'Trust the People! Populism and the Two Faces of Democracy', *Political Studies 47*, XLVII, 2–16.

32. Populists often appeal to the 'united people', the nation or country, as against the parties and factions that divide it. Merging with this stress on unity is the appeal to 'our people', often in an exclusive sense that distinguishes 'our people' from those who do not belong – alien immigrants, for example. P. Taggart. 1996. *The New Populism and the New Politics: New Protest Parties in Sweden in a Comparative Perspective*, London: Macmillan, 33–35.

33. F. Domela Nieuwenhuis to E. Douwes Dekker [Multatuli], 16 March 1884, in Multatuli. 1989. *Volledig Werk*, vol. 23, Amsterdam: Van Oorschot, 124. In original: 'Ik mag mijn arme lijdende broeders niet aan hun lot overlaten. … Is niet eigen lijden veelal een oorzaak die drijft tot medelijden voor anderen?'

34. According to Weber charisma is not compatible with the routine of economic profit, which is not the same as the ownership of fortune or other material property. Weber, *Wirtschaft und Gesellschaft*, Vol. 1, 140–42, vol. 2, 663.

35. F. Domela Nieuwenhuis to C. De Paepe, The Hague, 9 January 1880, IISH (International Institute of Social History), Archives, César De Paepe.

36. K. Marx to F. Engels, 8 November 1882, in *Marx Engles Werke*. 1985. Berlin: Dietz Verlag, Vol. 35, 105.

37. Velde, 'Charismatic Leadership', 47.

38. On myths as mobilizing schemes Claude Lévi-Strauss points out: 'what gives the myth an operational value is that the specific pattern [i.e., combination of elements] is timeless; it explains the present and the past as well as the future'. So, the French Revolution constitutes a 'timeless pattern which can be detected in the contemporary French social structure and which provides a clue for its interpretations, a lead from which to infer future developments'. C. Lévi-Strauss. 1955. 'The Structural Study of Myth', *The Journal of American Folklore* 68, 430 cited in Willner and Willner, 'The Rise and Role of Charismatic Leaders', 84.

39. Cited in R. Bell. 1986. 'Charisma and Illegitimate Authority', in R. Glassmann and R. Swatos (eds), *Charisma: History and Social Structure*, New York: Greenwood Press, 57–70, 64.

40. Willner and Willner, 'The Rise and Role of Charismatic Leaders', 84.

41. See more specifically Ringer, *Max Weber*, 186–87.
42. Mommsen, *The Age of Bureaucracy*, 78.
43. See in general Ellis, 'Explaining the Occurrence of Charismatic Leadership in Organizations', 305–19. Aaron Wildavsky even suggests that charismatic leadership only occurs in egalitarian organizations that reject formal authority. A. Wildavsky. 1984. *The Nursing Father: Moses as a Political Leader'*, Alabama: University of Alabama Press, 197–99.
44. Mommsen, *The Age of Bureaucracy*, 80.
45. *Tagträume vom aufrechten Gang, Sechs Interviews mit Ernst Bloch*. 1977. Republished and introduced by A. Münster, Franfurt am Main: Suhrkamp, 83. E. Bloch. 1967. *Naturrecht und menschliche Würde*, Frankfurt am Main: Suhrkamp.
46. On this issue, see M. Löwy and R. Sayre. 1992. *Révolte et Mélancolie. Le romanticisme à contre-courant de la modernité*, Paris: Editions Payot.
47. G. Roth. 1987. *Politische Herrschaft und persönliche Freiheit. Heidelberger Max Weber-Vorlesungen 1983*, Frankfurt am Main: Suhrkamp, 146–50.
48. E. Gentile. 2005. 'Political Religion: a Concept and Its Critics – a Critical Survey', *Totalitarian Movements and Political Religions* 6(1), 19–32, 20.
49. Velde, 'Charismatic Leadership', 47. See also H. te Velde, 'Charismatic Leaders, Political Religion and Social Movements: Western Europe at the End of the Nineteenth Century' in this volume.
50. The first attempt to interpret modern political movements, from Jacobinism to Stalinism and national socialism, with the concept of political religion was made by the libertarian Rudolf Rocker, who used the concept in his book *Nationalism and Culture*, published in the USA in 1937. R. Rocker. 1937. *Nationalism and Culture* [Original title: *Die Entscheidung des Abendlandes*], New York: Covici Friede.
51. J. Loreck. 1978. *Wie man früher Sozialdemokrat wurde. Das Kommunikationsverhalten in der deutschen Arbeiterbewegung und die Konzeption der sozialistischen Parteipublizistik durch August Bebel*, Bonn and Bad Godesberg: Neue Gesellschaft, 212–13. Cf. Velde, 'Ervaring en zingeving in de politiek', 523.
52. In *Wirtschaft und Gesellschaft* Weber wrote: 'Der Begriff des Charisma (Gnadengabe) ist altchristlicher Terminologie entnommen. Für die christliche Hierokratie hat zuerst Rudolph Sohms Kirchenrecht der Sache, wenn auch nicht der Terminologie nach den Begriff, andere (z.b. Karl Holl in 'Enthusiasmus und Buszgewalt' [1898] haben gewisse wichtige Konsequenzen davon verdeutlicht)'. M. Weber. 1976. *Wirtschaft und Gesellschaft. Grundrisz der verstehenden Soziologie*, ed. J. Winckelmann, 5th ed., Tübingen: Mohr, 124. Cf. F.H. Tenbruck. 1988. 'Max Weber und Eduard Meyer', in W.J. Mommsen and W.G. Schwentker (eds), *Max Weber und Seine Zeitgenossen*, Göttingen: Vandenhoeck & Ruprecht, 337–80.

I. The Charismatic Family

CHAPTER 1

A NEW KIND OF FORCE

Examining Charisma in the Light of Gandhi's
Moral Authority

Dilip Simeon

Our first duty is to preserve the noble presence of moral responsibility in nature: of a being who is able to recognise the good-in-itself as such.[1]

The Dilemma of Detachment

Max Weber is renowned for advocating the idea of a value-free science of culture. It was Nietzsche for whom an irrational 'will to truth' became aware of itself as a problem, and who characterized modern culture as one in which the 'highest' values had withdrawn from the public sphere. The phenomenon of the autonomous individual developed within this culture. For Weber, the world is objectively meaningless and visible only through the perspectives of ideal-types. Value-perspectives are created by the dynamic of charisma and routinization, which confronts and displaces prevalent forms of culture.[2] Charismatic individuals are those whose devotion to a calling gives them a capacity to create a *community of judgement*.[3] Charisma is thus a grievous matter for Weber; it is the source of norms, standards and meaning bestowed upon society by dominant personalities. Hence,

> charisma, in its most potent forms, disrupts rational rule as well as tradition altogether and overturns all notions of sanctity. Instead of reverence for customs that are ancient and hence sacred, it enforces the inner subjection to

the *unprecedented and absolutely unique and therefore Divine*. In this purely empirical and value-free sense charisma is indeed the specifically creative revolutionary force of history.[4]

Years before his embarkation on a scholarly quest for value-free truths about society, Weber had stated his motivational force in the form of a pedagogical ideal: 'We do not want to train up feelings of well-being in people, but those characteristics we think constitute the greatness and nobility of our human nature.'[5] The work of the cultural scientist expresses the immanent political goal of evoking the noble side of human character. Political morality remained an abiding concern for him, as reflected in his comments on the dialectic of the ethics of conviction and responsibility. Weber seems stranded between scientific detachment and political commitment. There is a further problem. To the extent that the personality of the law-giver (and one who creates a community of judgement is a law-giver) appeals to an ideal of nobility, the charismatic person must appear, intuitively, to be a bearer of noble qualities. But perceptions of nobility change over time. Charisma is unstable. The greater the degree of stability, the closer the charismatic figure is to being noble; that is, representing the Absolute in popular consciousness – hence the attempt to harness charisma to the functions of state.[6] Stability in charisma signifies that the perception is acknowledged over time, unlike Hitler's for example, which dissipated rapidly during the Second World War. But placed as we are in history, how do we theorize a historically fluctuating perception?

This could be an intractable problem, but we must think about it. A political system that relies increasingly upon tyranny to preserve itself, whose functionaries seek to secure its civilization via increasing doses of intimidation, is a system on the edge of disintegration. In its last phase the British colony in India was reverting to its foundational violence, a fact that both reflected and accelerated the erosion of its hegemonic legitimacy. In the face of rising nationalist sentiment during and after the Great War, the British elite became radicalized: the 1919 Amritsar massacre was a deployment of state terror designed to educate a rebellious populace.[7] The colonial animus towards Gandhi and the Congress was deeply felt at the highest levels of government. During the Second World War, Winston Churchill was reportedly in favour of letting Gandhi die in case he went on a hunger strike. This was also the view held by Lord Linlithgow, Viceroy from 1936 to 1943, who took India to war without consulting the Indian political leadership.[8] This radical imperialism could be countered by radical nationalism, as indeed it was, but the consequences were likely to be destructive. Gandhi invented a form of resistance that was radical precisely on account of its moderation – this despite the official depiction of him as an anarchist and Bolshevist. It was his firm rejection of imperial arrogance combined with moderation in conduct that gave rise to Gandhi's political authority. And this authority was based on an alternative perception of public virtue.[9]

Actions, Outcomes and Justifications

Gandhi's politics and his moral philosophy were inseparable, so they bear comparison with the pessimism and ethical nihilism rampant in his time. Nihilism and annihilationism are closely related. Gandhi's rejection of militarism and the terrorists' martyr cult had a great deal to do with his charisma, especially in light of the fact that the nationalist-minded public were fascinated with patriotic terrorists. Let us see where such an inquiry can lead us.

If nihilism be defined with Nietzsche as the belief in the world's valuelessness, and hence in an extraneous source of value or justification, then all religious-minded persons are nihilists along with those who sought meaning but did not find it, or who believed in traditional values but discovered that value had evaporated. Nietzsche believed we are all bound to be conscious or unconscious nihilists, and that humans will remain in this condition for the immediate future, measured in centuries.[10] However, historicists also derive purpose, if not from an afterlife, from a future whose contours are known to them via their foreknowledge of history.[11] This imaginary state of affairs is distinguished from the ordinary optimism of lesser beings by virtue of an anticipatory self-exoneration from moral standards. Historicism as a source of value encompasses the perspectives of imperialists, nationalists, communists and fascists, and places them (whether they be religious-minded or not) beyond ordinary norms.

Thus it is not merely the religious-minded who derive their purposes from an extraneous or transcendental source. Self-styled atheists are capable of doing the same. We are obliged to ask therefore, whether it is really a belief in Heaven or History that defines the nihilist, or something more fundamental. Gandhi was a religious person and believed in a higher purpose. Was he therefore a nihilist? Or was his philosophy the very antithesis of nihilism? In my view, the central issue with nihilism does not arise from the purported source of justification, but from the nature of the answers derived from metaphysical thought. There are three aspects to our current nihilist predicament:

1. Anomie, the liberation from justifications; or the easy flitting from one justification to another by those who place themselves beyond good and evil. The question is *what activities* appear as justified to the doer, rather than the *fact* of their needing a justification.

2. The decline of dialogue and the divorce between reason and goodness. Absolute truths, whether secular or theological, lead to the conceit that all truths are interpretations. In this sense, totalitarianism and relativism mirror each other. If 'real' truth can only be produced by mathematical sciences, ethics must retire to the realm of speculation. One ethical standard is as good as another. This is a nihilist condition.
3. Nihilism's annihilationist character is manifest in the metaphysic of glory, which is inextricably linked to violently virile pursuits.

Gandhi's language was straightforward, and he could admit to being perplexed. He was not a relativist, and whilst criticizing modernity, did not believe that modernity had resulted in a transvaluation of all values. To the contrary, he held that certain truths transcended history and a democratic political edifice could be built upon them. *Ahimsa*, or nonviolence, was such a transcendent truth. He delivered radical demands in conventional language, all the while telling Indians and anyone who would listen about the reasonableness of nonviolence. He refused to accept the normless pretensions of science and I doubt he would have understood Weber's value-free social science. Gandhi's wisdom retained the connection between truth and virtue. Thus in 1947 he said, 'I regard the employment of the atom bomb for the wholesale destruction of men, women and children as the most diabolical use of science'.[12]

In contrast to the Semitic theodicy of misfortune, which imbues a metaphysically defined vocation with the promise of future redemption, Gandhi's nonviolent *satyagraha* was a confrontation with, rather than an appeal to the theodicean reconciliation of good and evil.[13] Whatever his theological beliefs (his interpretation of the Bihar earthquake of 1934 as chastisement for untouchability was an invocation of the divine origins of a natural disaster),[14] Gandhi was convinced that violence was evil, even when committed for the sake of a good cause. No good could come of evil wrought by human agency. As he said, 'What difference does it make to the dead, the orphans and the homeless, whether the mad destruction is wrought under the name of totalitarianism or the holy name of liberty or democracy?'[15]

Gandhi's politics confronted semantic anomie as well as militarist exterminism. His engagement with alterity was couched in terms of acceptance rather than annihilation. Totalitarian ideologies and democratic dialogue mutually exclude one another. Totalitarianism can oscillate between dogma and relativism – when affinity is enforced and world-views are upheld at the point of a knife, one truth is as good as another. Or as good as the amount of force it brings to the field. Democracy can only be built upon truths that are discursively arrived at, and nonviolence is a prerequisite of discourse. Intimidation contaminates conversation and leads to the political abolition of truth. Gandhi had a dialogic approach to truth, and hence his epistemological stance was open-ended rather than absolutist or teleological. This enabled him to communicate meaningfully with people including intellectuals of vastly differing traditions; a discursive skill essential for a democratic movement in a society as complex as India.

Gandhi's Impact

A central issue in the debate about Gandhi's charisma has to do with courage and manliness, and their redefinition. These ideals were the small change of colonial discourse that defined certain communities as unmanly and others as martial. Such characterizations were used in colonial ethnography in the nineteenth century and became more central to it after the rebellion of 1857, after which the upper castes of North India were excluded from military service. The extremist wing of nationalism from the late nineteenth century onwards was obsessed with manliness and relied upon texts such as the Bhagwad Gita to incorporate a sense of military mission among upper-caste patriotic youth. Symbolic issues of masculinity and strength were even more marked among communities such as the Sikhs and Pathans. Gandhi played upon the popular significance of these themes by giving them a fresh meaning all his own. We can understand the resonance that his message carried within popular consciousness. Yet the new direction and meaning that he gave to the ideals of strength and courage was remarkable. The same can be said of Abdul Ghaffar Khan, also known as the Frontier Gandhi, a follower of the Mahatma till his last days. What took place was a transmutation of masculine consciousness on a nation-wide scale, inviting those who prided themselves on their bravery to face the violence of the colonial state without flinching. It was a form of self-assertion that appealed to large numbers of helpless people, empowered them with the capacity to resist, gave them a chance to participate in a great cause, and drew humble persons into mainstream politics. In this sense Gandhi's charisma was profoundly democratic and ethically novel, even revolutionary. And it stands in complete accord with Weber's understanding of it as 'the specifically creative revolutionary force of history'.

Given the difficulty of defining charisma, I shall attempt to evoke it via descriptions of certain crucial episodes in India's national movement. These descriptions are culled from secondary sources and eyewitness accounts, and in one case from a fictional representation. All of them show a populace deeply affected by a new kind of moral force, to the point where they became bearers of Gandhi's truth.

The Akali Movement and the Guru Ka Bagh
Agitation of 1922

The period following the first noncooperation movement (1918–22) was marked by violence in Punjab. Much bitterness was generated by the massacre at Jallianwala Bagh in Amritsar in 1919. What caused particular outrage was the pro-British attitude of the head priests of the *gurudwaras*, and thereafter an agitation was launched to reclaim the Sikh holy places from these men. The government upheld their control over the lands surrounding the shrines. On 20 February 1921 about 150 Sikh volunteers, or Akalis, were killed at the holy shrine of Nankana Sahib, fifty miles from Lahore, when they attempted to take possession of one of its five gurudwaras from the *mahant* Narandas. Writing about this incident, Gandhi drew attention to the fact that although the volunteers were carrying ceremonial arms, they upheld their pledge to refrain from violence, and allowed themselves to be brutally cut down by the mahant's armed guards.[16] Another site, known as Guru Ka Bagh, lies a few miles from Amritsar, and contains gurudwaras linked to Tegh Bahadur (the ninth Guru) and Arjun Dev (the fifth Guru). In August 1921 the site fell formally under the control of the Shiromani Gurudwara Parbandhak Committee or SGPC, constituted in 1920. On 8 August 1922, five Akalis were arrested for the theft of firewood, long considered a conventional right for the communal kitchen. From 25 August till 13 September 1922 the local government stopped the volunteers, many of whom were demobilized soldiers of the British Indian Army, and assaulted them, accusing them of unlawful assembly. On duty were English police and military officers and their Indian subordinates. The Congress Party's inquiry into these events recorded statements by eyewitnesses, including journalists, lawyers, retired teachers and ex-policemen.[17] Testimonies spoke of assaults with brass-tipped *lathis* (wooden staves) on volunteers who calmly took their punishment without flinching or retaliating. The brutality of these beatings indicates a level of animus that does not emerge from official reports. The Akalis were often beaten on their private parts, dragged by their hair, stomped upon by horses, and even thrashed after they had collapsed. They were reported to be praying as all this went on, and several Sikh women and onlookers were moved to tears at the scene. The Reverend C.F. Andrews, a Cambridge missionary and Gandhi's confidante, wrote an eyewitness account dated 12 September 1922.[18]

> When I ... stood face to face with the ultimate moral contest I could understand the strained look and the lips which silently prayed. It was a sight I never wish to see again, a sight incredible to an Englishman. There were four Akali

Sikhs with their black turbans facing a band of about a dozen police, including two English officers. They had walked slowly up to the line of the Police … and were standing silently in front of them …. Their hands were placed together in prayer. Then without the slightest provocation on their part, an Englishman lunged forward the head of his lathi which was bound with brass. The blow which I saw was sufficient to fell the Akali Sikh and send him to the ground. He rolled over, and slowly got up once more and faced the same punishment over again. Time after time one of the four … was laid prostrate by repeated blows, now from the English officer and now from the police …[;] the police committed certain acts which were brutal in the extreme – I saw with my own eyes one of these police kick in the stomach a Sikh who stood helplessly before him …[. W]hen one of the Sikhs … was lying prostrate, a police sepoy stamped with his foot upon him, using his full weight …. The brutality and inhumanity of the whole scene was indescribably increased by the fact that the men who were hit were praying to God and had already taken a vow that they would re-main silent and peaceful in word and deed. The Akali Sikhs who had taken this vow, both at the Golden Temple and also at the shrine of Guru Ka Bagh, were … largely from the Army. They had served in many campaigns in Flanders, in France, in Mesopotamia and in East Africa …. Now they were felled to the ground at the hands of English officials serving in the same government which they themselves had served …. But each blow was turned into a triumph by the spirit with which it was endured …. The vow they had made to God was kept to the letter. The onlookers too … were praying with them … and for them …. It was very rarely that I witnessed any Akali Sikh who went forward to suffer, flinch from a blow when it was struck. The blows were received one by one without resistance and without a sign of fear ….

There has been something far greater in this event than a mere dispute about land and property. It has gone far beyond the technical questions of legal pos-session or distraint. A new heroism, learnt through suffering, has arisen in the land. A new lesson in moral warfare has been taught to the world.

Spearheaded by the Shiromani Gurudwara Parbandhak Committee, the Gurudwara Reform Movement carried on for three years. Agitations were attended by Sikh *jathas* arriving from as far afield as Canada and China. Each foray towards a major gurudwara (such as Gangsar at Jaito, in the princely state of Nabha in 1924) was marked by an oath of nonviolence administered publicly by religious superiors.[19] Gandhi remained in close communication with the leadership of the movement, which explicitly named itself a religious satyagraha.[20] In June 1925, the government re-lented and handed over control of Sikh shrines to elected managing com-mittees under a revised Sikh Gurudwara and Shrines Bill.[21]

The Red Shirts of the North West Frontier

The Pathan leader Abdul Ghaffar Khan, also known as Badshah Khan and the Frontier Gandhi, was born into a small khan family in 1890, and educated in a Christian missionary school in Peshawar. Education as the instrument of social elevation and political transformation remained the obsession of his life. His earliest efforts were to set up village schools on charitable contributions. Their syllabi included studies of the Koran, designed to liberate villagers from the hidebound interpretations of their mullahs. The Anjuma-i-Islahul-Afaghina (Society for the Reform of Afghans) was founded in 1921, during the first noncooperation movement. It encouraged social reform, the learning of skills and sanitation – statements of self-assertion against a background of acute colonial neglect of education and social infrastructure. Among its achievements was an impetus to modern Pashto literature and political journalism. For his participation in the nationalist upsurge of 1919–21, Badshah Khan spent three years in rigorous imprisonment (1921–24) partly in proximity with Akali activist Baba Kharak Singh, imprisoned during the Guru-ka-Bagh agitation, from whom he gained inspiration about nonviolence. He met Gandhi and Jawaharlal Nehru in 1929, the year he founded the Khudai Khidmatgars or Servants of God, a political organization that also worked for social and educational uplift.[22] The movement was quintessentially Gandhian, being deeply imbued with the motive of social transformation.

It is noteworthy that Ghaffar Khan's belief in nonviolence derived from his own experience, which taught him that 'it was useless to start digging a well after the house was on fire'. Combining the status of a tribal chief with that of saint, he was perhaps even closer to his people than Gandhi, and achieved the 'miracle' of transforming his fractious and violence-prone Pathan volunteers into a nonviolent mass movement. In his own words, 'My non-violence has become almost a matter of faith with me. I believed in Mahatma Gandhi's *ahimsa* before. But the unparalleled success of the experiment in my province has made me a confirmed champion of non-violence.'[23] Convinced that peace was the coping stone of Islam, and that the greatest figures in Islam's history were known for their forbearance and restraint, he remains an enigmatic figure in the history of the Pathans. The enigma lay in the fact that a community known for its ferocity could produce and hoist such a man as their standard-bearer in battle with its most powerful adversary; and that he appeared to them as a revolutionary whilst remaining rooted in traditional culture. He appealed to religious sanction on the ground that Islam meant tranquillity and striving after righteousness, and convinced his people that it was more courageous to die than to kill. The Turkish scholar Halide Edib, who visited the Frontier in the 1930s, wrote of Ghaffar Khan's achievements:

Although he based his simple ideology on religion, his interpretation of it was so universal, that instead of separating the Muslims from the rest of the world, he tried to make them so that they could co-operate with their fellow-men for the good of all ...[. H]is supreme importance lies in his having brought the simplest and truest conception of Islam into the lives of a most elemental people.[24]

Gandhi's description of his own exhortations to the Pathans bears out my point about the resonance between traditions of courage and the novel direction that this strange new agitator gave them:

At every meeting I repeated the warning that unless they felt that in non-violence they had come into possession of a force infinitely superior to the one they had and in the use of which they were adept, they should have nothing to do with non-violence and resume the arms they possessed before. It must never be said of the Khudai Khidmatgars that once so brave, they have become or been made cowards under Badshah Khan's influence. Their bravery consisted not in being good marksmen but in defying death and being ever ready to bare their chests to the bullets.[25]

The commitment of the Khudai Khidmatgars to nonviolence was based on the culture of *Pukhtunwali* and Islam. The Congress leadership, susceptible to stereotypes about Pathan ferocity, remained anxious about the Red Shirts' commitment to ahimsa. Yet in 1942 the movement obliged the government to station thirty thousand troops in the North West Frontier Province (NWFP) (a threefold increase over 1941) and this served to lessen the burden of repression upon the rest of India. When it came to the Pathans, the British excelled themselves in cruel punishment and psychologically designed torture including forcing activists to make counter-oaths upon the Koran, violating the sanctity of the women's quarter in Pathan homes; public exposures of private parts, insertions of tent pegs into anuses and even sexual mutilation. The Peshawar massacre in April 1930 (over two hundred killed) and the Bannu shooting in August (seventy dead) shocked the country, whilst arousing admiration for the Pathans' patriotism and nonviolent spirit. After touring the Frontier, British journalist Robert Bernays wrote that 'some of the stories of the wholesale shootings and hangings made me hang my head in shame'.[26] All the while Badshah Khan insisted on patience and restraint as the greatest Koranic and patriotic virtue: 'abstain from violence and do not defame your nation, because the world will say how could such a barbarous nation observe patience'.[27] The Khidmatgar movement grew from one thousand members in 1930 to twenty-five thousand in 1931, with numbers of women entering public life for the first time. It was not lost on the nationalist public that the Englishmen on a civilizing mission were behaving like mad dogs, and the volatile Pathans were teaching their rulers a lesson in restraint.

The Khudai Khidmatgar's openness to non-Pathans and non-Muslims alarmed the British. Government reports noted that 'probably at no time since British influence was first extended to the Frontier have conditions given rise to such acute anxiety ...[;] acts of lawlessness and defiance of authority increased with extraordinary speed, and organisations affiliated to the Congress gained greatly in prestige and popularity'.[28] The authorities were especially concerned to prevent nationalist agitation in the NWFP. Khidmatgar prisoners were often made to wear saffron clothes to ridicule their association with the 'Hindu' Congress. Officials encouraged the Khan landlords to support the Muslim League and spread rumours about tribal raids on the small Hindu minority. They consistently excluded Badshah Khan from the tribal areas, although Jinnah was allowed a visit in 1936. And they subsidized the clergy to support the League and denounce the Red Shirts as Bolsheviks and enemies of Islam. Today, the dominant stereotype of the Pathan frontier is dictated by the activities of the Taliban. We would do well to remember that the people whom colonial ethnography depicted as being addicted to violence produced one of the staunchest Gandhian movements in Indian nationalism. The Khidmatgars dominated the Frontier from 1930 till 1947. Badshah Khan instilled among his followers a practice of restraint based upon Pakhtun culture and Islam. Halide Edib felt that the 'psychological aspect of the movement was more interesting than its political significance'. She suggested that the Pathans had developed 'a new interpretation of force, which is very unexpected'. In her words, 'non-violence is the only form of force which can have a lasting effect on the life of society .... And this, coming from strong and fearless men, is worthy of study'.[29]

A bitter opponent of the Partition of India, Badshah Khan was the last of those Gandhian stalwarts who could walk across three international boundaries in post-1947 South Asia and be treated by the citizens of four countries as one of their own. He died in 1988 at the age of ninety-eight in Jalalabad, and the antagonists in the Soviet-Afghan War ceased fire for a day to allow his funeral to take place. The Peshawar-Jalalabad border was opened and thousands joined the procession. 'In his death Badshah Khan bore witness to the possibility of a closed border becoming an open frontier, restoring to the North West Frontier its open character of past centuries.'[30] Badshah Khan's life exemplified the spirit of satyagraha that stayed alive in India during the darkest years of the twentieth century, proof that the dignified self-assertion of oppressed peoples not only creates a new community of judgement, but can carry a charisma all its own.

Chander Singh Garhwali, the Hero of Peshawar

That a Hindu soldier in the colonial British Army should have become part of nationalist folklore in the heart of Pathan territory sounds unlikely today, but testifies to the mood of the times. In 1930, at the height of the civil disobedience movement, large gatherings of Pathan satyagrahis took place in Peshawar, and for a while succeeded in setting up a parallel administration. On 23 April 1930, not just the police but the army was on duty to quell the disturbances. At one demonstration, it deployed a battalion of the Garhwal Rifles, Platoon 4 of which was under the command of *Havildar* Chander Singh Garhwali. The streets of Kissa Khani Bazaar were full of nationalist flags, and a Sikh agitator was rendering a patriotic speech in Pashto and Urdu. Slogans such as 'Allah-ho-Akbar' and 'Mahatma Gandhi ki jai' resounded in the air. The English officer present, Captain Rickett, decided to disperse the crowd. Upon hearing his order to fire, the havildar pronounced a countermanding order to cease fire. He was reported to have turned to the Englishman and said, 'Sir, these are all unarmed people. How can we shoot them?' Soldiers of two other platoons followed suit, and one soldier reportedly offered his rifle to the demonstrators.[31] Officials were shaken by this 'betrayal'. As a civil servant later described it, 'Hardly any regiment of the Indian Army won greater glory in the Great War than the Garhwal Rifles, and the defection of part of the regiment sent a shock through India, of apprehension to some, of exultation to others.'[32] Chander Singh was cashiered and, along with his fellow-mutineers, sentenced to several years' rigorous imprisonment.

Some years later, interviewed in prison by the famous left-wing writer Rahul Sankrityayan, Chander Singh recounted his first-ever meeting with Mahatma Gandhi, in the temple town of Bageshwar, in Uttaranchal in June 1929. Gandhi was staying at a Dak Bungalow, reportedly performing acts of penance. Chander Singh attended his public discourse wearing his army hat. The hat caught Gandhi's attention, and he made a light-hearted comment about not being intimidated by army uniform. The havildar responded that he was ready to cast the hat aside if someone gave him some other headgear. A member of the audience pulled out what was then known as a Gandhi cap, popular with nationalist volunteers, and gave it to Chander Singh. He in turn threw it in the direction of the platform, saying, 'Main boodhe ke haath se topi loonga' (I'll take it from the hands of the old man). Gandhi then flung the cap back at Chander Singh, who took it respectfully, stood up, and with tears in his eyes, saluted the Mahatma with the promise that he would bring honour to the cap one day.[33]

The Brahmin Convert

One of the most moving evocations of Gandhi's charisma is contained in a work of fiction, the 1938 novel *Kanthapura*, by Raja Rao. Narrated as the stream-of-consciousness of an old village woman, the novel has been hailed by some critics as the first major English novel written by an Indian. It deals with the impact of the national movement on the humble inhabitants of a small village in Karnataka Province. Issues such as Gandhi's appeal for social reform as part of the freedom movement, the brutality of colonialism's lesser functionaries such as revenue collectors and the police, and the intertwining of religious feeling and symbols with popular mobilization are made visible almost effortlessly. The experiences of lower-caste migrant workers on fields and plantations are brought to life, as is the crisis of conscience of the young Moorthy, only surviving son of the Brahmin widow Narsamma, who dreamt of his becoming 'a Sub-Collector at least'.

> But Moorthy would have none of this. For, as everyone knew, one day he had seen a vision, a vision of the Mahatma, mighty and God-beaming, and stealing between the Volunteers, Moorthy had got on to the platform, and he stood by the Mahatma, and the very skin of the Mahatma seemed to send out a mellowed force and love, and he stood by one of the fanners and whispered, 'Brother, the next is me', and the fanner fanned on and the Mahatma spoke on, and Moorthy looked from the audience to the Mahatma and from the Mahatma to the audience, and he said to himself, 'There is in it something of the silent communion of the ancient books,' and he turned again to the fanner .... And Moorthy stood by the Mahatma and the fan went once this side and once that, and beneath the fan came a voice deep and stirring that went out to the hearts of those men and women and came streaming back through the thrumming air, and went through the fan and the hair and the nails of Moorthy into the very limbs, and Moorthy shivered and then there came flooding up in rings and ripples, 'Gandhi Mahatma ki jai!' – 'Jai Mahatma!', and as it broke against Moorthy, the fan went faster and faster over the head of the Mahatma, and perspiration flowed down the forehead of Moorthy. Then came a dulled silence of his blood, and he said to himself, 'Let me listen,' and he listened, and in listening, heard, 'There is but one force in life and that is Truth, and there is but one love in life and that is the love of mankind, and there is but one God in life and that is the God of all,' and then came a shiver and he turned to the one behind him and said 'Brother,' and the man took the fan from Moorthy and Moorthy trembled ... and sought his way out to the open, but there were men all about him and behind the men women, and behind them carts and bullocks and behind them the river, and Moorthy said to himself 'No, I cannot go'. And he sat beside the platform, his head in his hands, and tears came to his eyes, and he wept softly, and with weeping came peace. He stood up, and he saw there, by the legs of the chair, the sandal and

the foot of the Mahatma, and he said to himself, 'That is my place.' And suddenly there was a clapping of hands and shoutings of 'Vande mataram, Gandhi Mahatma ki jai!' and as there was fever and confusion about the Mahatama, he jumped onto the platform, slipped between this person and that and fell at the feet of the Mahatma, saying, 'I am your slave'. The Mahatma lifted him up and before them all, he said, 'What can I do for you my son?' and Mahatma said, 'You wear foreign clothes my son' – 'It will go, Mahatmaji.' 'You perhaps go to foreign Universities' – 'It will go', Moorthy said, 'I am ignorant, how can I seek Truth?' – and the people around him were trying to hush him and to take him away .... 'You can help your country by going and working among the dumb millions of the villages' – 'So be it Mahatmaji,' and the Mahatma patted him on the back, and through that touch was revealed to him as the day is revealed to the night the sheathless being of his soul; and Moorthy drew away, and as it were with shut eyes groped his way through the crowd to the bank of the river. And he wandered about the fields and the lanes and the canals and when he came back to the College that evening, he threw his foreign clothes and his foreign books into the bonfire, and walked out, a Gandhi's man.[34]

Towards the end of the book, the narrative relates to North India, as the nationalist volunteers attempt to raise the morale of the villagers. They describe the events in Peshawar:

And suddenly, across the Bebbur Mound, we saw shapes crawl along and duck down and rise up, and we said, 'Perhaps soldiers – soldiers,' but 'In Peshawar,' says the city boy, 'you know they would not shoot,' and we said we too are soldiers, and we are the soldiers of the Mahatma, and this country is ours, and we said to ourselves, a day will come, a day when hut after hut will have a light at dusk, and flowers will be put on the idols, and camphors lit, and as the last Redman leaps into his boat, and the earth pushes him away, through our thatches will a song rise like a thread of gold, and from the lotus-navel of India's earth the Mahatma will speak of love to all men. 'Say Mahatma Gandhi ki jai!' – 'Inquilab Zindabad, Inquilab Zindabad!' – and the Police lathis showered on us, and the procession-throne fell, and the gods fell, and the flowers fell, and the candelabras fell, and yet the gods were in the air, brother, and not a cry nor lamentation rose, and when we reached the village gate, suddenly from the top of the pipal someone swings down and he has a flag in hand, and he cries out,

Lift the flag high,
O Lift the flag high,
Brothers, sisters, friends and mothers,
This is the flag of the Revolution,

and the Police rush at him, and he slips in here and he slips out there and the boys have taken the flag, and the flag flutters and leaps from hand to hand, and with it the song is clapped out:

O Lift the flag high,
Lift it high like in 1857 again.[35]

What is striking about *Kanthapura* is the depiction of the psychological transformation of the villagers – an overcoming of the fear of officialdom and the first halting confrontation with deep-rooted caste prejudice. All this takes place as part of the nationalist awakening, and is inspired by the Mahatma's message. Gandhi's charisma is palpable in its pages, in the elemental forms that it might have assumed for humble Indians.

Gandhi during Partition

The year 1946 had seen the worst outburst of communal killing in the decade before partition. It took place in Calcutta as a result of Jinnah's call for direct action on 16 August. (The Muslim League was then in power as a provincial government under Chief Minister Husain Suhrawardy.) There were reports of between five and ten thousand people being killed and fifteen thousand injured between 16 and 19 August. The presence of the chief minister and his associates, as well as his intemperate speeches made in the course of the run-up to Direct Action Day gave rise to suspicions about deliberate political instigation of the massacre. No single event served to embitter communal relations and the political atmosphere more than this event, which came to be known as the Great Calcutta Killing of 1946.[36] The months following the riots were perhaps the most tense the city had experienced in its recent history. From November 1946 till the end of February 1947, Gandhi spent his time walking in the district of Noakhali, in North Bengal, which had been badly affected by communal violence. This was a Muslim majority area, soon to become part of East Pakistan. This pilgrimage for peace became legendary as his prayer meetings and public discourses healed the public psyche, encouraging Hindus to return to their villages and Muslims to discard their animus. The area still has a Gandhi Museum, and memories of the Mahatma's visit there still linger among the elderly.[37]

For contemporary observers, therefore, it was nothing short of a miracle that Hindus and Muslims in their thousands attended Gandhi's prayer meetings and even celebrated Eid together on 18 August 1947. For once, British officialdom was much relieved at Gandhi's presence. On 26 August, Viceroy Mountbatten sent him a telegram stating: 'My dear Gandhiji, In the Punjab we have 55 thousand soldiers and large-scale rioting on our hands. In Bengal our forces consist of one man, and there is no rioting ....
As a serving officer may I be allowed to pay my tribute to the One Man

Boundary Force.' For its part, the Muslim League fraction in the Constituent Assembly in Delhi passed a resolution expressing its 'deep sense of appreciation of the services rendered by Mr Gandhi to the cause of restoration of peace and goodwill between the communities in Calcutta'.[38]

Less than a month later, on 31 August 1947, Calcutta witnessed a renewed outbreak of violence, which prompted Gandhi to cancel his much-awaited trip to the Punjab and remain in the city. On the evening of 1 September, he announced his decision to fast against violence. He stayed in the abandoned Hydari Mansion in a Muslim part of the city. Within a day, students began to take part in peace processions, and even the north Calcutta police force, including Europeans and Anglo-Indians, wore armbands and fasted on duty in sympathy with Gandhi. The following day, bands of hooligans came to him to surrender their weapons and plead with him to cease endangering his life. Gandhi is reported to have commented that it was the first time he had set eyes on a Sten gun.[39] On 4 September 1947 he was paid a visit by a senior delegation of politicians, including members of the business community, the Muslim League-led Seaman's Union, the Hindu Mahasabha and Chief Minister Suhrawardy. He made them swear they would give their own lives before allowing another outbreak of communal violence to take place. This unprecedented oath was then written down and signed by the entire delegation. The prominent Tamil Congressman Chakravarthi Rajagopalachari, who became independent India's second governor general, remarked that not even the successful struggle for independence was 'as truly wonderful as his victory over evil in Calcutta'.[40] In an editorial on 1 September, the colonial-minded English editor of *The Statesman* made a point of announcing that henceforth 'Mr Gandhi' would be referred to in his columns as the Mahatma.

Confronted by the violence of 1946, Gandhi had said:

> It has become the fashion these days to ascribe all such ugly manifestations to the activities of hooligans. It hardly becomes us to take refuge in that moral alibi. Who are the hooligans after all? They are our own countrymen, and so long as any countryman of ours indulges in such acts, we cannot disown responsibility for them consistently with our claim that we are one people .... Mankind is at the crossroads. It has to make its choice between the law of the jungle and the law of humanity.[41]

And at the height of the violence of 1947 he said, 'it is time for peace-loving citizens to assert themselves and isolate *goondaism*. Non-violent non-cooperation is the universal remedy. Good is self-existent, evil is not. It is like a parasite living in and around good. It will die of itself when the support that good gives it is withdrawn.'[42] If we were to use Gandhi's logic to describe the situation he confronted in 1947 we could say that the struggle between violence and ahimsa was going on in every soul, and was not merely demarcated by the social distance between goondas and polite society.

Gandhi's Charisma

Charisma is not reducible to an aspect of an individual personality, though personal strength and style are essential to it. Nor is it a quality bestowed upon the charismatic figure by an adoring public. It lies, rather in the resonance between leader and followers, and signifies an awareness of historical needs. These needs include psychic expectations that may take many forms, some of them conflicting with others. But howsoever substantial be the public mood, the emergence of a charismatic personality remains a fortuitous event, irreducible to objective determinations. It would be a travesty of historical method to say that had there not been Gandhi, someone like him would have appeared on account of historic necessity.

I find it noteworthy that the word 'resonance' carries an acoustic meaning. This means that certain emotions and ideas are awakened in the followers, who in turn will the leader to nurture those feelings and ideas in furtherance of the cause. Charisma is a psychological power and expresses self-recognition on the part of everyone involved, a recognition of qualities of head and heart of which they were previously unaware, or only dimly aware. It was Gandhi's capacity to pierce the hearts of everyone, including those who were personally engaged in violence and killing, that lay at the heart of his charisma.

Gandhi's charismatic influence has not waned, despite the iconization, cynicism and hostility directed at him by the Indian middle classes. The latter has ebbed recently with the appearance of films such as *Lage Raho Munnabhai* (2006) that popularized the idea of *Gandhigiri*,[43] although it was a depoliticized Gandhi that was presented here. Aside from the middle class, if there are still thousands of humble citizens who visit the site of his assassination every day, this is because he touched an unshakeable chord in the hearts and minds of ordinary Indians. We need also to take note of Gandhi's stature in the world outside India, which perhaps respects him more than do his compatriots. What is the reason for this lasting impact? I suggest the following:

1. His reputation as a tireless worker for communal harmony. Since the subcontinent has been plagued by communal strife, and since a com-

munal Partition took place despite Gandhi's best efforts, a nostalgic memory of those efforts persists.

2. His stature as the man who prised India's freedom from the grip of the mighty British Raj.

3. The people's experience of Gandhi as a leader who remained physically close to his most humble compatriots, scorning police protection, who did not flinch from placing himself in dangerous places.

4. His insistence on the secular character of public space in independent India. His charisma lent legitimacy and weight to the norms he wanted to see inscribed in the Indian Constitution.

5. A renewed interest in Gandhi's critique of modern technology.

But there is something more. In a country so conscious of local and caste identity, Gandhi is perceived as one who left vernacular identity behind him. He was a *bania* by caste, and a Gujarati-speaking and English-trained lawyer. However, he surpassed these identities and obtained the allegiance of so-called 'virile' ethnic groups as well as poor, 'outcaste' rural communities. Banias, traditionally the caste-cluster engaged in commerce, are typecast as instrumentalist in outlook, disinclined to engage in confrontation. For a bania to command the unstinted respect of Pathans and Sikhs was remarkable. It is noteworthy that by his demeanour, Gandhi was almost unconsciously democratic. As Orwell said of him:

> he was not afflicted by envy or by the feeling of inferiority. Colour feeling, which he first met in South Africa, seems to have astonished him. Even when he was fighting what was in effect a colour war, he did not think of people in terms of race or status. The governor of a province, a cotton millionaire, a half-starved Dravidian coolie, a British private soldier were all equally human beings, to be approached in much the same way.[44]

Gandhi bore the identity of a renunciator, someone who cannot be summed up in terms of caste or linguistic identity, but whose character has risen above it all. He was no populist, and never bothered to adjust his ideas and convictions to shifting public moods and perceptions. In the midst of the most bitter public recriminations, especially during the dark and tragic days of Partition, Gandhi endured vicious barbs from people who had lost everything, including their loved ones, to communal hatred and cruelty. In this upsurge of bitterness, he asked people to retain their faith in humanity, comforted the inconsolable, and silently suffered the barbs, even abuse of humans damaged by grief. A young Punjabi judge, himself a refugee from Lahore, who met Gandhi in October 1947 to discuss mundane matters pertaining to evacuee property, noticed his calm, practical and matter-of-

fact demeanour as they spoke, but then felt constrained to observe, 'Reali-
sation came to me that this man had only one sentiment in his heart and
that was the sentiment of love. When he looked at me I noticed a softness
in his eyes and I felt ashamed.'[45] The wife of the American journalist Upton
Close expressed it as follows: 'In his presence I felt a new capability and
power in myself rather than a consciousness of his power. I felt equal, good
for anything – an assurance I had never known before, as if some consciousness within me had newly awakened.'[46]

At a prayer meeting on 29 November 1947, Gandhi decried the conversion of mosques into temples, and demanded they be returned to their
original status. He then observed, 'But when someone commits a crime
anywhere I feel I am the culprit. You too should feel the same .... Let
us all merge in each other like drops in an ocean.'[47] This utterance hints
at the ontological root of his nonviolence.[48] It was his sense of being at
one with all Indians – indeed, all humanity – that lay at the root of Gandhi's charisma. Indians could not get away from him for good or ill; he
manifested what was best in them, even when they hated him. A people
obsessed with virility was bemused by his combination of gentleness and
courage. That is why his fasts worked best when they were directed at
the conscience of his compatriots. He had no official protection at a time
when he had already become a target for assassination. He died on his
feet, standing up, God's name on his lips, having taken three bullets fired
from close range into his chest and stomach. His unique blend of nonviolence and moral force represented a remarkable detachment of manliness
from ferocity and militarism. There is no doubt that the Indian people
sensed how different he was from virtually all the leaders in the contemporary world.

Gandhi remains recalcitrant, a character indissoluble in the language
and practices of political cynicism. There has been no routinization of his
personality, he had no inheritors, there is no organization that can claim
his mantle. He is known to have desired the dissolution of the Congress
Party because its main goal – Indian independence – had been attained.
There were and there remain powerful ideological currents opposed to
him, and some that even take pride in his assassination. The ideology of
Pakistan needs to portray him as a Hindu leader, nothing more, and the
radical Left takes issue with his unabashed use of religious metaphors;
even though he insisted on a secular state for independent India. His
insistence on nonviolence continues to cause unease even amongst his admirers. His life and ideals raise profound questions, although he did not
care to place them philosophically.[49] Contrary to the modernist political
tradition exemplified by Machiavelli and Robespierre that held violence
essential to the act of political foundation, Gandhi made the prescient ob-

servation that 'what is granted under fear can be retained only as long as the fear lasts', an insight that calls into question the decisionist metaphysics of revolutionary political theory from the Jacobins to the Bolsheviks.[50] If routinization is something more than and other than iconization (of which there has been a great deal), Gandhi's charisma retains something of its magical and passionate quality, impossible to grasp completely, replicate or reduce to a humdrum dimension, yet impossible to remain unmoved by.

I began this essay by posing a question about the place of nobility in what is called charisma. If indeed there is no conceptual account of nobility, which must remain accessible to us only as a perception, the fact remains that even his severest critics intuitively grasped that Gandhi's historic stature was rooted in a profound nobility of spirit. And so it remains. If we cannot deduce nobility from axioms and logical principles, we can only understand it by recourse to example, and one example that will surely command widespread acceptance is the personality of the man whom Indians came to refer to as *Mahatma* – the Great Soul – or simply *Bapu*, Father. Mohandas Gandhi was undoubtedly a strong man and a towering political leader. But he was simultaneously full of gentleness, love and compassion. That is why his life and fearless final sacrifice became a foundation stone for the constitutional edifice of the Indian Union. That is why Indians can never forget him, and the recognition of his greatness by people the world over continues unabated.[51]

Notes

1. From Lawrence Vogel's introduction to H. Jonas. 1996. *Mortality and Morality: A Search for the Good after Auschwitz*, Evanston: Northwestern University Press, 17.
2. D. Owen. 1994. *Maturity and Modernity: Nietzsche, Weber, Foucault and the Ambivalence of Reason*, London and New York: Routledge, 91–93, 101, 96.
3. Owen, *Maturity and Modernity*, 130–31.
4. M. Weber. 1978. *Economy and Society: An Outline of Interpretive Sociology*, 4 vols, ed. G. Roth and C. Wittich, Berkeley: University of California Press, vol. 2, 1117. Emphasis added.
5. From 'The Nation State and Economic Policy' (Freiburg Address); cited in Owen, *Maturity and Modernity*, 98.
6. I refer to the Absolute not as an eternally valid and unquestionable Order, but as a manifestation of law and social stability.
7. D. Rothermund. 1991. *Mahatma Gandhi: An Essay in Political Biography*, Delhi: Manohar Publications, 34.
8. On 1 January 2006 the BBC cited newly published Cabinet papers showing that Winston Churchill favoured letting Gandhi die if he went on hunger strike. The prime minister thought India's leader should be treated like anyone else if he stopped eating while in custody. His ministers persuaded him against the tactic, fearing Gandhi would become a martyr if he died in British hands. (Accessed 9 April 2009.)

9. 'Nobility is a perception, not a concept. Or – what comes to the same thing – our concept of nobility is rooted in a perception, not in another concept …[;] nobility is a value, an estimation, a ranking, and therefore it is an ambiguous mixture of aesthetic and moral qualities that may be named and understood but that must in any given case be recognized directly.' S. Rosen. 1989. *The Ancients and the Moderns – Rethinking Modernity*, New Haven and London: Yale University Press, 12.
10. See A. White. 1990. *Within Nietzsche's Labyrinth*, New York: Routledge, 15–25; and K. Carr. 1992. *The Banalization of Nihilism: Twentieth Century Responses to Meaninglessness*, Albany: SUNY Press, 13–22.
11. I use the term *historicism* to refer to the belief in a teleologically determined end of history; or that history possesses an immanent purpose. An interesting account of this concept may be read in S. Rosen. 1969. *Nihilism: A Philosophical Essay*, New Haven and London: Yale University Press, 56–93. See also Vogel's introduction to Jonas, *Mortality and Morality*, 1–40.
12. See Rothermund, *Mahatma Gandhi*, 114.
13. 'In this theodicy of the disprivileged, the moralistic quest serves as a device for compensating a conscious or unconscious desire for vengeance …. [O]nce a religious conception of compensation has arisen, suffering may take on the quality of the religiously meritorious.' M. Weber, in *The Sociology of Religion*, cited in Owen, *Maturity and Modernity*, 104. Owen observes that 'indeed, the emergence of the theodicy of misfortune is tied by Weber to the movement from a militarised peasantry to a de-militarised plebeian strata: "Here and only here plebeian strata become exponents of a rational religious ethic"' (104). The strongly devotional elements in nationalist mobilizations plus the presence in Punjab of demobilized soldiers from the British Indian Army gives Weber's depictions a strong correspondence with Indian political reality in 1918–21.
14. For the correspondence between Gandhi and Tagore on the Bihar earthquake, see S. Bhattacharya (ed.). 2008. *The Mahatma and the Poet: Letters and Debates between Gandhi and Tagore 1915–1941*, New Delhi: National Book Trust India, 158–61.
15. *Harijan*, 29 September 1940. M. Gandhi. 1999. *The Collected Works of Mahatma Gandhi*, New Delhi: Publications Division Government of India, vol. 79, 257. Henceforth, *CWMG*.
16. Gandhi, 'Sikh Awakening', 13 March 1921. O.P. Ralhan and S.K. Sharma. 1994. *Documents on Punjab*, vol. 6, part 1, *Sikh Politics (1919–1926)*, New Delhi: Anmol Publications, 42–48.
17. See 'Report of the Congress Guru-ka-Bagh Inquiry Committee', in O.P. Ralhan and S.K. Sharma, *Documents on Punjab*, vol. 7, *Sikh Politics (Guru-ka-Bagh Morcha)*, New Delhi: Anmol Publications, 13–25.
18. From Andrews' press communiqué, in Ralhan and Sharma, *Documents on Punjab*, vol. 7, 1–8.
19. Ralhan and Sharma, *Documents on Punjab*, vol. 6, part 1, 233, 101.
20. See correspondence between Mahatma Gandhi and the SGPC, in Ralhan and Sharma, *Documents on Punjab*, vol. 6, 126–51.
21. Ralhan and Sharma, *Documents on Punjab*, vol. 6, 243.
22. R. Gandhi. 2004. *Ghaffar Khan: Nonviolent Badshah of the Pakhtuns*, New Delhi: Penguin-Viking, 83.
23. J.V. Bondurant. 1965 (1958). *Conquest of Violence: the Gandhian Philosophy of Conflict*, Berkeley: University of California Press, 139.
24. Bondurant, *Conquest of Violence*, 143.
25. D.G. Tendulkar. 1961. *Mahatma: Life of Mohandas Karamchand Gandhi*. New Delhi: Government of India, Ministry of Information and Broadcasting, Publications Division, vol. 4, 303–304.
26. Bondurant, *Conquest of Violence*, 138.
27. See M. Banerjee. 2000. *The Pathan Unarmed: Opposition and Memory in the North West Frontier*, Karachi and New Delhi: Oxford University Press, 145–66.

28. Bondurant, *Conquest of Violence*, 136.
29. Bondurant, *Conquest of Violence*, 140.
30. Banerjee, *The Pathan Unarmed*, 2.
31. R. Sankrityayan. 1957. *Veer Chandra Singh Garhwali*, Allahabad: Kitab Mahal, 129–31.
32. Bondurant, *Conquest of Violence*, 138.
33. Sankrityayan, *Veer Chandra Singh Garhwali*, 113.
34. R. Rao. 2007. *Kanthapura*, Delhi: Orient Paperbacks: 39–41. I am indebted to my friend Abhishekara, Ph.D. student from Jawaharlal Nehru University, for calling my attention to this novel.
35. Rao, *Kanthapura*, 170–71.
36. See C. Markovits. 2007. *The Calcutta Riots of 1946*, retrieved 10 April 2009 from Online Encyclopedia of Mass Violence, http://www.massviolence.org/The-Calcutta-Riots-of-1946. My late father, Lt. Col. E.J. Simeon, was an Indian Army officer stationed in Fort William, Calcutta in August 1946, and a witness to these events. He was convinced of the responsibility of the political leadership.
37. See the interviews with residents of Noakhali in R. Gandhi. 2006. *Mohandas: A True Story of a Man, His People, and an Empire*, New Delhi: Penguin-Viking, 591–93.
38. D. Dalton. 1970. 'Gandhi during Partition: A Case Study in the Nature of Satyagraha', in C.H. Philips and M.D. Wainwright (eds), *The Partition of India: Policies and Perspectives 1935–1947*, London: George Allen and Unwin, 222 to 244, fn. 5 and 6, 234.
39. See R. Gandhi, *Mohandas*, 636–37; and Philips and Wainwright, *The Partition of India*, 235–38.
40. *The Statesman*, 6 September, 1947.
41. Speech at prayer meeting in Bombay, 11 March 1946; *CWMG*, vol. 90, 64.
42. Extract from a conversation in Calcutta on 4 September 1947, reported by N.K. Bose in *Harijan*, 14 September 1947; *CWMG*, vol. 96, 335. *Goonda* is the Hindi word for hooligan.
43. A neologism that can roughly be translated as 'Gandhi-like behaviour'.
44. G. Orwell. 1949. *Reflections on Gandhi*, retrieved 10 April 2009 from: http://orwell.ru/library/reviews/gandhi/english/e_gandhi
45. From the memoir of G.D. Khosla, cited in R. Gandhi, *Mohandas*, 654.
46. Cited in R. Gandhi, *Mohandas*, 633.
47. M.K. Gandhi, *CWMG*, vol. 97, 420.
48. 'Gandhi rejected violence on four grounds: the ontological, the epistemological, the moral and the practical. Being a manifestation of *Brahman*, every living being was divine. Taking life was therefore sacrilegious and a form of deicide.' B. Parekh. 1989. *Colonialism, Tradition and Reform: An Analysis of Gandhi's Political Discourse*, New Delhi: Sage Publications, 155.
49. 'To write a treatise on the science of ahimsa is beyond my powers. I am not built for academic writings. Action is my domain, and what I understand, according to my lights, to be my duty, and whatever comes my way, I do. All my action is actuated by the spirit of service. Let anyone who can systematise ahimsa into a science do so, if indeed it lends itself to such treatment .... The world does not hunger for shastras. What it craves, and will always crave, is sincere action .... No man has ever been able to describe God fully. The same is true of ahimsa.' Gandhi, *Harijan*, 3 March 1946; *CWMG*, vol. 90, 1–2.
50. M.K. Gandhi. 2003 (1909). *Hind Swaraj, or Indian Home Rule*, Ahmedabad: Navjivan Publishing House, 60.
51. In a millennium poll in 2000, Mahatma Gandhi was voted the greatest man of the past thousand years by readers of the BBC News website – BBC report dated 14 November 2005.

CHAPTER 2

AN UNLIKELY CHARISMATIC LEADER
D.F. Malan in a Weberian Light

Lindie Koorts

Introduction

It was a May night in 1948. The winter chill was setting in, as all across South Africa people huddled around their radio sets, listening intently to the election results pouring in, from one constituency to the next. The picture that emerged led to euphoria and astonishment. *Time* magazine reported: '[i]n rural Burghersdorp a pro-Malan voter had got so excited over the election returns on his radio that he ran out firing his rifle in the air, accidentally shot down his antenna. A Smuts supporter kicked his radio to smithereens and had to be given sedatives by the doctor'.[1]

As the news reached London:

> politicians, bankers and bureaucrats, answering an insistent jangle of telephones, turned pale at what they heard. South African gold shares broke wide open on the stock exchange, tumbled more than $300 million. Winston Churchill augustly gloomed: 'a great world statesman has fallen, and with him his country will undergo a period of anxiety and perhaps a temporary eclipse'.[2]

Field Marshall Jan Christiaan Smuts, hero of the Anglo-Boer War, signatory to the Treaty of Versailles, member of the British war cabinet, international statesman and co-founder of the United Nations, was defeated.[3] It was the end of an era, 'The age of the Generals'.[4]

The podgy-looking man, who felled the great oak tree that was Jan Smuts, could not have been further removed from this image. Dr Daniël

---

Francois Malan seemed stern and severe. His eyes were obscured by thick black-rimmed glasses. He looked anything but a warrior. To historians, his victory seemed inexplicable.

And thus, international observers and the scholars who followed them scrambled to explain Smuts' defeat. And there were explanations aplenty. The most popular explanation was that the slogan of apartheid, pandering to the Afrikaners' 'inherent' racism, was responsible for the Nationalists' victory. Nelson Mandela immortalized this assumption in his autobiography, *Long Walk to Freedom*:

> The Nationalists, led by Dr Daniel Malan, a former minister of the Dutch Reformed Church and a newspaper editor, were a party animated by bitterness – bitterness towards the English, who had treated them as inferiors for decades, and bitterness towards the African, who the Nationalists believed was threatening the prosperity and purity of Afrikaner culture .... [During the 1948 election] the National Party's campaign centred on the 'swart gevaar' (the 'black danger'), and they fought the election on the twin slogans of 'Die kaffer op sy plek' ('the nigger in his place') and 'Die koelies uit die land' ('the coolies out of the country') – coolies being the Afrikaner's derogatory term for Indians.[5]

But, as was later pointed out, according to a survey of newspaper articles and election materials, there never were such slogans.[6]

Scholarly analyses of the election results pointed to the fact that Malan's National Party did not win a majority of the votes cast, but a majority of parliamentary seats. This was as a result of the electoral system. Smuts' predominantly English-speaking supporters were concentrated in the cities, while the sparsely populated rural constituencies, where Afrikaans-speaking Malan supporters resided, weighed more in parliament, since rural constituencies did not require as many voters as those in the urban areas.[7] However, this explanation became problematic in the light of the twofold swing that enabled Malan's victory: Transvaal farmers, who had previously voted for Smuts, deserted him, giving Malan fifteen new rural constituencies, as did Afrikaner mine and steel workers in Johannesburg and Pretoria, who were responsible for Nationalist victories in eight new urban constituencies.[8]

Other factors were added to the mix, such as irritations about wartime measures that were still in place.[9] It was noted that the National Party machine was far more efficient in its campaigning than Smuts' complacent and overly confident United Party.[10] These and a myriad of other smaller factors, which are not listed for the sake of brevity, resulted in the 1948 election being perceived as not so much a victory for Malan as a defeat for Smuts. The event became an aberration, an opportunity to speculate on the 'what ifs'.

None of these analyses paid attention to the man who won the 1948 election. Scholars failed to historicize Malan's leadership style and public persona, with the result that he has never been considered as a charismatic leader. However, Weber's description of the charismatic leader brings his character to life. It enables us to shed a completely new light on the matter, adding a new dimension to the event and facilitating a reappraisal of Malan and the Afrikaner nationalist movement. In addition to this, Malan's grim public persona forces us to re-examine our connotation of 'charisma'.

Weber's Description of the Charismatic Leader

Weber's remarks on the charismatic leader are scattered throughout his various publications. None of these contains a single, authoritative definition and they encompass a number of contradictions.[11] However, for the purposes of biography, a theory needs to provide a framework, not a cage. In spite of Weber's vagueness, the biographer can use his theory of the charismatic leader to enlighten our understanding of a particular character, without compromising on uniqueness or context.

This is particularly true in the case of D.F. Malan. It is difficult to grasp how, in a post-Second World War context, the South African population could support a policy behind which pariah-status loomed. However, if we consider the fact that the Afrikaners' experience of the war's horrors was extremely limited and that the policy was presented to them by a charismatic leader, a man whom they trusted above all else, their acceptance of the policy of apartheid becomes more comprehensible.[12]

The concept of a charismatic leader begs definition, especially in an age when the word *charisma* evokes images of glittering and highly likeable celebrities. In contrast, Weber's description seems rather sobering. Charismatic authority is:

> the authority of the extraordinary and personal *gift of grace* (charisma), the absolutely personal devotion and personal confidence in revelation, heroism, or other qualities of individual leadership. This is 'charismatic' domination, as exercised by the prophet or – in the field of politics – by the elected war lord, the plebiscitarian ruler, the great demagogue, or the political party leader.[13]

The figure of the prophet is the key to understanding Malan's leadership style in general and is, in particular, the link that binds him to Weber's charismatic leader. It is therefore necessary to understand Weber's conception of the prophet. According to Weber, the prophet is 'a purely individual bearer of charisma, who by virtue of his mission proclaims a religious doctrine or divine commandment'.[14] This, along with his conscious identification with the Biblical prophet, Elijah, formed the basis of Malan's approach to politics.

Weber added further clarity to the image by providing a list of characteristics that typified the charismatic leader. Charismatic leaders are natural leaders who emerge during times of distress. They are outsiders, being neither office holders nor incumbents. They have special gifts of body and spirit which are regarded as supernatural. They demand obedience and support by virtue of their mission. Charismatic leaders do not engage in their mission for economic gain and often reject rational, but undignified, economic conduct. For this reason, Weber believed that the prophet provided the ideal metaphor for the charismatic leader: a person who exudes heavenly grace and godlike strength. Such a leader is not concerned with leading his people through the peaceful struggle of humankind against nature, but rather the violent struggle between human communities.[15]

In practical terms, charismatic leaders are likely to present themselves in religious language, as people who have been given a mission by higher powers. They feel called to their task and dedicate their lives to its service. They have the ability to play on slumbering dissatisfaction. There is an important dynamic between the leader's own originality and the appeal to existing beliefs and prejudices. Such a person, who promises calm in a world of chaos, answers an unfulfilled need. However, there is a tragic element: the charismatic leader's diagnosis of a problem is often oversimplified, creating the impression that he is more capable of effecting change than reality determines.[16] This description seems to run like a narrative of Malan's career, which challenges us to revise our perception of charisma. Could a 'dour, unsmiling man'[17] like Malan have been a Weberian charismatic leader? Does this change our connotation of 'charisma'?

The Calling

D.F. Malan was born on 22 May 1874 in the Cape Colony. By birth he was a British subject, by background, an Afrikaner nationalist. His ancestors were French Huguenots, a heritage of which both he and his deeply religious family were very proud. The family practised the Evangelical Reformed faith and were members of the Dutch Reformed Church.[18] The Cape Colony of the late-nineteenth century was decidedly Evangelical and a number of religious revivals swept through its towns, including Malan's home town.[19] Children were encouraged to dedicate their hearts to the Lord, regardless of their age, and an emotional display of their deeply felt faith was encouraged.[20] In this atmosphere, Malan's parents raised him with the belief that every person had a unique, God-given calling.[21] Unlike his peers, Malan never recounted a particular moment during which he dedicated himself to God. But he did experience an intense awareness of having a special mission to fulfil.[22] This awareness would remain with him throughout the years. The twin concepts of 'calling' and 'mission' became the driving forces behind his career.

Apart from religious fervour, Malan's world was one in which Afrikaner nationalism was stirring. Through the course of the nineteenth century, the Afrikaners of the Western Cape, to whom he belonged, became increasingly anglicized and were generally tolerant of the British. Mastery of the English language was regarded as the hallmark of good breeding, giving one entry into polite society. However, the 1870s, which marked the beginning of South Africa's Industrial Revolution in the wake of the discovery of diamonds and later gold, were a turning point. The Cape Afrikaners became more aware of their blood ties to the *Voortrekkers*, their fellow Afrikaners who had moved to the northern interior, where they established the two Boer Republics, the Orange Free State and the Transvaal. These two states were locked in perpetual conflict with the British Empire. The Cape Afrikaners now began to realize the extent to which their own cultural traditions had been forced into the background.[23] This moved the young Malan, a theology student in the town of Stellenbosch, to take up the cause of Afrikaner nationalism and, in so doing, to make passionate pleas for the Afrikaners' identity to be upheld in the face of British cultural domination:

> Let us stand together, let us preserve our nationality and with our nationality our national character .... To preserve then our nationality and national character it is absolutely necessary that we keep in honour our history and our language, holding to our own to the very last, struggling to get our rights acknowledged and granted to the full, not from any sense of race hatred or prejudice to which some will ascribe our activity, but from a true sense of patriotism.[24]

Coming from a British subject, these were strong words indeed. They were a sign of the Afrikaner nationalist leader who was to come. As a student, Malan seemed apart from the crowd. He refrained from effusive displays of emotion, appearing as composed and balanced as 'a small scale in the chemistry laboratory'. He did not play any sport and he refused to read novels. He also showed no interest in the opposite sex.[25] This was due to a combination of intense youthful shyness and a continued awareness of the special calling that he had to fulfil. His self-imposed celibacy would last until the age of fifty-two and was strengthened by his identification with St Paul, who chose to remain celibate in order to devote his undivided attention to the Lord's work.[26] Even after his eventual marriage and the birth of his children, Malan was surrounded by women who gladly took the bulk of familial obligations upon themselves, thus enabling him to devote himself to the leadership of his political party.[27] This initial aversion to matrimony formed part of Weber's portrait of the charismatic leader. Because he is not bound to the routine of family life, the charismatic leader enjoys a greater measure of freedom in the pursuit of his cause. According to Weber, those who hold a prophetic charisma are often single.[28]

It is also important for the charismatic leader to possess the gift of rhetoric in order to rally his supporters to his call. In spite of his reserved nature, Malan was blessed with this special talent, which began to manifest itself during his student years.[29] As a result, he was elected as the president of his debating society[30] and would in later years be hailed as one of South Africa's greatest orators.[31]

When the Anglo-Boer War broke out in October 1899, the two Boer Republics tried to enlist the support of their kinsmen to the south by invading the northernmost regions of the Cape Colony and effectively forcing the Afrikaans-speaking inhabitants to join the Republican forces. Without this coercion, the Cape Afrikaners, torn between loyalty to queen or kinsman, did not dare to join their northern brothers, as they faced confiscation of property and death for treason if caught by the British.[32]

The outbreak of the war coincided with Malan's completion of his studies. Joining the war as a rebel was not a consideration. In 1900, instead of joining the church, he left South Africa to study at the University of Utrecht, where he obtained a Doctorate in Divinity. His absence during the war would set him apart from the men who would lead South Africa for the first half of the twentieth century.

It was in the Netherlands that Malan refined his ideals with regards to leadership, as well as his calling. In the house of his mentor, Professor J.J.P. Valeton junior, he found his role model: the prophet Elijah. Thus, like Weber, Malan began to look to the prophet as the ideal leader. Valeton's description of Elijah formed the basis of this model:

> Elijah is the narrow man, one who has but one end in mind and who sacrifices everything for its sake. Elijah is intolerant and hard, yes, great and impressive, but in a manner which inspires respect but also indignation. He sacrifices everything for an idea, human lives are nothing to him, think of the 400 prophets he had executed at Carmel; also the interests of the state are nothing

to him. What a man! A gale wind, a bolt of lightning, all-conquering and all-destroying, to be admired from a distance and when close by, to be avoided as far as possible.[33]

The image of such a figure found resonance with Malan, the student of theology. It permeated his perceptions of leadership and manhood. In 1911, Malan formulated the image of an ideal man, which bore the mark of the prophet:

A man is a personality, one who is not like the tide moved and swayed by every wind, but who can assert himself on every terrain. A man is someone who can leave his mark on others, because he has his own character. He is someone who has beliefs, who knows what he wants, who is aware that he stands for something. A man is someone who knows that there are principles that he must hold on to, no matter what the costs, and who will, if necessary, willingly give his life for his principles. That is a man.[34]

That Elijah was the model for this portrait was clear from another speech Malan delivered a mere two months later, in which he called Elijah the 'man of steel', who refused to compromise any of his principles and who did not flinch in the face of Ahab's power and Jezebel's fury, in spite of being alone and unarmed.[35] It was with the image of the lone, but fearless prophet in mind, that Malan formulated his own divine mission, which would remain unchanged throughout the four decades that spanned his political career:

I have undertaken to myself to use my weak powers to work for the Afrikaner nation and not to budge one inch from my path. To make it clear to the nation that God is also the Sovereign of its history and that He needs to be recognized as such in the national life, is as much an extension of God's kingdom as it is to preach the Gospel to the heathens. But lately nothing has become clearer to me than that the man who wants to work for the Afrikaner nation's ability to develop itself on its own terms, so that it can be an own nation with its own history, language, character and ideals, that would in its own manner embody the Kingdom of God in itself, that that man would be held up by heavy resistance, not least from his own nation. He will be seen as an extremist, a fanatic, one who is narrow-minded.[36]

Malan's words were prophetic indeed. He accurately predicted the manner in which his persona would be regarded by his opponents and by successive generations.

The Crisis

Malan returned to South Africa in 1905 and entered the church. Two years later, Afrikaners in the two former republics, which were now British colonies, were enfranchised. In the elections that followed, they elected men who had fought as generals in the Anglo-Boer War, the most prominent being Generals Louis Botha and Jan Smuts from the Transvaal, and General J.B.M. Hertzog from the Orange River Colony.[37] When, in 1910, the four British colonies were amalgamated into the Union of South Africa, General Louis Botha became Prime Minister, with Generals Smuts and Hertzog as members of his cabinet.[38] These three generals would hold power in South Africa until D.F. Malan's ascension in 1948.

Botha's first years as head of the South African government were characterized by a general sense of optimism, as he sought to bring the English and Afrikaans-speaking communities together through a policy of conciliation. It was not to last. His cabinet was torn apart only two years after its formation – by his fellow Boer War general, Barry Hertzog. Hertzog's campaigns for equal language rights, which existed on paper but were disregarded in practice, as well as his controversial statements about South Africa's relationship with the British Empire, caused unwanted tension in a government that was trying to smooth over differences of opinion. As a result, Hertzog was forced from the cabinet in late 1912.[39] In January 1914, Hertzog established the National Party in the Free State Province, hoping that the other provinces would follow suit. Afrikaner nationalists in the Transvaal followed Hertzog's example, but there was no response in the Cape or Natal. With his tiny party showing no growth, Hertzog felt despondent and ready to abandon all efforts to build the organization.[40] It was the crisis sparked off by the First World War that generated support for the party and brought D.F. Malan into politics.

Louis Botha's government, in an effort to prove its loyalty to the British Empire, agreed to invade German South West Africa. To large sections of the Afrikaner population, still bitter about their defeat at the hands of the British only twelve years earlier, fighting in Britain's war against a power that had been sympathetic towards them in their own struggle was unacceptable. A number of highly respected Boer War generals now led a rebellion against the government, which became known as the 1914 Rebellion. Louis Botha's decision to use only Afrikaner troops against the rebels caused an outcry, as fellow Afrikaners were forced to fire on each other. The Rebellion was soon squashed, but not without leaving enormous rifts within the Afrikaner community and producing a number of martyrs, the most prominent of whom was Jopie Fourie: an officer in the government forces who failed to resign his commission before rebelling. His band of rebels inflicted casualties on government troops and therefore, after his capture, he was taken to Pretoria where he was tried and sentenced to death.[41]

Fourie's end marked D.F. Malan's beginning. Malan had begun to draw attention to himself through his widely publicized travels to visit Afrikaner congregations north of the Limpopo River,[42] and especially as a language activist. However, the Second Afrikaans Language Movement, which lobbied for the replacement of Dutch with Afrikaans, was the most politicized activity that Malan could engage in. Dutch Reformed clergymen were not allowed to participate in party politics.[43]

On the day that Fourie's sentence was to be announced, Malan was in Pretoria and agreed to draw up a petition pleading for clemency and to lead a delegation to General Jan Smuts. However, attempts to locate Smuts proved futile and Jopie Fourie was executed. In the eyes of most Afrikaners, the act of executing one of their own became an even greater sacrilege because the sentence was carried out on a Sunday.[44] Malan's attempt to plead for Fourie's life added to his moral stature and would be played upon throughout his political career.

However, Malan's opening hour was not over yet. News came pouring in that the Dutch Reformed Church, the most prominent of all Afrikaner institutions and the only one to have survived the Anglo-Boer War, faced a schism. Some congregations were censuring the rebels, while others did the same to government troops. Following the initiative of Malan and a few other clergymen, the churches of the four provinces agreed to a national meeting in order to prevent such a catastrophe and to provide clear guidance to their followers. Malan was asked to draw up resolutions for the meeting to adopt,[45] which were accepted and prevented the church from being torn apart.[46]

Malan's resolutions exhorted the nation to respect worldly authorities in accordance with the Biblical maxim (except for extenuating circumstances) and called on the worldly authorities to investigate the grievances that compelled its citizens to take up arms. He called on ministers of the church to refrain from political involvement (except in extenuating circumstances) and also on the church not to censure any of its members.[47] But he also used the opportunity to impart to the church its divine mission:

> [O]ur Dutch Reformed Churches in South Africa, apart from their general calling as Christian churches, have also received a particular calling from God for the Dutch-speaking Afrikaner nation with whose existence they are so intimately bound. Therefore they must always regard it as their duty to be national themselves, to guard over our particular national interests and to teach our nation about its history and formation at the hand of God and, furthermore,

to keep the realization of a national calling and destiny alive within the Afrikaner nation. Only therein is the spiritual, moral and material advancement and strength of a nation to be found.[48]

Malan was now a prominent figure on the national stage, a nationalist voice of reason at a time of crisis. By the end of 1914, Afrikaner nationalists in the Western Cape, particularly those in Cape Town and Stellenbosch, began organizing themselves. They were determined to advance their cause and to gain legitimacy by placing a formidable and respected figure at the head of their movement. Their first step was to establish a pro-Hertzog newspaper in the Western Cape and they decided that Malan, who was widely respected as a theologian-philosopher, had to become its editor.[49] The second step would be the establishment of a National Party in the Cape, with Malan as its leader. However, persuading Malan to rescind his vows to the church and leave the pulpit proved to be difficult. Initial attempts failed.[50] Determined to add his stature to the movement, they launched a letter-writing campaign. Respected politicians, clergy, intellectuals and the like responded by writing a flood of letters to Malan, asking him to rescue the nation during its hour of need.[51] These letters portrayed Malan as a Messiah figure; '[f]rom all sides, people are asking for a leader and everywhere you are being pointed out as the only one to have displayed the gifts of determination, knowledge of human nature, discernment and tact at a time of crisis'.[52]

Finally, as a result of pleas from fellow ministers of the church as well as prominent Afrikaner leaders such as the former president of the Orange Free State, M.T. Steyn,[53] and the imprisoned rebel leader, General C.R. de Wet,[54] Malan relented and agreed to become the first editor of *De Burger* and to enter politics. He left the pulpit with a dramatic farewell sermon, in which he stated the ultimate aim of his mission: '[That] the entire Afrikaner nation will stand before the face of God, just as we so dearly wish to see it, Christian and national and free. And then it will be united in its innermost being. But it will be a unity that is, above all, to the glory of God.'[55]

His decision was welcomed enthusiastically and, of course, the sacrifice of his career in the church added even more weight to the occasion. However, there was somewhat less enthusiasm from General Hertzog and his inner circle. Malan entered their ranks as a political outsider, but his background as a clergyman and language activist gave him instant legitimacy, to which was added his double power base as newspaper editor and leader of the Cape National Party, which was established in the course of 1915. Malan brought a new element into the party, one that would draw a new generation of Afrikaner intellectuals to him and finally overtake Hertzog and his allies: an integration of the Christian faith and Afrikaner nationalism, which, for our purposes, can loosely be described as Christian nationalism.[56]

Under Malan's guidance, *De Burger* was so Christian national that it was regarded as suitable for Sunday reading. It attracted the talents of idealistic young Afrikaner intellectuals who had recently graduated from universities in Europe. *De Burger* became a 'views paper', rather than a newspaper, publishing regular contributions by the language activists of the Second Afrikaans Language Movement.[57] However, Malan played hardly any role in its administrative management. After his parliamentary career took off, he did not even have an office at the paper and seldom wrote editorials. The general public was blissfully unaware of this state of affairs. Malan's moral stature reassured *De Burger's* subscribers that the newspaper was of a sound and wholesome origin. In effect, Malan himself became a valuable 'brand name'.[58] This remained the case throughout his political career. Malan's involvement in administration was always extremely limited. A survey of the minutes of his party's purely administrative meetings over a period of two years reveals that he was absent as often as he present.[59] He was elected to a myriad of committees and organizations, but the purpose of his election was limited to the use of his 'brand name'.[60] Instead, he would appear on the political stage at crucial moments, deliver a rousing and inspiring speech and then leave the inspired to turn the ideal into a reality.

The Sacrifice

For nearly two decades after his entry into politics, Malan built his power base, which served to strengthen Hertzog's position. When the National Party won the general elections in 1924, Malan became a member of Hertzog's cabinet. But it was yet again another national crisis that thrust him to the fore and set him on the road to his victory in 1948. When the New York stock market crashed in October 1929, it dragged the rest of the world along with it into the Great Depression. South Africa's position was exacerbated by a devastating drought in the early 1930s. In what became known as the 'Gold Standard Crisis', Prime Minister J.B.M. Hertzog, in a politically motivated attempt to demonstrate South Africa's independence, refused to follow Britain's example in abandoning the Gold Standard, thus effectively strangling an already weakened agricultural sector, which was unable to compete on the export market due to the strength of the South African pound.[61]

Hertzog's decision proved to be disastrous and in the political crisis that ensued, the South African government was finally forced to abandon the Gold Standard in December 1932. In the aftermath of the crisis, Hertzog became convinced that his position was so damaged that the party would not survive the next election. He thus engaged in secret negotiations with the Leader of the Opposition, General Jan Smuts, to form a coalition – without consulting his own party caucus.[62] When Hertzog finally revealed his plans, Malan not only regarded such a move as unthinkable on principle, but was also furious at being presented with a *fait accompli*. He opposed coalition, regardless of his cabinet seat, which he had to sacrifice.[63]

As Weber noted, in order for a politician to live for his cause, it is best not to be financially dependent on the income generated by politics.[64] Malan, however, faced financial peril, as the forfeit of his cabinet seat left him dependent on his relatively meagre parliamentary income, which he could lose at the next election. It did not deter him from leaving the cabinet. It was much to his relief and gratitude that, after taking the plunge, he discovered that a wealthy friend had begun to deposit money in his account. This income, which would later come from a trust fund after his friend's death, would enable Malan to navigate the political wilderness.[65] Malan's personal sacrifice of his position for the sake of his principles added to his moral authority, in the same manner that his sacrifice of his career in the church had done in 1915.

However, Malan was also an intelligent politician. He was able to risk the financial repercussions of sacrificing his cabinet seat, but the same could not be said of the average member of parliament – especially during an economic depression. They had to choose between principles and survival and would doubtlessly pick the latter. Malan therefore decided to support the coalition officially, but under protest, while appointing himself as a watchdog. Only once his followers were assured of their parliamentary salaries for another term, could he dare to break away.[66]

The 1933 elections therefore took place under the banner of coalition. The two major parties, Hertzog's predominantly Afrikaans-speaking National Party and Smuts' predominantly English-speaking South African Party, agreed not to oppose each other in the various constituencies, thus returning the majority of candidates to parliament unopposed.[67] Once parliamentary salaries were no longer a concern, Malan could rely on the unequivocal support of those who had brought him into politics: the Cape nationalists. He also commanded the support of *Die Burger*, which had become a powerful press organ and which remained loyal to him, instead of Hertzog.[68] As Weber noted, 'every politician of consequence has needed influence over the press'.[69]

From his position as self-appointed watchdog, Malan kept a close eye on the coalition, making it clear that he would not accept a fusion of the two parties. However, as coalition inevitable evolved into fusion and Malan and Hertzog's final attempts at reconciliation failed, the only option, as far as the Cape nationalists were concerned, was to break away and to form a new party. But once again, they knew that it was impossible without Malan's moral authority. After much soul searching, which replicated his inner battle when he left the church nineteen years before, Malan reprised the role that he had played in 1915, insisting that the Afrikaners needed a party that would preserve their language, their faith and their traditions.[70] It was during such moments, at a time of crisis, when the need for a new direction was keenly felt, that his star shone brightest. The new party, which became known as the Purified National Party, was almost entirely composed of Malan's power base in the Cape, which would continue to dominate the broader organization until his retirement in 1954.[71] Malan's followers from the northern provinces were members of a younger generation who had not experienced the Anglo-Boer War and who did not possess their elders' reverence for the Boer War generals. Within a mere fourteen years, the fledgling party would grow large enough to take control of the country.[72]

The Movement

These events coincided with the establishment of a number of Afrikaner cultural organizations during the late 1920s and early 1930s, which would mushroom into a broad Afrikaner nationalist movement through the course of the next two decades. Hertzog welcomed these organizations at first, but his ardour soon cooled when he realized that they leaned in a Christian national direction and did not regard cultural issues as distinct from politics.[73]

The organizations were led by a new generation of young Afrikaner intellectuals, fresh from their studies on the European continent.[74] They constituted an intellectual elite and rallied around Malan and his new party in the same manner as the young intellectuals who had gathered around his newspaper after its establishment in 1915. These young men would spearhead and drive the Afrikaner nationalist movement into a swelling wave for the next two decades by forming a nationalist coalition with the Afrikaner working class and tackling pervasive Afrikaner poverty as a nationalist project.[75]

The movement manifested itself in the form of various organizations which encompassed nearly every conceivable public sphere. It had two major prongs: cultural and economic. Thus, on the cultural front, a range of organizations busied themselves with wide-ranging issues, from the practical implementation of Afrikaans as one of the country's two official languages (in practice, English was still dominant) to an Afrikaner alternative to the Boy Scouts. These cultural organizations attracted a significant number of teachers, who would in turn teach an entire generation of young Afrikaners a sacralized version of their national history.[76] In effect, Malan's ideal that the nation be taught to see God's hand in its history was realized in classrooms across the country.

The cultural movement reached its height during the 1938 centenary celebrations of the Great Trek. The celebrations took the form of a symbolic ox-wagon trek, which began in Cape Town and moved northwards. The wagons eventually parted ways; one group headed for Pretoria, where the foundation stone of the *Voortrekker* monument would be laid, while the other group would gather at Bloodriver, the site of a historic battle between the *Voortrekkers* and the Zulus. This was scheduled for 16 December 1938, a hundred years to the day that the Battle of Bloodriver took place.[77]

The celebrations evoked feverish euphoria that bordered on mass hysteria. The intellectual elite's ideals were embraced by the masses. Speeches made in cities, towns and villages across the country carried the same themes: Afrikaner unity and the rescue of the Afrikaner poor, especially in the face of African urbanization, behind which loomed the 'threat' of miscegenation.[78] Malan's National Party managed to seize the initiative from Hertzog's government and became associated with the spirit and ideals of the celebrations.[79] It was especially obvious as the celebrations neared their climax on 16 December. Hertzog and the governor-general were to attend the laying of the foundation stone in Pretoria. But their presence meant that *God Save the King* had to be sung at the occasion. This evoked a storm of protest and Hertzog was bombarded by letters, telegrams and petitions imploring him not to defile the day through the singing of the British national anthem.[80] Hertzog eventually boycotted the event and spent the day on his farm,[81] while at Bloodriver, Malan gave one of the most rousing speeches of his career, taking up the cause of the Afrikaner poor. He implored them, in the face of rapid Afrikaner urbanization, to regard the cities as their new battleground, their second Bloodriver, where the most impoverished of Afrikaners would have to fight for the entire nation's survival against overwhelming African numbers.[82]

The 1938 centenary provided an impetus to the second aspect of the Afrikaner nationalist movement: the economic movement. Within months after the celebrations, an economic congress was organized to address Afrikaner poverty. It was decided not to resort to classical Victorian-style charity, but rather to capture the economic sphere for the Afrikaner by transforming the liberal-individualistic nature of capitalism into an ethnic system that would benefit the people. Capitalism became *volkskapitalisme* or 'people's capitalism'. This was done, yet again, by establishing a myriad of organizations: an investment house, a bank, a chain store enabling Afrikaners to 'buy Afrikaans', a chamber of commerce catering to Afrikaner businessmen, trade unions operating on the basis of Christian national principles and an institute that mobilized funds to address pervasive Afrikaner poverty and dispensed bursaries to Afrikaner students to study trades and commerce.[83]

The significance of these organizations lay in the values they propagated: they were thoroughly Christian national, in keeping with the principles and ideals that Malan espoused, which stood in stark contrast to those of Hertzog and Smuts. The process was not uncomplicated and rivalry did ensue, especially as the clouds of war drew nearer.

In the wake of the Third Reich, a number of Afrikaner organizations, which drew their inspiration from Nazi Germany and effectively combined National Socialist Party principles with Christian nationalism, entered the political arena. Malan recognized them as competitors and set out to destroy them, making it clear that the National Party was to be the only political representative of Afrikaner unity. In yet another of his rousing speeches at a party conference, Malan took ownership of Afrikaner nationalism in its entirety and made it clear to his followers that the National Party was the 'Mother', without whom none of the other Afrikaner organizations could have existed. And as the 'Mother', the party was more than a political organization; 'we embody the two founding ideas without which an Afrikaner nation would never have been possible. The one is the Nationalist idea and the other is the idea of our restored Afrikaner-unity. It is we who have taken the idea of an own South African nationhood as a holy inheritance from the hands of our courageous ancestors.'[84]

The battle between the rival political organizations would last for at least another year, during which Malan displayed his skills as a master strategist in outmanoeuvring his competitors. By the end of the war, the National Party emerged as the sole representative of Afrikaner nationalism and, in effect, Malan became the figurehead of the entire Afrikaner nationalist movement in all its various manifestations.[85]

Malan the Prophet

Malan was the icon and personification of the value system of his time. His oratorical ability was legendary and even his critics acknowledged that he was one of South Africa's foremost speakers: a man with 'a deep vibrant voice',[86] an outstanding parliamentarian and one who could keep his Afrikaner audiences spellbound for up to two hours at a time.[87] Malan's speeches were characterized by an astounding clarity of thought. Equally impressive was his ability to formulate slogans and catchphrases that encapsulated his ideals and resonated with his followers, especially his famous: '*Glo in God, glo in u volk, glo in uself*' (Believe in God, believe in your nation, believe in yourself).[88]

His public persona was one of remoteness, much like the Biblical prophet, Elijah, whom he admired so much. An English journalist succeeded in capturing his image:

> As he rises from his desk to welcome you, slowly, gravely, you find yourself in the presence of a sombrely dressed elderly gentleman of medium height and running to weight; a tight-lipped man with powerful head, now bald, and pale: heavy, expressionless, clean-shaven features. He fixes you rather disconcertingly with flickering eyes through his glasses; a slow-moving man of sedentary habits ...[;] the general impression is rather formidable. It is one of solemnity, even severity. It does no injustice to the man or his philosophy. Stern Calvinist that he is, in unrelenting warfare against the world, the flesh and the devil. Publicly and privately, his reputation is one of uniform patience and courtesy to friend and foe, but he remains distant and unbending. He smiles rarely – and wanly – and the only indulgence he permits himself in his speeches is an occasional exercise in elaborate irony. Nevertheless, in a land of sunshine, where men laugh loudly, none – not even Smuts – enjoys higher prestige among his own people than this stern, implacable, isolated man of God.[89]

To his inner circle, Malan was renowned for his dry wit, but this talent was rarely employed on a political stage. With the expansion of the mass media in South Africa, a need was felt for political leaders to endear themselves to their followers. This was evident from a smattering of 'human interest' articles on Malan that appeared during the late 1940s and early 1950s. These articles would coincide with Malan's birthday and carry titles such as 'The Dr Malan whom most members of the public do not know: he loves animals, gardening ... and ice cream'[90] or 'The man behind the grim mask: anecdotes about South Africa's Prime Minister on the occasion of his eightieth birthday'.[91] They contained anecdotes from Malan's childhood or mundane details about his pets. Instances of his dry humour would be recounted, such as the occasion when an unnamed person wrote a letter to him, offering the party one hundred thousand pounds in return for adopting a particular point of policy. Malan circulated the letter to his party's members of parliament with a brief note in the margin: 'The £100,000 would also be all that we'll have.'[92] The articles abounded with tales about his inability to make small talk and his absent-mindedness while he concentrated on national affairs. In effect, attempts to reveal Malan's 'ordinariness' only served to emphasize his 'extraordinariness'. In so doing, the persona that Malan had built into an institution through the course of nearly four decades was strengthened.

By the 1948 election, Malan and the National Party had become the embodiment of the Afrikaners' ethnic identity and they voted accordingly.[93] The apartheid policy, as Malan presented it to his electorate, was directly linked to their holy calling and identity as Afrikaners. As Malan later explained, 'apartheid is mainly a positive and non-oppressive policy as implemented in our enlightened day and it is based on what the Afrikaner regards as his godly calling and privilege – to convert the heathens to Christianity without wiping out their national identity'.[94]

Unfortunately a discussion of the apartheid policy, and the perceptions of race that underlie it, is beyond our scope. It is important to note that scholars have concluded that in 1948, apartheid meant different things to different interest groups, each of which had its own expectations of the benefits they would derive from it. The word and the policy itself were ambiguous enough to accommodate these conflicting interests and versions and, contrary to popular belief, Malan and his party did not take office with a 'Grand Plan' of apartheid in hand.[95] Apartheid, as propagated by Malan, was based on a value system that had its origins in the Western Cape's slave society, the paternalism of British colonial rule and the Dutch Reformed Church's missions policy, which argued that Christianity did not necessitate cultural assimilation; rather, it was best that the different races be kept separate in order to preserve their God-given uniqueness.[96] It was the faith in which Malan was raised, in which he was educated and which he espoused throughout his career.[97] Malan succeeded in making apartheid a part of the Christian national value system, in the same manner that he had united Afrikaner nationalism and the Christian faith. The words he used to describe the policy gave reassurance to the average Afrikaner voter who might have had qualms in the face of a changing international context with a new international value system. Malan's election manifesto even sounded noble:

> The party's policy is based on the two fundamental principles of apartheid and trusteeship. As the words themselves indicate, this does not mean the oppression of the non-whites at all, but on the contrary, the eradication of racial tension through the recognition of their right to exist, their freedom to develop, paired with the nurturing of a spirit of self-respect and independence and providing them with the necessary support – but all on their own terrain and under the rule and guidance of the whites.[98]

Thus, the tragedy of the charismatic leader did indeed come to pass through an oversimplified solution to a very complex problem.

Conclusions

With the hindsight of a post-apartheid context, it is difficult to compre-
hend the Afrikaners' support for the policy of apartheid and their trust
in the unsmiling man who sold it to them. Weber's theory has enabled
us to historicize Dr D.F. Malan's leadership of the Afrikaner nationalist
movement. For the first time it has become clear that in 1948, it was a
Weberian charismatic leader who won the watershed election. Malan was
a representative of his followers' value system, a system that he consistently propagated for nearly four decades.

Malan built his leadership style on the Biblical prophets – the same
figures to whom Weber turned as a model of charismatic leadership. Malan's ideal of prophetic leadership was based on a personal recognition of
and identification with these figures and was driven by an inner belief of
having a divine mission to fulfil. His career followed the patterns of charismatic leadership that Weber identified: he was an outsider who entered
the political arena at a time of crisis. His exuded integrity and evoked
the trust of his followers, whom he was able to inspire with his mission
and rally to his call through his exceptional rhetoric. He remained aloof
from familial relations for a great part of his life in order to devote himself
to his calling and did not hesitate to make personal sacrifices that were
deemed by others to have adverse professional and financial implications.
Most importantly, Malan tapped into his followers' spiritual faith, a faith
which he shared with the utmost conviction and which he extended into
the realm of politics. His grim demeanour was not a handicap, but rather
contributed to his prophetic image, which worked to his political advantage. It set him apart and made him exceptional. In D.F. Malan's case, a
humourless façade formed part of his charisma. D.F. Malan might have
won the 1948 election on a technicality, but the results of this seeming
aberration would not be reversed for more than four decades. Instead,
support for Malan, his party and its policy grew and continued to grow,
long after he had exited the stage.

While Weber's picture of the charismatic leader has proven to be an
ideal tool in understanding the nature of D.F. Malan's leadership, a biographical study of Malan also exposes the shortcomings in Weber's un-
synthesized theory. Weber's description of the charismatic leader focuses
on the leader's inner conviction and his public image. It does not account
for changing circumstances which might warrant a new approach to a political issue – political leaders who are unable to move with the times disappear overnight. Weber also failed to consider the more prosaic realities
which a leader faces: power politics and internecine fighting, which are to
be found in most organizations and within political parties in particular.

In this respect, Weber does not necessarily provide the ideal framework for studying politics, but rather the ideal point of departure when examining leadership.

Notes

1. 'To Relieve the People', *Time*, 28 June 1948.
2. 'These Things Happen', *Time*, 7 June 1948.
3. T.R.H. Davenport and C. Saunders. 2000. *South Africa: A Modern History*, London: Macmillan, 223, 225, 229–32, 284, 342–43, 516–17.
4. D.W. Krüger. 1958. *The Age of the Generals: A Short Political History of the Union of South Africa, 1910–1948*, Johannesburg: Dagbreek Book Store, 8.
5. N. Mandela. 1995. *Long Walk to Freedom*, Johannesburg: Macdonald Purnell, 104.
6. H. Giliomee. 2003. 'The Making of the Apartheid Plan, 1929–1948', *Journal of Southern African Studies* 29(2), 373–92.
7. R. Ross. 1999. *A Concise History of South Africa*, Cambridge: Cambridge University Press, 114.
8. D. O'Meara. 1983. *Volkskapitalisme: Class, Capital and Ideology in the Development of Afrikaner Nationalism, 1934–1948*, Cambridge: Cambridge University Press, 226.
9. 'South African Elections', *The Times*, 26 May 1948.
10. Davenport and Saunders, *South Africa*, 370–71.
11. M.A. Toth. 1981. *The Theory of the Two Charismas*, Washington D.C.: University Press of America, 17–18.
12. Another factor that should be considered was white South Africa's fear of Africans' overwhelming numbers. The quest for 'survival' as the driving force behind Afrikaner politics has formed the underlying theme of H. Giliomee. 2004. *The Afrikaners: Biography of a People*, Cape Town: Tafelberg. D.F. Malan was able to play on this latent fear.
13. M. Weber. 1970. 'Politics as a Vocation', in H.H. Gerth and C.W. Mills (eds), *From Weber: Essays in Sociology*, London: Routledge & Kegan Paul, 79.
14. M. Weber. 1968. 'The Prophet', in S.N. Eisenstadt (ed.), *Max Weber on Charisma and Institution Building*, Chicago: University of Chicago Press, 253.
15. M. Weber. 1968. 'The Sociology of Charismatic Authority', in Eisenstadt, *Max Weber on Charisma and Institution Building*, 18–25.
16. M. Becker. 2006. 'Charisma tussen analyse en overgave, een inleiding', in M. Becker (ed.), *Charisma: de fascinatie van leiders*, Nijmegen: Damon Budel, 7–18.
17. C. Saunders and N. Southey. 2001. *Dictionary of South African History*, Cape Town: David Phillip, 107.
18. University of Stellenbosch, J.S. Gericke Library (herafter called US Library), Document Centre, D.F. Malan collection (hereafter called DFM), 1/1/32689, Danie Malan, 'Herhinneringe aan my Vader', 3.
19. P.B. van der Watt. 1980. *Die Nederduitse Gereformeerde Kerk*, Pretoria: N.G. Kerkboekhandel, 4, 15–20; P.G. Thirion. 1993. 'Die Nederduitse Gereformeerde Kerk van Riebeek-Wes, 1858–1948: 'n Ondersoek na standpunte wat ingeneem is en invloede wat uitgeoefen is', D. Theol. Thesis. Stellenbosch: University of Stellenbosch, 137, 143.
20. W.K. Hancock. 1962. *Smuts: The Sanguine Years, 1870–1919*, Cambridge: Cambridge University Press, 10–11; University of the Free State, Institute for Contemporary History (hereafter called INCH), PV 141, Oumatjie Stoffberg collection, File 37, 'Oumatjie Stoffberg vertel', 3.
21. US Library, DFM 1/1/84, D.F. Malan, 'Beweegredenen'; DFM, 1/1/32689, Danie Malan, 'Herhinneringe aan my Vader', 6.
22. US Library, DFM 1/1/32689, Danie Malan, 'Herhinneringe aan my Vader', 6.

23.   T.R.H. Davenport. 1966. *The Afrikaner Bond*, Cape Town: Oxford University Press, 2–3, 5–6, 8–9, 11.
24.   US Library, DFM 1/1/117, D.F. Malan, 'Our Situation'.
25.   G.G. Cilliers. 1955. 'Doktor Gawie Vertel...', *Die Stellenbosse Student: D.F. Malan uitgawe*, 22–23.
26.   US Library, DFM 1/1/32689, Danie Malan, 'Herhinneringe aan my Vader', 24; L. Korf. 2008. 'Behind Every Man: D.F. Malan and the Women in his Life, 1874–1959', *South African Historical Journal* 60(3), 403–4.
27.   Korf, 'Behind Every Man; US Library, H.B. Thom collection, 191. M.1. (2) Notes on conversation with D.F. Malan junior, 30 May 1978, Stellenbosch.
28.   Weber, 'The Sociology of Charismatic Authority', 21–22.
29.   US Library, DFM 1/1/3271, T.H. le Roux to B. Booyens, 7 November 1964.
30.   *Stellenbosch Students' Annual, 1897*, 17.
31.   M.E. Rothman. 1972. *My Beskeie Deel: 'n Outobiografiese Vertelling*, Cape Town: Tafelberg, 216; Giliomee, *The Afrikaners*, 414; US Library, DFM 1/1/2472, J.A. Gray, 'South Africa's New Voice', 23 April 1949.
32.   J.H. Snyman. 1979. *Die Afrikaner in Kaapland, 1899–1902*, Pretoria: Argief Jaarboek vir Suid-Afrikaanse Geskiedenis, 10–13, 61–62, 68, 72, 74.
33.   J.J.P. Valeton. 1909. 'De strijd tusschen Achab en Elia: voordracht gehouden in de paedagogische vereeniging van Christelijke Onderwijzers, te Utrecht 24 April 1900', in J.J.P. Valeton, *Oud-testamentische Voordrachten IV*, Nijmegen: Firma H. ten Hoet, 27 (translated from the original Dutch).
34.   US Library, DFM 1/1/303, D.F. Malan, 'Taal en Nationaliteit, 7 April 1911' (translated from the original Dutch).
35.   US Library, DFM 1/1/308, D.F. Malan, 'De Profeet Elia en zyne beteekenis voor den tegenwoordigen tyd', 16 June 1911, Stellenbosch.
36.   US Library, DFM 1/1/986, C.V. Nel to D.F. Malan, 2 March 1933: Excerpt from letter from D.F. Malan to C.V. Nel, 9 April 1903 (translated from the original Dutch).
37.   This was the name given to the Orange Free State after the Anglo-Boer War.
38.   Davenport and Saunders, *South Africa*, 254–55, 267.
39.   Davenport and Saunders, *South Africa*, 267–69.
40.   Giliomee, *The Afrikaners*, 370.
41.   Giliomee, *The Afrikaners*, 33, 380–82. It is important to note that recent research has uncovered a discrepancy between the rebel leaders' prevalent, but politicized, interpretation of the rebellion as a revolt against participation in Britain's war and the more prosaic reality of the rank-and-file rebels, who were impoverished Afrikaners, motivated by a combination of material factors and republican nostalgia, taking up arms against a government from which they felt alienated. See A. Grundlingh and S. Swart. 2009. *Radelose rebellie? Dinamika van die 1914–1915 Afrikanerrebellie*, Pretoria: Protea Boekhuis, 23–41, 53–66. D.F. Malan shared the leaders' interpretation and acted accordingly.
42.   D.F. Malan. 1913. *Naar Congoland: een reisbeschrijving*, Stellenbosch: Christen Studentevereniging.
43.   Davenport and Saunders, *South Africa*, 246–47.
44.   D.F. Malan. 1961. *Afrikaner-Volkseenheid en my ervarings op die pad daarheen*, Cape Town: Nasionale Boekhandel Beperk, 19–25.
45.   Malan, *Afrikaner-Volkseenheid*, 20–21, 26–27.
46.   *De Kerkbode*, 18 Maart 1915, 245–47.
47.   US Library, DFM 1/1/342, D.F. Malan, 'Concept Voorstellen'.
48.   US Library, DFM 1/1/342, D.F. Malan, 'Concept Voorstellen' (translated from the original Dutch).
49.   C.F.J. Muller. 1990. *Sonop in die Suide: Geboorte en Groei van die Nasionale Pers, 1915–1948*, Cape Town: Nasionale Boekhandel, 137–38.

50. B. Booyens. 1969. *Die lewe van D.F. Malan: die eerste veertig jaar*, Cape Town: Tafelberg Uitgewers, 298–301.
51. Muller, *Sonop in die Suide*, 138–39.
52. US Library, DFM 1/1/358, Dormehl to Malan, 21 April 1915 (translated from the original Afrikaans).
53. US Library, DFM 1/1/355, Steyn to Malan, 19 April 1915.
54. US Library, DFM 1/1/377, De Wet [e.a.] to Malan, 8 May 1915.
55. D.F. Malan. 1964. 'Dan kom ek om', in S.W. Pienaar (ed.), *Glo in U Volk: Dr. D.F. Malan as Redenaar, 1908–1954*, Cape Town: Tafelberg Uitgewers, 17 (translated from Afrikaans).
56. Muller, *Sonop in die Suide*, 150–51, 162, 184; L. Korf. 2007. 'Podium and/or Pulpit? D.F. Malan's Role in the Politicisation of the Dutch Reformed Church, 1900–1959', *Historia* 52(2), 214–38.
57. Muller, *Sonop in die Suide*, 138, 162, 183–84.
58. M.E. Rothman. 1972. *My Beskeie Deel: 'n outobiografiese vertelling*, Cape Town: Tafelberg Uitgewers, 215.
59. INCH, PV 27, File 1/3/2/2/1/1, 'Hoofbestuur en Daelikse Bestuur – Notule.
60. Such was his leadership of the *Afrikaanse Taal Vereniging* (Afrikaans Language Association) (ATV), his membership of the *Helpmekaar* (Mutual Assistance) Movement, as well as his membership of the *Afrikaner Broederbond* (Afrikaner Brotherhood).
61. O'Meara, *Volkskapitalisme*, 35–37; Giliomee, *The Afrikaners*, 404.
62. Davenport and Saunders, *South Africa*, 319–20.
63. Malan, *Afrikaner Volkseenheid*, 152–56.
64. Weber, 'Politics as a Vocation', 84–85.
65. Malan, *Afrikaner Volkseenheid*, 201–4.
66. Cape Archives Repository (hereafter called KAB), A.L. Geyer collection, A 1890/3, 'Persoonlike herinnerings uit die Koalisiestryd', 17–18.
67. H.B. Thom. 1988. *Dr. D.F. Malan en Koalisie*, Cape Town: Tafelberg Uitgewers, 138–42.
68. KAB, A.L. Geyer collection, A 1890/3, 'Persoonlike herinnerings uit die Koalisiestryd', 18–19.
69. Weber, 'Politics as a Vocation', 97.
70. For a comprehensive account of the Coalition and Fusion Crisis, see L. Korf. 2010. 'D.F. Malan: A Political Biography', D.Phil. Thesis. Stellenbosch: University of Stellenbosch, 294–349.
71. Giliomee, *The Afrikaners*, 408–9.
72. Davenport and Saunders, *South Africa*, 333.
73. T.D. Moodie. 1980. *The Rise of Afrikanerdom: Power, Apartheid and the Afrikaner Civil Religion*, Berkeley: University of California Press, 146.
74. Moodie, *The Rise of Afrikanerdom*, 154.
75. Giliomee, *The Afrikaners*, 415, 418.
76. Moodie, *The Rise of Afrikanerdom*, 151–53.
77. Moodie, *The Rise of Afrikanerdom*, 177–79, 197.
78. Moodie, *The Rise of Afrikanerdom*, 179–81; Afrikaanse Taal- en Kultuurvereniging. 1940. *Gedenkboek van die Ossewaens op die Pad van Suid-Afrika, Eeufees: 1838–1939*, Cape Town: Nasionale Pers Beperk, 64–70, 79–80, 101, 381–89.
79. Giliomee, *The Afrikaners*, 432–33.
80. National State Archives of South Africa (hereafter referred to as SAB), J.B.M. Hertzog collection, A32/47/160.
81. Giliomee, *The Afrikaners*, 433.
82. US Library, DFM, 1/1/1336, 'Die Bloedrivier Eeufees: Toespraak van Dr. D.F. Malan, 16 Des. 1938.'
83. Moodie, *The Rise of Afrikanerdom*, 202–6.

84. D.F. Malan. 1964. 'Die Party is die Moeder', in S.W. Pienaar (ed.), *Glo in U Volk: Dr. D.F. Malan as Redenaar, 1908–1954*, Cape Town: Tafelberg Uitgewers, 37–38 (translated from the original Afrikaans).

85. For a thoroughly researched and comprehensive account of the rivalry between the National Party and the Oxwagon Sentinel, see C. Marx. 2008. *Oxwagon Sentinel: Radical Afrikaner Nationalism and the History of the Ossewabrandwag*, Pretoria: University of South Africa Press; Korf, 'D.F. Malan', 401–13.

86. US Library, DFM 1/1/2472, J.A. Grey, 'South Africa's New Voice', 23 April 1949.

87. Giliomee, *The Afrikaners*, 415.

88. D.F. Malan. 1964. 'Boodskap vir die Toekoms', in S.W. Pienaar (ed.), *Glo in U Volk: Dr. D.F. Malan as Redenaar, 1908–1954*, Cape Town: Tafelberg Uitgewers, 238.

89. US Library, DFM 1/1/2472, J.A. Gray, 'South Africa's New Voice', 23 April 1949.

90. J.J.J. Scholtz. 1947. 'Die Dr. Malan wat die meeste lede van die publiek nie ken nie: Hy is lief vir diere, tuinmaak … en roomys', *Die Burger*, 24 May (translated from the original Afrikaans).

91. S.J. Kleu. 1954. 'Die man agter die stroewe masker: Staaltjies oor SA se Eerste Minister by geleentheid van sy tagtigste verjaardag', *Die Burger*, 22 May (translated from the original Afrikaans).

92. Scholtz, 'Die Dr. Malan wat die meeste lede van die publiek nie ken nie' (translated from the original Afrikaans).

93. J.P. Brits. 1993. 'Apartheid en die politieke grondverskuiwing van 1948', *Historia* 38(1), 81.

94. D.F. Malan. 1954. *Apartheid: Suid-Afrika gee sy antwoord op 'n groot probleem*, Pretoria: Staatsinligtingskantoor, 4 (translated from the original Afrikaans).

95. D. Posel. 1987. 'The Meaning of Apartheid before 1948: Conflicting Interests and Forces within the Afrikaner Nationalist Alliance', *Journal of Southern African Studies* 14(1), 123–39.

96. Giliomee, 'The Making of the Apartheid Plan', 373–92; H. Giliomee. 2003. 'The Weakness of Some: The Dutch Reformed Church and White Supremacy', *Scriptura* 83, 212–44.

97. Korf, 'Podium and/or Pulpit?', 214–38.

98. US Library, DFM 1/1/2390, D.F. Malan, 'Verkiesingsmanifes', 5.

CHAPTER 3

BEARDED, ATTRACTIVE AND BELOVED

The Charisma of Ferdinand Domela Nieuwenhuis
(1846–1919)

Jan Willem Stutje

'suffering for truth's sake/ Is fortitude to highest victory' (Milton, *Paradise Lost*)

Max Weber's celebrated essay on charismatic leadership appeared post-humously in 1922.[1] Weber observed that in situations of crisis the public endow a charismatic leader with the supernatural powers necessary for the fundamental social changes they want. Loaded with extraordinary gifts Ferdinand Domela Nieuwenhuis probably was the most charismatic leader ever in the Dutch labour movement.[2]

In the 1880s and the beginning of the 1890s Domela and his followers shared an '*emotionale Vergemeinschaftung*' [emotional communality]: a bond that can be considered as a creative cultural community in opposition to the ruling social order, which was to be turned upside down.[3] The public did believe Domela was able to make breakthroughs. 'Our redeemer is coming!', a follower literally exclaimed: it seemed only a matter of time for a new world to be created.

It is interesting to consider how Domela earned this reputation. Were his gifts sufficient for him to be selected for leadership or were the social and cultural crises at the end of the nineteenth century a preponderant influence? What can we say about the nature of Domela's charisma and what about the interaction between the leader and his followers?

In general the revolutionary passion cools down after some time. It is a matter of '*Veralltäglichung des Charisma*' [routinisation of charisma], a phase Weber defined as the process of trivializing due to the impact of a rational bureaucratic framework. In this chapter I will show how Domela embraced discipline, hierarchy and organization, which decisively contributed to trivializing his charisma and which finally provoked his political downfall.

Moreover I will discuss the conflict of Domela Nieuwenhuis and his political rival Pieter Jelles Troelstra, who in 1894 became the prominent leader of the Dutch reformist Social Democratic Workers Party (SDAP), using Weberian terminology: each of them representing and emphasizing one side of the entanglement of charisma and reason, Domela the example of a more or less spontaneous charisma and Troelstra the example of vulgarization into a kind of pseudo-charisma.[4] I will link their different roles to the specific motives that inspired them: Domela led a romantic revolt against modernity conditioned by precapitalistic values and Troelstra, the representative of anticapitalism, criticized the dominant social order in terms of modern rational values.

The Theatre of Charisma

Domela was born in a religious family: his father was a pastor and professor of theology at the Lutheran seminary in Amsterdam. Domela became a clergyman too, an office he held for ten years. He could draw on abundant religious experience when he started his political career in the 1870s.

Domela's pure and authentic attitude was remarkable. His longing for purity originated in his experience with impurity, with misery and decay, in what Weber called the spirit of calculation and selfishness and Marx in his *Early Writings* described as alienation and commodity fetishism, the pathological symptoms of an expanding industrial society.[5] After he resigned as a Lutheran minister in 1879, Domela succeeded in transposing the ideal of purity into a socialist-inspired utopia: a world full of harmony and community without a need for profit and unlimited consumption.

For the sake of his ideal Domela preached the truth of asceticism, of total abstinence and vegetarianism.[6] From 1878 onwards he stipulated the consumption of only the natural and the pure. At workers meetings he addressed, he did not accept the consumption of alcohol. In the Netherlands the consumption of alcohol by the working class was far more fatal than in neighbouring countries where one used to drink beer and not the very cheap and destructive jenever.[7] But Domela did more than fight alcohol abuse alone. In a more general way Domela's fight for total abstinence was also a sign of spirituality, proving the superiority of the mind over the body and the ability to resist worldly temptations. It was not only a demonstration of restraint, but also a well considered revolt

against modernity; a revolt to which the masses during the social crisis at
the end of the nineteenth century were strongly attracted.[8]

Thanks not only to this spiritual attitude, but also to an eye-catching
performance, Domela gained great popularity. He was an eloquent
speaker, dignified rather than agitated. His father – himself a very popular
preacher – taught him that a modest speech heightens authority.[9] Domela
was influential since he knew how to approach the audience. As a former
preacher he was used to reading the realm of emotions and thoughts and
to giving redemption without bowing.[10] With illustrative metaphors he
tried to convince the workers to organize themselves, stipulating that they
had to emancipate themselves as nobody else would do this for them.

Domela fiercely rejected all hierarchy and authority. At a very early
stage Domela even denied the idea of Jesus as the son of God, performing
miracles. Instead he identified with a more humanized Jesus-figure, the
prototype of an independent and inspiring thinker. Even after he turned
his back on the church at the end of the 1870s, Domela did not stop
referring to and comparing himself to this humanized Jesus.[11] This might
seem somewhat exalted but at the end of the nineteenth century there
was still a close relation between religion and politics. In an article for
the German socialist theoretical journal *Die Neue Zeit* Domela himself
explained, 'The atmosphere in the meetings is quite spiritual. One seems
to preach a new religion.'[12]

In the socialist movement at that time form was still important.[13] Quasireligious rituals and symbolism kept people together, at least as effectively as the rational, ideological content of the party they joined. One
only has to look at the photographs in their houses or in the meeting
halls to be convinced on this point. On the walls one could see portraits
of bearded prophets such as Marx and Domela Nieuwenhuis, sometimes
even next to paraphernalia of Christian origin. Many people harboured
high eschatological hopes; the day of redemption was near. Socialist Sunday schools prepared the children for the new times, teaching them 'the
truth, the right and the justice'. Together with the mass singing, the ceremonial celebration of the First of May and the solemn consecration of
flags and banners, these forms expressed the new socialist ideology in the
familiar terms of religious experience. Anticlericalism, an always strengthening phenomenon in the second part of the nineteenth century, did not
imply automatically antireligiousness.[14] Strong messianism demanded a
prophet-like figure, gifted with rhetorical talents, who was prepared to
die at the stake as an offering for the liberation of the oppressed proletariat: Domela Nieuwenhuis.

The evaluation of Domela's *Imitatio Christi* varied. Eleanor Marx
sneered at Domela, 'that Jesus Christ mal tourné', whose crucifixion 'as they

did Christ at the age of 30' would have been a blessing to mankind.[15] Even more patronizing, her father qualified the ex-minister as '*das holländische Pfäfflein*' [that little Dutch vicar].[16] But in general Domela was treated with respect. Many contemporaries were impressed by his physical resemblance to Jesus. In speeches and writing the resemblance was as remarkable. When he was detained in 1887 after he was sentenced for offending the king (lese majesty), he said farewell to his followers with a phrase Jesus spoke at Golgotha: 'don't weep for me, but for yourself and for your children'.[17]

The working-class people who were until then kept out of politics and were longing for restoration of their dignity recognized in Domela their champion of honour and virtue – the right person to testify to their communal ideals. They expressed a political loyalty combined with a near religious affection. Illustrative of this was a small article in a popular Frisian weekly in November 1882. It announced: 'He comes! Who? Domela Nieuwenhuis!! The social-minded minister!!!'[18] The example shows a firm conviction that religion was about justice and purity and that these virtues were reproduced in socialism.

Domela was not selected as leader because he wrenched the masses out of their apathy as the well-known socialist poet Henriette Roland Holst wants us to believe.[19] In the 1880s and the 1890s the masses were far from demoralized. Even Marx was struck by the spirit of their independence and militancy.[20] Domela achieved leadership because he was carried away by the enthusiasm of the masses, who pushed him to the forefront. In his memoirs, *Van Christen tot Anarchist*, Domela summarized his experiences, noticing that he was 'pulled into the labour movement. .... I didn't seek affiliation, on the contrary the circumstances took me to it'.[21] Or in the words of a rather subtle eyewitness: not so much a leader, Domela seemed to be led, in particular by the passion of the masses.[22]

Domela's rise to leadership was not the result of an organizing impetus. No party or trade union had the capacity to facilitate it. The process of social change differed strongly in time and tempo depending on place, region and trade sector.

Counterculture and the Social Democratic League

From 1885 to 1893 the Social Democratic League (Sociaal Democratische Bond, SDB) became a more or less nationally orientated organization.[23] From that time on the SDB was no longer the exclusive domain of artisans. It expanded its influence to broad layers of the unskilled, industrial working class, to casual labourers, farm workers, peat-workers and seasonal workers and to the dockers in Amsterdam and Rotterdam.

But despite this breakthrough the SDB lacked a central authority and retained a rather informal, undisciplined character.[24] Although the league inspired
an enormous popular movement in the 1880s and 1890s – tens of thousands
overcrowded the meetings and the journal *Recht voor Allen* (Justice for All)
was sold in even greater numbers – the organization failed to stabilize.[25] Membership of the league stagnated at some four thousand in 1886 (half of them in
Amsterdam and the surrounding areas such as the Zaanstreek) and about five
thousand in 1893 (half of them in the north, in Friesland and Groningen).

The modest membership illustrates that the vast majority of the lower
classes was not yet interested in organized politics and debate. Their integration in civil society had been limited. The efforts to discipline and
manage these groups, which were 'rough' and 'uncivilized', had failed.
The success of the liberal civilizing offensive was reduced to the upper
strata of the working class and to the new middle classes.[26]

Periodically the lower classes were in revolt, often without a clear political perspective or programme.[27] In their neighbourhoods the masses kept
to what their adversaries coined as 'old fashioned' traditions: the customs
of solidarity and mutual aid, a counterculture, which was the beginning
of a fierce class consciousness.[28] With their energetic consciousness – developed in the realm of cultural and social segregation – the workers faced
new and strict regulations, discipline and alienation, by-products of the
growing industrialization since 1865 and the birth of large-scale enter-
prises. Workers who were used to managing their own jobs found themselves more and more degraded to commodities.[29] Anger about social
insecurity and mass unemployment and rage about the loss of traditional
rights and customs resulted, in the beginning of the 1880s, in a first wave
of strikes and actions in Amsterdam, The Hague and the Zaanstreek. The
actions were spontaneous and above all unorthodox in the values that
inspired them. It was not the 'decent', socialist artisans who took the lead
but the unskilled factory workers, casual labourers and the unemployed
in the overcrowded neighbourhoods.

These working-class districts were dominated by men and women who
had their own beliefs and customs, their own argot and clothes, their own
songs and legends. They were less attracted by organization than by passion and were not afraid to use violence. The streets were transformed
into theatres of agitation: arrests and verdicts were considered as titles of
honour and martyrdom assessed by the duration of penalty. It was part of
a stubborn and obstinate culture which the veterans of the more artisan
tradition were not accustomed to and which seriously irritated the moderate wing of the party apparatus.

They disliked seeing Domela supporting this kind of radicalism and
abhorred the increasingly aggressive and hateful calls for revenge in the

columns of the journal *Recht voor Allen*. Domela had to know that cursing and swearing only helped to provoke animal instincts. He was pressed to stop his indulgence and was urged to fight the 'damned anarchists'. If not, (the best) militants would probably leave the organization, his opponents claimed.[30]

In the middle of the 1880s, the party seemed to be divided into two different tendencies.[31] The disputed question, however, had nothing to do with the assessment of revolutionary tactics or parliamentarianism. The question was how to integrate the 'unpolished' and 'uncivilized' groups into the party? How to do justice to the various cultural communities and traditions?

According to A.H. Gerhard (1858–1948), one of the leaders of the Amsterdam branch, the mass of ordinary people was wholeheartedly anarchist in the bad sense of the word. In his opinion social democracy demanded a stronger moral attitude.[32] There was hardly any enthusiasm to integrate these so-called anarchists into the party ranks. It is not surprising to learn that a lot of them left the SDB soon after the turmoil in 1885 and 1886 (The Eel Riots) in the Jordaan, a working-class district of Amsterdam, where twenty-six people were killed and more than one hundred wounded.[33] Their resignation was due to disappointment with the lack of success, but also to an aversion to the arrogance of leaders who considered themselves more civilized. One distrusted the intentions of these bourgeois gentlemen who were almost invariably supporters of parliamentary tactics. The party lacked the natural solidarity the people were accustomed to. All kinds of contradictions, between skilled and unskilled, rich and poor, town and countryside, divided the ranks sufficiently for the denigrating pressure of role and social standing to be felt.

To this pattern there seemed to be only one exception: Ferdinand Domela Nieuwenhuis. Domela embodied the ambition to develop an egalitarian community in which everyone could feel at home whatever their social background or profession. And what is more: he helped to build the community even against the current.

This attitude was rewarded by a promotion to leadership – a leadership which could be endowed with an unrestricted, dynamic charisma because the movement was not yet hindered by discipline and filled with rules and procedures. Domela earned his prestige not by formal authority but by courage and by a willingness to sacrifice, competences he was able to demonstrate amply during the period of fierce turmoil between 1885 and 1887.

The young agitators sympathized with the harsh tones in *Recht voor Allen*, the journal which Domela edited. He was admired for his courage, stubbornness and straightforward attitude. He was sentenced for insulting the crown, in itself the ultimate proof that Domela did not deny his convictions. Thousands bade him farewell when he left to be detained (1887). He was adored as the leader, as the symbolic image of the new times. Domela answered this adoration with the words of Pilatus: 'Either my deeds are human, then they will vanish, or my deeds are from God, then they will be preserved, in spite of all persecution.'[34] Was this empty rhetoric? Not at all, as contemporaries observed: Domela had the power to lead the masses as he wished.[35]

A leader who was endowed with such a supernatural grace had to accept suffering. Domela refused to go abroad, against advice which was given by some of his friends.[36] The martyrdom offered him a prestige he did not want to give up. This was a practical consideration, as 'the trial aroused a wonderful propaganda and was of more benefit than most of the addresses I had made. And this in all parts of the country.'[37]

Suffering was essential to Domela's charisma. Impressed by the suffering of the working class and participating in their struggle, he was fully prepared to sacrify himself. Sacrificing himself – he confessed – brought satisfaction. He loved to quote John Milton's phrase: 'that suffering for truth's sake is fortitude to highest victory'.[38] That point of view proved itself easily. Suffering helped Domela to promote identification with and by his followers. It created an extraordinary amount of energy among them. The capacity to stir up these mystical forces illustrates the intensity of Domela's charisma. Domela was more than a leader who only dictated the course of events; he was like Gideon, who changed the mentality of his followers and inspired them to unexpected decisiveness. He was trusted blindly and his followers did not begrudge him his luxurious home, his journeys to Paris or to the exciting Swiss Alps. Did he not sacrifice everything, even a wealthy and careless existence? By financially supporting the party, Domela confirmed Weber, who said that the true charismatic person refuses any regular benefit.[39] A faithful socialist, Domela said, wants to be compensated only by the pleasure of having done the right things.[40]

The Crumbling of Charisma

Charisma is by definition unstable. The hero does not receive it by heritage, tradition or rules; he or she wins authority by personal power and as soon as the power fades away, the hero will lose the ability to enchant. To safeguard his charisma, Domela had to prove that he was able to unite people behind a programme of egalitarian values again and again. The chances for success, however, slowly deteriorated during the last decade of the nineteenth century.

Until the 1890s the SDB preserved a rather undisciplined and loose character. Without very many rules to obey, Domela was in a good position to unfold his charisma. As soon as the party became more professional, however, charisma and discipline proved to be uneasy partners.

Professionalization was instigated by two circumstances: in the first place by the expansion of the party's influence to the northern rural provinces Friesland and Groningen, due to the agrarian crisis and the extension of social conflicts from 1888 on, when the number of local branches increased spectacularly;[41] and in the second place by the affiliation of the SDB to the Socialist (Second) International, which was founded in Paris in 1889. Both occasions called for coordination and centralization on a more daily basis and this tended to harm Domela's position. The expanding apparatus, the growing discipline, the rules and fixed procedures made the charismatic playground smaller. From that time on the Amsterdam branch became more and more the ideological and organizational centre, dominated since 1887 by affiliated trade unions that silenced the radical branches in the neighbourhoods and the independent women's and youth organizations.[42] This process of organization and control did not yet reach the northern provinces. Here the party preserved its open character and demonstrated a warm, militant atmosphere, stimulated by a spectacular wave of strikes from 1888 till 1892. Here Domela's charisma gained a second life.

The Free Country

Domela was very popular in the countryside. The towns, however, Leeuwarden for example, were dominated by radical liberals, representatives of the suffrage movement, such as the editor of *Het Friesche Volksblad* Oebele Stellingwerf, the teacher Vitus Bruinsma and the lawyer Pieter Jelles Troelstra. Troelstra started his career in the Friesche Volkspartij (The Frisian People's Party), a broad coalition of radicals and socialists coming from the SDB, which at its height united more than one hundred clubs and numbered more than five thousand members.[43]

Although their ideological outlook differed, all representatives spoke the Frisian language. The ordinary peat- and agricultural labourers did not understand Dutch very well. This was a serious impediment for Domela, who did not speak Frisian and who strongly depended on the spoken word. Mass meetings in particular offered workers the opportunity to identify with him. But Domela commanded more ways to express himself. The gatherings where he spoke were a true spectacle and this seemed to compensate for a lot, bearing in mind the many testimonies of adoration. Admiration needed dissociation. Like an actor in a *commedia dell'arte* Domela showed a blank mask, enabling his followers to project their hopes and longings onto him: 'The worshipping was immense ... but Domela did not show any emotion, no sparkling in his eyes, no signs of pride or satisfaction, nothing at all! .... Had he asked them to offer their lives, thousands would have done so. Everyone felt he was the leader', an eyewitness remembered.[44] By maintaining distance from his followers, emotionally and physically, Domela was able to create a fascinating and even mysterious image of himself.

Although Domela enjoyed an outstanding reputation, the need for native spokesmen from Frisia and Groningen remained. In these regions one distrusted the centralist ambitions of the national leadership and their representatives were not taken very seriously.

Since the mid-1880s the movement in these districts could supply their own spokesmen, often schoolteachers, self-confident people, who had not been recruited to the socialist movement by Domela himself. Gifted with common sense, mostly of freethinker origins and inspired by Multatuli's criticism of social conformism, they were very radical.[45] They had to be so in order to outflank the militant liberals.[46] They respected Domela highly, but they did not hesitate to criticize him, not in the least when their hero deemed it acceptable to ridicule everyone outside the SDB as 'a reactionary mess'. The real object of this ridicule was the Friesche Volkspartij whose leaders Domela envied.[47]

Until 1890 Domela's position was undisputed; thereafter it changed. Two years earlier he was elected as a member of parliament. Despite strong efforts he did not succeed in contributing to any social legislation. Whatever he put forward (an eight-hour working day, an end to the war in Atjeh [Aceh], the independence of the colonies, a ban on the truck system, etcetera), his proposals were received with exclamations of derision. This did not help to strengthen his reputation; he lost the aura of sacrosanctity. Not having any success in a period full of new hope was considered a sign of weakness.

Domela was usually very self-controlled, but he lost his patience when his companions showed their independent ambitions more and more openly. He did not hesitate to blame them for marching under the same moderate banner as the Friesche Volkspartij. Domela feared the creation of a new, reform-minded, parliamentarian socialist party besides the SDB. He could not be more explicit as he warned in the journal *Recht voor Allen*: 'We social democrats, the mightiest workers party, will never be exploited, not by anyone'.[48] A rupture was imminent, as he declared that an ongoing cooperation with other organizations would inevitably result in the socialist momentum petering out and proclaimed that the strength of the party had to be found in isolation.[49]

The price for this political purity was high. The number of dissidents increased. This was an indication that Domela's charisma was losing its attraction. To his followers, Domela appeared more and more dependent on rational procedures and other bureaucratic instruments, a situation Weber had qualified as *Veralltäglichung des Charisma* (trivialization).[50]

This attitude proved to be a fatal paradox. The more he appealed to the apparatus, the more Domela undermined the charismatic bond with his followers. Although he hoped to sustain radicalism by rejecting moderate parliamentary tactics, this did not prevent Domela from becoming alienated from his local confidants. The losses were difficult to overcome. The press organs could not compensate for these deficiencies. Especially in the northern provinces, Domela missed the friends who were able to explain and translate his ideas to the ordinary public. This was a serious handicap, as the masses of illiterates were not able to discuss political issues from written texts, journals and brochures without these mediators. In the countryside the loss of discipline was felt very directly. Here he missed the friends who enjoyed his confidence. From 1892 onwards the parliamentarians gained their first strengths not in Amsterdam or in The Hague, but in these northern provinces.

Domela had become powerless; his charisma atrophied. No more than an ordinary politician, he only dispensed modest sanctions. The magician in the man, who was able to move mountains, vanished forever.

Troelstra and Domela

The term *charisma* is used whether it is relevant or not. Any eloquent politician with support from the public is labelled charismatic. But being popular is not the same thing as being gifted with charisma. Pieter Jelles Troelstra, Domela's great adversary, was considered to have been trusted unconditionally – a claim made in 1922 by the well known historiographer of the early Dutch labour movement Willem Vliegen. This raises the question of whether Domela and Troelstra were peers in the love the masses conferred on them.

Although Troelstra belonged to a younger generation, there were certainly some similarities: both were adored by their followers and were eloquent speakers. Although neither was able to show any personal intimacy, in meetings each demonstrated great emotional warmth. Each was eager to wear the Messiah's mantle and loudly proclaimed his message of 'suffering and struggling together'.[51]

But despite the similarities, did they share the same charisma? Did Troelstra equal Domela Nieuwenhuis as an original, nonconformist leader representing an independent, revolutionary counterculture? Or should we characterize Troelstra, the rationalist, as the sheer embodiment of social democracy, dominated by the ambition to gather the masses in the party – convinced of the so-called inevitable collapse of capitalism? A tragic leader at most, who showed charisma only at one specific moment during the revolutionary turmoil in November 1918[52] – a moment, however, when he had to deal with such strong opposition within and outside the party that his enthusiasm was immediately made use of in order to cool down the masses.[53] Troelstra was definitely a dominant party leader, but did he also create a new set of traditions? He always gave reason for an atmosphere of distrust, not only with the followers of Domela or the Marxist party opposition around the journal *De Nieuwe Tijd*, but even with other loyal social democrats, such as Henri Polak, the Amsterdam leader of the international diamond workers, or Willem Vliegen, the outstanding party organizer and historiographer.[54] Not everybody had forgotten Troelstra's liberal origins – and his complete absence from the growing class struggle in the period from 1880 to 1890.[55]

It did not bother Vliegen to attribute to Troelstra the talent 'to live in symbiosis with the masses and to share their emotions at least as strongly as they felt them'. He displayed a 'crusader's passion', Vliegen said.[56] And although he was not unique in this (a reference to Domela Nieuwenhuis), only a few leaders were as realistic as he was. He inspired the crowd with enthusiasm but he also knew how to deal with the mounting passions. The domestication of the so-called wild socialism was seen as Troelstra's highest virtue.[57]

If paternalism was the secret of Troelstra's leadership, this had nothing to do with charisma in the Weberian sense of the word.[58] Paternalism had no harmful effect whatsoever on hierarchy. Politics continued to be a gentlemen's affair; at most the experience of the masses was no longer neglected. Weber considered charisma to be more than a strong plebiscitarian leadership.[59] Charisma was a social relation in which the masses kept their autonomy. They had to be awakened and convinced, but emancipation had to be their own work and not that of an almighty redeemer.

Unlike Troelstra, Domela Nieuwenhuis really displayed charisma: he lived in a symbiotic relation with a loosely structured movement, and was not – as Troelstra was – the organizer of a disciplined, modern party who believed in an organic and deterministic route to socialism, as Kautsky puts it.[60] In this perspective, wishes, dreams and ideals were of secondary importance, as they were individual emotions with not the slightest effect on the collapse of capitalism. Domela, however, did worry about these emotions, more than about the party or its ideology alone.

The legitimacy of Domela was his magical, religious inspiration. From this his followers derived an unexpected strength, which they used to discover their own individuality and the meaning of their existence. Domela drafted a set of humanistic values with a reference far beyond socialism. Purity and authenticity were the organizing principles. These qualities, Domela said, divided the world into 'wholes' and 'halves', into good and bad. Together with 'suffering and struggling', these principles, originating in a renunciation of modern capitalism, modelled his charisma. His longing for what was lost complied with the perceptions of the rank and file, shocked by the loss of basic values like integrity, equality and a sense of community; it complied with the perceptions of the poor labourers in the northern provinces who were convinced that they were living in a false world, a world which had to be turned upside down – a longing of which Domela only knew one outcome: 'the sixth continent, which had not yet found its Columbus ..., a continent listening to the harmonious name of "mankind"'.[61]

Always kept outside official politics, this man and his experiences suddenly were important and became the elemental material of one's (self-) emancipation.[62] Domela's socialist ideas were characterized – to paraphrase the French sociologist Michael Löwy – by strong utopian, humanistic leanings.[63] Apart from materialistic needs, stimulating, harmonious ideas were of the utmost importance: the solidarity of interests, the idea of community, which would restore the just proportion between duties and rights.

The symbiosis of the leader and his followers, the intense relationship with the rank and file: these were elements Troelstra was totally deprived of. He only had in mind the 'respectable' members of the working class; the 'sane elements' in his view: the serious wage labourers to whom the future belongs, not the failures, not the noise-makers, who could not feel at home in a liberal society, nor the unemployed, the sick, the drop-outs, in short the lumpen proletariat, trash of the old society. But even those he saw as the true, serious workers, who sustained the future, needed a strong leadership, Troelstra believed, because 'these wretched people' – he frankly said – 'do not have any talent at all to understand the most important national and international issues'.[64]

Essential in Domela's repugnance for a parliamentarian road to socialism was the tension between charisma and the belief in progress based on structural economic and social changes taking place at the end of the nineteenth century. In the context of accelerating industrialization and deployment of capitalist relations, a new parliamentarian party (SDAP) was born. The SDAP was the expression of a 'modern' working class which tried to formulate rational, scientific solutions to explosive social problems; a party which, as Frank van der Goes, one of the founders of the SDAP claimed, 'tried to promote class-socialism into a neutral, impartial science'. Connecting science and the 'true' working class, a new philosophical attitude was born which considered the concrete suffering of human beings as of secondary importance to the abstract suffering of mankind.[65] The individual had to submit to progress, being its victim at the same time. Socialism was alienated from this 'man' and trivialized more and more, as was the professional activity of leaders such as Troelstra.

Conclusions

A charismatic leader distinguishes himself by his ability to provoke loyalty independent of any formal status or position whatsoever. He manifests himself in periods of turmoil, breaks with traditions and is attributed with extraordinary gifts. This Weberian concept suits Domela Nieuwenhuis better than Troelstra.

Domela's charisma did not originate in his personality. However notable his performance may have been, it was not his actions but his perception by his followers which was decisive in validating his charisma.[66] Domela's influence was at its peak in the period 1885 to 1891, when the movement was a loose structure and the rank and file sociologically represented the proletariat as a whole and not just the artisans or the more respectable, skilled members of the working class. These were circumstances specific to the initial period of industrialization, when the modern capitalist market and labour relations, characterized by strong discipline and commercialization, had not yet totally destroyed the preindustrial autonomy.

Domela and his followers lived in a symbiotic relation with each other. Domela was not just an ordinary politician. Neither a party organizer nor a delegate, he was above all the champion of the people, who tried to make an egalitarian, socialist counterculture. He tried to use values like purity and authenticity to enter the world of the rank and file. His use of religious symbolism facilitated the sublimation of anger into hope and expectations. It was no coincidence that this took place at the end of the nineteenth century, when politics and religion were closely connected.[67]

The party, or rather the movement or counterculture, was not only an apparatus to defend material interests. In the world of the singing and drama clubs, the debating societies, the women's and youth organizations, everyone used his own idiom and showed his own mentality. Taking part was meaningful; it proved one's identity and created a common feeling, where congeniality was just another word for brotherhood. Whoever wanted to participate, Domela supported morally and if necessary even financially; the relations were not yet commodified.

The party officials played a crucial role in popularizing ideas; Domela, from bourgeois origins, however, earned the status of hero because he succeeded in fraternizing uninhibitedly with the ordinary people. At mass meetings he accentuated this role with his tall stature and impenetrable face. However exalted, Domela was not worshipped as a person but as the embodiment of shared values. This image languished as Domela's entourage, first in Amsterdam but soon in the northern districts as well, started to plead for a more moderate course when the movement remained unsuccessful in parliament and was afflicted by heightened repression after 1887. Domela tried to save the revolutionary project by replacing loyalty and purity with discipline. With this, however, he reduced his own playground and undermined his charisma. He was contaminated by the triviality of organization, the procedures, the uniform rules and order. By exercising power and demanding sacrifices he castrated the essence of his prophet figure: the readiness to be vulnerable and to make sacrifices. His performance did not answer the expectations of his followers any longer. Domela had become an ordinary politician who in the conflict with Troelstra could no longer count on the natural support of the rank and file.

Notes

1. 'Die drei reinen Typen der legitimen Herrschaft' was posthumously published by Marianne Weber in the *Preußischen Jahrbüchern* vol. 187, 1922 (pp. 1–12). The essay was included in M. Weber. 1956. *Wirtschaft und Gesellschaft, Grundriss der verstehende Soziologie*, 4th ed., 2 vols, Tübingen: J.C.B. Mohr (Paul Siebeck), vol. 1, 140–48, vol. 2, 662–90.
2. *Van christen tot anarchist. Gedenkschriften van F. Domela Nieuwenhuis*. 1910. Amsterdam: Van Holkema & Warendorf; J. Meyers. 1993. *Domela, een hemel op aarde*, Amsterdam: Arbeiderspers; B. Altena (ed.). 1979. *'En al beschouwen alle broeders mij als den verloren broeder', de familiecorrespondentie van en over Ferdinand Domela Nieuwenhuis, 1846–1923*, Amsterdam: Stichting Beheer IISG; J.W. Stutje. 2008. 'Ferdinand Domela Nieuwenhuis (1846–1919). Revolte en melancholie: romantiek in Domela's kritiek op de moderniteit', *Tijdschrift voor Sociale en Economische Geschiedenis* 5(2), 3–28.
3. Weber, *Wirtschaft und Gesellschaft*, vol. 1, 140–41.
4. Pieter Jelles Troelstra was born in Leeuwarden in 1860. He came from a liberal background. In 1894 he was one of the founders of the Social Democratic Workers Party (SDAP). He belonged to the leadership until 1925. In 1897 he was sent to the Second Chamber of the States General for the first time. He figured as one of the prominent leaders of the Second (Socialist) International during the period from 1889 to 1914. He died in The Hague in 1930.
5. M. Weber. 2006. *Die protestantische Ethik und der Geist des Kapitalismus*, republished and introduced by D. Käsler, Munich: Beck; K. Marx. 2004. *Die Frühschriften*, ed. S. Landshut, 7th ed., Stuttgart: Kröner.
6. 'F. Domela Nieuwenhuis to Adriaan Domela Nieuwenhuis, Den Haag, 9 December 1876', in IISH, F. Domela Nieuwenhuis Archives, XI A 1. D. de Clercq. 1916. 'Domela Nieuwenhuis en het vegetarisme', in *Gedenkboek ter gelegenheid van den 70sten verjaardag van F. Domela Nieuwenhuis, 31 December 1916*, Amsterdam.

7.   P. Wielsma. 1988. 'Working Class Culture: Alcohol Abuse or Abstinence', in L. Heerma
     van Voss and F. van Holthoorn (eds), *Working Class and Popular Culture*, Amsterdam:
     Stichting Beheer IISG, 122. After a stable liquor consumption in the 1850s and 1860s
     (between seven and eight litres) the consumption increased to ten litres per head a year in
     the 1870s. After it reached a maximum at the end of the 1870s it decreased, slowly at first,
     to seven litres in 1909. At the end of the 1930s the consumption figures did not rise above
     two litres.
8.   For the cultural crisis, see A. Labrie. 2001. *Zuiverheid en decadentie. Over de grenzen van
     de burgerlijke cultuur in West-Europa, 1870–1914*, Amsterdam: Bert Bakker, 30; E.J. Hobs-
     bawm. 1995. *The Age of Empire, 1875–1914*, New York: Pantheon Books, 10.
9.   'F.J. Domela Nieuwenhuis to C. Domela Nieuwenhuis, Amsterdam 15 March 1858', Na-
     tional Archives, Archives of the Family Domela Nieuwenhuis, 34.
10. J. Romein and A. Romein-Verschoor. 1971. *Erflaters van onze beschaving. Nederlandse gestal-
     ten uit zes eeuwen*, 9th ed., Amsterdam: Querido, 802–3; H. te Velde. 2002. *Stijlen van leider-
     schap. Persoon en politiek van Thorbecke tot Den Uyl*, Amsterdam: Wereldbibliotheek, 88.
11. See B. Altena. 1989. 'Domela's beeld van de Jezusfiguur', *De AS, anarchistisch tijdschrift*
     17(87), 1–6.
12. F. Domela Nieuwenhuis. 1890. 'Die sozialistische Bewegung in Holland', *Die Neue Zeit*
     9(2), 51–57.
13. E.J. Hobsbawm. 1959. *Primitive Rebels: Archaic Forms of Social Movement in the 19th and
     20th Centuries*, Manchester: Manchester University Press, 151.
14. For secularization in the Netherlands, see J.P. Kruijt. 1933. *De onkerkelijkheid in Neder-
     land, haar verbreiding en oorzaken, proeve ener sociografiese verklaring*, Groningen and Ba-
     tavia: P. Noordhoff; H. Faber. 1970. *Ontkerkelijking en buitenkerkelijkheid in Nederland,
     tot 1960*, Assen: Van Gorcum; J.G.A. ten Bokkel. 2003. *Gidsen en Genieën. De dageraad
     en het vrije denken in Nederland 1855–1898*, Haarlem: FAMA, 225; and J. Giele. 1976.
     'Arbeidersbestaan, levenshouding en maatschappijbeeld van de arbeidende klasse in Ne-
     derland in het midden van de negentiende eeuw', in J. Giele et al. (eds), *Jaarboek voor de
     geschiedenis van socialisme en arbeidersbeweging in Nederland*, Nijmegen: SUN, 55–56.
15. 'E. Marx to Franc van der Goes. 29 December 1893', in IISH, Van der Goes Archives,
     1784. Cf.: S. Bloemgarten. 1981. 'De Tweede Internationale en de geboorte van de
     SDAP (1889–1896)', *Tijdschrift voor Sociale Geschiedenis* 7(22), 124.
16. 'K. Marx to F. Engels, 8 November 1882', in K. Marx and F. Engels. 1967. *Werke 35*,
     Berlin: Dietz Verlag, 104–6.
17. 'H. Hiebink to C. Domela Nieuwenhuis, Zutphen 6 March 1887', in National Archives,
     Archives of the Family Domela Nieuwenhuis, 34. Altena, *'En al beschouwen ...'*, 340. A.A.
     de Jong. 1966. *Domela Nieuwenhuis*, The Hague: Kruseman, 20.
18. J.J. Kalma. 1978. *Er valt voor recht te strijden. De roerige dagen rond 1890 in Friesland*, The
     Hague: Boekencentrum, 21.
19. H. Roland Holst. 1919. 'F. Domela Nieuwenhuis' Uitvaart', *De Nieuwe Tijd* 24, 747.
20. About the vitality of Dutch socialism Domela said: 'Although the start was late, we soon
     caught up. Socialism in the Netherlands is as strong as in Germany'. Domela Nieuwenhuis,
     'Die sozialistische Bewegung in Holland', 53.
21. *Van Christen tot Anarchist*, 54.
22. S. de Wolff. 1951. *En toch...! Driekwart eeuw socialisme in vogelvlucht*, Amsterdam: G.J.A.
     Ruys, 71.
23. The SDB was the first socialist party in the Netherlands, founded in 1881. Domela Nieu-
     wenhuis and his journal *Recht voor Allen* (Justice for All) soon joined. P. van Horssen and
     D. Rietveld. 1975. 'De Sociaal Democratische Bond. Een onderzoek naar het ontstaan van
     haar afdelingen en haar sociale structuur', *Tijdschrift voor Sociale Geschiedenis* 1, 19–20. P.
     van Horssen and D. Rietveld. 1977. 'De Sociaal Democratische Bond. Een onderzoek naar
     het ontstaan van haar afdelingen en haar sociale structuur', *Tijdschrift voor Sociale Geschie-*

denis 7, 50–52. D. Bos. 2001. *Waarachtige volksvrienden. De vroege socialistische beweging in Amsterdam 1848–1894*, Amsterdam: Bert Bakker, 264–68.

24. Bos, *Waarachtige volksvrienden*, 176, 180–81.

25. Exact circulation figures are difficult to give. At the end of 1886 *Recht voor Allen* gives a figure of 30,000 to 50 /60,000 copies; see *Recht voor Allen*, 22 December 1886. A police informer reports of 34,000 copies in September 1885; 6,000 of these were sold in Amsterdam only. 'Verslag cursusvergadering, 8 September 1885 in Walhalla', in Secret Archives, Ministry of Justice, 6470. The number of subscribers in 1886 amounted to 2,000. In 1887 the average circulation figure spectacularly decreased to 13,200 and the number of subscribers to 1,500. Horssen and Rietveld, 'De Sociaal Democratische Bond', 7, 37–38.

26. B. Sanders and G. de Groot. 1988. 'Without Hope of Improvement: Casual Labourers and Bourgeois Reformers in Amsterdam, 1850–1920', in Heerma van Voss and Holthoorn, *Working Class and Popular Culture*, 227–43. B. Kruithof. 2006. 'Godsvrucht en goede zeden bevorderen. Het burgerlijk beschavingsoffensief van de Maatschappij tot nut van 't Algemeen', in N. Bakker, R. Dekker and A. Janssens (eds), *Tot burgerschap en deugd. Volksopvoeding in de negentiende eeuw*, Hilversum: Verloren.

27. Giele, 'Arbeidersbestaan, levenshouding en maatschappijbeeld', 37–38, 47–52. J. MacLean. 1979. 'Arbeidsconflicten in de periode 1813–1872, gegevens uit het kabinet des Konings', *Tijdschrift voor Sociale Geschiedenis* 5(16), 292–312.

28. Giele, 'Arbeidersbestaan, levenshouding en maatschappijbeeld', 82–86.

29   J.L. van Zanden and A. van Riel. 2000. *Nederland 1780–1914. Staat, instituties en economische ontwikkeling*, Amsterdam: Balans, 277–88, 315.

30. 'H.H. van Kol to F. Domela Nieuwenhuis, Eindhoven 7 November 1885', in IISH, F. Domela Nieuwenhuis Archives, II C 9.

31. As Bymholt said: 'denying or neglecting these tendencies would be like burying one's head in the sand'. B. Bymholt. 1976 (1894). *Geschiedenis der arbeidersbeweging in Nederland*, Amsterdam: Van Gennep, 355 (n. 1).

32. 'A.H. Gerhard to F. Domela Nieuwenhuis, 20 November 1887', in IISH, F. Domela Nieuwenhuis Archives, II C 6.

33. Bos, *Waarachtige volksvrienden*, 207–22. P. de Rooy. 1971. *Een revolutie die voorbij ging: Domela Nieuwenhuis en het Palingoproer*, Bussum: Van Dishoeck.

34. W. Havers and S.W. Coltof. 1916. 'Ferdinand Domela Nieuwenhuis', in *Gedenkboek ter gelegenheid van den 70sten verjaardag van F. Domela Nieuwenhuis, 31 December 1916*, Amsterdam, 166.

35. Havers and Coltof, 'Ferdinand Domela Nieuwenhuis', 170.

36. 'H. van Kol to F. Domela Nieuwenhuis, Den Haag, 18 June 1886', in IISH, F. Domela Nieuwenhuis Archives, II C 9. 'N. van Kol to F. Domela Nieuwenhuis, Den Haag, 18 June 1886', in IISH, F. Domela Nieuwenhuis Archives, II C 9. 'Ed. Anseele to F. Domela Nieuwenhuis, 11 June 1886', in IISH, F. Domela Nieuwenhuis Archives, II C 1.

37. 'F. Domela Nieuwenhuis to C. de Paepe, Den Haag, 1 July 1886', in IISH, César de Paepe Archives. Cf. Domela Nieuwenhuis, 'Die sozialistische Bewegung in Holland', 57.

38. S. Orgel and J. Goldberg (eds). 2004. *J. Milton, Paradise Lost*, Oxford: Oxford University Press, book XII.

39. According to Weber charisma is not compatible with the routine of economic profit, which is not the same as the ownership of fortune or other material property. See Weber, *Wirtschaft und Gesellschaft*, vol. 1, 140–42, vol. 2, 663.

40. F. Domela Nieuwenhuis to C. De Paepe, 'Gravenhage, 9 January 1880', in IISH, César De Paepe Archives.

41. The number of local branches in the northern provinces increased by fifty between 1891 en 1893. Horssen and Rietveld, 'De Sociaal Democratische Bond', 1, 30–31.

42. Horssen and Rietveld, 'De Sociaal Democratische Bond', 7, 9–11, 13–14. F. Dieteren and I. Peeterman. 1984. *Vrije Vrouwen of Werkmansvrouwen? Vrouwen in de Sociaal-Democratische Bond (1879–1894)*, Utrecht: Fischluc, 34.

43.   J. Frieswijk. 1992. 'The Labour Movement in Friesland, 1880–1918', *Tijdschrift voor Sociale Geschiedenis* 18(2/3), 388; A.F. Mellink. 1968. 'Een Poging tot Democratische Coalitie-vorming: de Nederlandse Kiesrechtbeweging als Volkspartij (1886–1891)', *Tijdschrift voor Geschiedenis* 81(2), 174–96.

44.   W.H. Vliegen. 1921. *De Dageraad der Volksbevrijding*, vol. 1, Amsterdam: Ontwikkeling, 50–52.

45.   Multatuli is the pseudonym of Eduard Douwes Dekker (1820–1887), author of *Max Havelaar of de koffieveilingen der Nederlandsche Handelsmaatschappij* (1859), a very influential indictment against the colonial abuses by the Dutch in the East Indies.

46.   Cf. O.S. Knottnerus.1988. 'Het anarchisme als geseculariseerde bevindelijkheid', *Bulletin Nederlandse Arbeidersbeweging* 18, 47.

47.   A.F. Mellink. 1988. 'Domela Nieuwenhuis en de voormannen van de Friese Volkspartij', in J. Frieswijk, J.J. Kalma and Y. Kuiper (eds), *Ferdinand Domela Nieuwenhuis. De apostel van de Friese arbeiders*, Drachten: Friese Pers Boekerij, 122. *Van Christen tot Anarchist*, 175, 178.

48.   Vliegen, *De Dageraad der Volksbevrijding*, vol. 2, 279.

49.   Vliegen, *De Dageraad der Volksbevrijding*, vol. 2, 286.

50.   Weber, *Wirtschaft und Gesellschaft*, vol. 1, 124–48, vol. 2, 669.

51.   In 1898 Troelstra published a volume of socialist poetry, entitled: 'Pain and Fighting'. P.J. Troelstra. 1898. *Van leed en strijd. Verspreide stukken (1892–1898)*, Amsterdam: Poutsma.

52.   Troelstra and other social democratic leaders did not believe the German November Revolution would stop at the Dutch-German border. They proclaimed the revolution on 12 November 1918. Their hope, however, proved to be too optimistic. The party did not really aim at revolution. It was satisfied with a few concessions. A defeated Troelstra lost much prestige.

53.   B. van Dongen. 1992. *Revolutie of Integratie. De Sociaal Democratische Arbeiders Partij in Nederland (SDAP) tijdens de Eerste Wereldoorlog*, Amsterdam: Stichting Beheer IISG, 725–28, 775–81.

54.   In 1909 the Marxist opposition founded the Social Democratic Party (SDP). This party joined the Communist (Third) International in 1918.

55.   A.F. Mellink. 1970. 'Het politiek debuut van mr. P.J. Troelstra (1891–1897)', *Tijdschrift voor Geschiedenis* 83(1), 38, 41. J.A. Nieuwenhuis. 1933. *Een halve eeuw onder socialisten. Bijdrage tot de geschiedenis van het socialisme in Nederland*, Zeist: De Torentrans, 95. P.J. Troelstra. 1927. *Gedenkschriften. Wording*, Amsterdam: Querido.

56.   W.H. Vliegen. 1930. 'Troelstra, de leider', *Het Volk*, 13 May. R. Hartmans. 1994. 'Pieter Jelles Troelstra: advocaat en agitator', in *Van Troelstra tot Den Uyl*, *Het jaarboek voor het democratisch socialisme* 15, 47.

57.   *De Telegraaf*, 17 May 1930. Cf. Hartmans, 'Pieter Jelles Troelstra', 21.

58.   Troelstra's pursuit of payment was significant for his conception of leadership. In 1890 he applied for membership of the editorial staff of *Recht voor Allen*, demanding a considerable fee. 'P.J. Troelstra to F. Domela Nieuwenhuis, 8 November 1890', in IISH, F. Domela Nieuwenhuis Archives, II C 15. One year later he still did not rank himself among the leaders, because he was as yet not serving the party officially. 'Sociaal-demokratie en Volkspartij', *Recht voor Allen*, 16 July 1891. Weber considered these kinds of ambitions not compatible with charismatic leadership. Weber, *Wirtschaft und Gesellschaft*, vol. 1, 140–42.

59.   For plebiscitarian leadership, see W.J. Mommsen. 1974. *The Age of Bureaucracy: Perspectives on the Political Sociology of Max Weber*, Oxford: Blackwell, 72–95.

60.   K. Kautsky, 1909. *Der Weg zur Macht*, Hamburg: Erdmann Dubber.

61.   IISH, F. Domela Nieuwenhuis Archives, IV B 1 a.

62.   H. te Velde. 1996. 'Ervaring en zingeving in de politiek. Het politieke charisma in de tijd van Abraham Kuyper', *Theoretische Geschiedenis* 23(4), 533.

63.   In *Thomas Münzer als Theologe der Revolution*, Ernst Bloch puts the social economic factor as detonator of social protest in perspective by emphasizing the force of chiliastic motives.

Bloch points out that Marx himself considered the potential of noneconomic elements to initiate resistance of utmost importance, especially in the beginning of revolutions. E. Bloch. 1960. *Thomas Münzer als Theologe der Revolution*, Berlin: Aufbau, 48–49. In an interview with Michael Löwy, Bloch argued that Marx's rejection of capitalism as an unfair social system was based on values going back to 'The Code of the Knights, to the Code of King Arthur's Round Table'. See M. Löwy. 1976. *Pour une sociologie des intellectuels révolutionnaires*, Paris: Presses Universitaires de France, 298; M. Löwy and R. Sayre. 1992. *Révolte et mélancholie. Le romantisme à contre-courant de la modenité*, Paris: Editions Payot.

64.　'P.J. Troelstra to J.F. Ankersmit, 5 December 1915', in Van Dongen, *Revolutie of Integratie*, 309–10.

65.　M. van der Linden. 2004. '"Normalarbeit" – das Ende einer Fiktion. Wie der Proletar verschwand und wieder zurück kehrte', *Fantômas* 6, 26–29.

66.　Weber, *Wirtschaft und Gesellschaft*, vol. 1, 140. Weber emphasized there were no objective qualities that mattered, but only qualities 'wie sie tatsächlich von den charismatisch Beherrschten, den Anhängern, bewertet wird'. Cf. A.R. Willner and D. Willner. 1965. 'The Rise and Role of Charismatic Leaders', *The Annals of the American Academy of Political and Social Society* 358(1), 77–88.

67.　H. te Velde. 2005. 'Charismatic Leadership, c. 1870–1914, a Comparative European Perspective', in R. Toye and L. Gottlieb (eds), *Making Reputations, Power, Persuasions and the Individual in Modern British Politics*, London and New York: I.B. Tauris, 47.

CHAPTER 4

ERRICO MALATESTA AND CHARISMATIC LEADERSHIP

Carl Levy

Introduction

This chapter will examine the role of charismatic leadership in the Italian anarchist and socialist movements in the period up to the *biennio rosso* (1919–1920).[1] It will focus on the role of Errico Malatesta (1853–1932) in the Italian anarchist movement. The Italian anarchists relied on informal leadership to maintain the continuity of their organizations. Even if Italian anarchism was a minority movement within the Italian Left by 1914, its symbols, repertoire of actions and geographically specific political cultures allowed it to exercise a notable effect during the social mobilization of the Red Week (June 1914) and the *biennio rosso*.[2] Malatesta was the embodiment of these forces.

In the following, I shall first discuss Max Weber's conception of charisma, Robert Michels' relationship to Weber and the Italian Left, and in a related fashion the role of the anarchist counterculture on both men's social theory. Then I will discuss charisma and Italian socialism, Malatesta and charisma and specifically the events surrounding the *biennio rosso*.

Charisma and Social Movements: Weber and Michels

For Weber, charisma is the irrational kernel, the article of faith, found at the heart of power.[3] In Weber's politics there is an unhealthy triangulation of nationalism, modernization and charismatic politics, which

---

Notes for this chapter begin on page 97.

however also left him intrigued by new social movements (socialism and anarchism) that invoked charismatic tropes, charismatic personalities and charismatic situations.[4] For Weber effective democratic politics in an age of bureaucracy depended on the emergence of individuals who could rule by virtue of their technical and charismatic abilities. In this respect, the anarchist, syndicalist or socialist 'conviction politicians' displayed the same irrational and vitalist quality as Weber's democratic 'Caesars' (William Gladstone, David Lloyd George or Woodrow Wilson): and he searched in vain for German equivalents at the end of his life.[5]

Weber never had any time for the followers of a certain a type of Nietzschean will to power he associated with the Pan-German literati, but as Wilhelm Hennis and others have demonstrated, Weber's Nietzsche is a reworked version of Kant's 'ethical personalism'. 'Conviction' politicians whether at the helm of the state or within utopian countercommunities and movements needed a dosage of *Persönlichkeit*.[6] In order to have 'personality' one maintained a 'pathos of distance' and displayed the traditional values of the patrician: chivalry (*Ritterlichkeit*), decency (*Anstand*), abhorrence of baseness (*Gemeinheit*), and a 'natural' sense of superiority (*Vornehmheit*).

The acceptance of anarchist and syndicalist arguments and individuals within his circle has been explained as an example of Weber's tolerance and intellectual curiosity.[7] I think it is more convoluted than that. Thus, ironically, as I have shown elsewhere, it was through his encounters with anarchism, syndicalism, pacifism and libertarian culture (mainly through Robert Michels and Otto Gross, his connections with that libertarian/ *völkisch* force field, Ascona, and later with a younger generation most notably Ernest Toller before and during the Munich Revolution of 1919) that Max Weber thought he detected reserves of 'ethical personalism' which would serve his project in power politics and thus save German power and culture from eclipse.[8]

Robert Michels was his main guide through Italian anarchism, socialism and syndicalism. Michels was also his wayward student, friend and alter ego.[9] Weber defended Michels when he was refused a professorial post in Imperial Germany due to his membership of the *Sozialdemokratische Partei Deutschlands* (Social Democratic Party of Germany, SPD). And both men used the *Archiv für Sozialwissenschaft und Sozialpolitik* for their major scholarly interventions. But for Weber, Michels remained an incurable romantic, whose complicated personal life drove him to distraction.

Michel joined the syndicalist wing of the *Partito socialista italiano* (Italian Socialist Party, PSI) and wrote extensively for syndicalist and anarchist journals, including the ones edited by Malatesta's 'intellectual' and right-hand man in Italy, Luigi Fabbri. Michels praised the domination of Italian socialism and anarchism by amateur refugees from the educated middle classes precisely because it allowed the rule of enthusiasts rather than that of self-interested social democratic bureaucrats.[10] Indeed in 1912, one year after the publication of *Political Parties* (which was foreshadowed by a series of essays in the *Archiv*), socialist Benito Mussolini would lament the passing of the era of the bohemian heroic leadership in Italy and the arrival of that of the grey professional.[11]

Later, Antonio Gramsci would mercilessly lampoon Michels as one of the lame positivists of the school of Achille Loria. Weber was placed in an entirely different category altogether by Gramsci. In turn Weber anticipated Gramsci's criticisms of Michels' encyclopaedic and laundry-list accounts of Italian anarchism and socialism. Indeed he felt that *Political Parties* and earlier essays were far too unilateral and positivist for his tastes. That Michels wrote quickly without thinking very deeply was essentially Weber's weary criticism of his alter ego.[12]

Central to Weber's friendship with Michels (or Gross, Toller etc. for that matter) was his juxtaposition of an ethic of ultimate ends (*Gesinnungsetik*) with an ethic of responsibility (*Verantwortungsethik*).[13] Now it may be the case that the bridging of these two ethics did happen in certain aspects of his life and affected some of his work. Certainly there are Weber's encounters with the anarchist sexual utopias of Otto Gross (who is the role model for a charismatic leader of a countercultural group, which Weber discusses abstractly in *Economy and Society*). Weber's own sexuality (his relationships with Mina Tobler and Elsa Jaffé) is related to the successive changes made to the *Sociology of Religion* and the core of the 'Intermediate Reflections' essay, in which the sexual and aesthetic spheres of life are increasingly given more extensive and sympathetic treatment and in which eroticism and love escape the processes of rationalization to attain the purity of unmediated relationships. But he had little time for those who mistook the realities of power politics for the anarchist rock-candy mountain.[14]

Hero Worship and *Sovversivismo*

In his study of Ferdinand Lassalle, Michels emphasized the hero worship which surrounded his person. Lassalle was considered a paladin of the people but not originating from the people. He represented their will and desires because of his articulate persona and educated personality. Thus similarly, when Michels studied the Italian socialist movement, the role of socialist or syndicalist notables was emphasized. More recent studies have noted that educated, middle-class professionals were disproportionately represented in the leadership of all factions of Italian socialism before 1914.[15] Reformist socialists such as Oddino Morgari, Camillo Prampolini or Filippo Turati, or radicals such as Enrico Ferri, or the first generation of syndicalists such as Arturo Labriola or Enrico Leone were usually educated professionals – lawyers, doctors, criminologists or professors – who relied upon a charismatic linkage with their constituents to maintain enthusiasm and continuity within their organizations. Some, such as Arturo Labriola and Enrico Ferri, were spellbinders who combined vulgarized scientific discourse with forensic debating skills, while others such as Camillo Prampolini or Claudio Treves were sentimental orators or invoked the imagery of the Sermon on the Mount, particularly Prampolini who gathered a group of 'apostles' around him to preach a new gospel to the landless labourers of the Po Valley. Events such as the '*La Boje* movement' around Mantua in the 1880s or the *Fasci siciliani*, which swept Sicily in the 1890s, displayed the fervour of the religious revival and lent themselves to the charismatic moment and the charismatic leader.[16]

By 1914 Mussolini, even less exalted and educated then the socialist and syndicalist professors and courtroom orators, who forged the movement, became known through his spellbinding oratory and flamboyant journalism. Indeed Mussolini was hailed as the new *Duce* of socialism who would impart the movement with a vibrant charismatic current, countering its bureaucratization. But what unsettled the mainstream socialists about Mussolini, even when he was socialist, was his mixture of Stirnerite and Nietzschean tropes, his open endorsement of Le Bon's crowd psychology, and his self-promotion as the 'exceptional personality', all announced through the techniques of modern advertising.[17]

Charismatic socialism was related to the notion of *sovversivismo*. I have dealt with this elsewhere, but put succinctly, sovversivismo was characterized by a form of Garibaldinian voluntarism, in which poorly structured social movements were rapidly mobilized by a charismatic figure such as Garibaldi (who, as Lucy Riall has shown, nurtured his fame in equal parts by an identification with religious charismatic currents in Italian culture and his own clever construction of a myth through the modern press).[18] Thus Gramsci argued that a Lassalle or the various tribunes of Italian socialism before 1914 would be tamed once a self-educated and disciplined working class was formed in Italy: sovversivismo would vanish as the Italians matured. 'So-called charisma in the modern world', Gramsci explained, 'always coincides with a primitive phase of mass politics, when doctrine presents itself to the masses as something nebulous and incoherent and there is need of an infallible pope to act as an interpreter.'[19] However, Gramsci was not immune to the syndrome he described, since he had started his career as a spirited advocate of a voluntarist Marxism, which identified its leader in the socialist radical Benito Mussolini. Slightly later, during the *biennio rosso*, Gramsci argued that the charismatic *capo* of the Russian Revolution, Lenin, grounded his 'science' of socialism in the modern factory and the transformative force of council communism. At the same time he and his youthful group condemned the mindless voluntarism of the maximalist socialists, the anarchists, and specifically Errico Malatesta.[20] In prison of course the major themes of the *Quaderni* are the collapse of the Left and the rise of the fascists in which charismatic, 'subversive' politics is one of the chief culprits and Benito Mussolini's political biography serves as the autobiography of the nation.[21] In any case, for Gramsci there were good and bad charismatic leaders. A contextual reading or perhaps, more cynically, Gramsci's political partisanship, swayed his final judgement.

Malatesta was suspicious of this subversive tradition and not least in Mussolini, whom he had met in the run-up to the Red Week of 1914, and thought was as unstable as Gustave Hervé, the French antinationalist demagogue with whom he had recently debated in London. Indeed Malatesta was never impressed by Mussolini, in fact far less than the camp follower Gramsci.[22] But I will also argue that the charismatic leadership which sovversivismo brought forth was also against the core beliefs motivating Malatesta's anarchism and his *modus operandi*.

Anarchism, Malatesta and the Italian Socialist Movement

After the decline of the First International in the early 1880s, Italian anarchism remained weaker than the rising socialists but through the themes of anticlericalism, antimilitarism and intransigent republicanism, libertarian socialism and anarchism shaped three generations of socialists before 1914. Anarchism had its heartlands in Tuscany, Emilia-Romagna, Liguria and Rome, in which the political culture of the First International was preserved by generational transfer and modernized by the newer political generations.[23] Meanwhile the socialist culture of sovversivismo was influenced by anarchist literature, poems and songs originating in this anarchist heartland. Equally, syndicalism acted as institutional cover for the anarchists. Thus the culture of sovversivismo was articulated by the *Camere del lavoro* (Chambers of Labour), which bound together the sentiments of localism and antistatism. The *Camere del lavoro* served as a counterpoint to the growth of parliamentary-based reformism of the PSI after 1900 when the Giolittian compromise was forged, as these institutions became increasingly involved in general strikes that sometimes developed into open insurrections (as was the case during the Red Week of June 1914).[24]

This anarchist-influenced socialist culture acted as an unofficial grapevine. During his fleeting returns to Italy, Malatesta's influence was radiated and magnified by its pathways and institutions.[25] Thus, paradoxically, anarchism relied on its leaders (local, national and international) to help preserve institutional continuity. Malatesta was in semipermanent exile from the 1880s to the First World War but he attracted three generations into the movement and thus even if the Internationalist generation had died, gone mad or betrayed the movement, newer circles of friends and militants replaced Carlo Cafiero, Andrea Costa and the rest.[26] Through Francesco Saverio Merlino initially and Luigi Fabbri later, Malatesta's type of anarchism remained significant in Italy even if Malatesta was not physically present.[27] But perhaps more important was the network of obscure 'cadres' of the anarchist 'party' who came from the traditional strongholds of Ancona, Massa-Carrara, Rome or Florence and who kept alive Malatesta's linkages with the Italian grassroots.[28] Thus through journalism, international meetings, correspondence and forays legally or clandestinely into Italy he recharged this network, even if he spent perhaps a cumulative total of just six years in Italy between 1885 and 1914. While it is undoubtedly the case that Malatesta was a superb journalist and organizer, was this network reliant on the charisma of his person? Or did the charismatic moment await Malatesta? And if the relationship was charismatic was it similar in style and feeling to the notables of Italian socialist and syndicalist stump politics?

Malatesta as Stump Speaker

It is questionable whether Malatesta was cut from the same cloth as the socialist and syndicalist notables discussed previously. Malatesta could use his noted forensic and Socratic debating skills to sway juries as he did in political trials in 1878 or later in 1921.[29] He was skilled at face-to-face meetings with comrades, as Luigi Fabbri and various police informers have testified.[30] In Ancona (1897–1898), where he exercised a personal power over the local movement, it was claimed by the local police that crime had decreased during his sojourn because criminals stopped preying on their neighbours and became political subversives.[31] Another police source in 1913 reported during a speech by Malatesta, that he possessed the 'qualities as an intelligent combative speaker who speaks to persuade with calm, and never with violent language'.[32]

But then there were other anarchists who combined Socratic skills with magnetic, charismatic oratory. Such was the case of the antiorganizationist Luigi Galleani, another exiled anarchist who spent much of the early twentieth century in the Boston area.[33] Paul Ghio, a French observer, was present on one occasion when Galleani was speaking to a group of Italian textile workers in Paterson, New Jersey. 'I never heard an orator more powerful than Luigi Galleani', he recalled. 'He has a marvellous facility with words, accompanied by the faculty – rare in any popular tribune – of precision and clarity of ideas. His voice is full of warmth, his glance alive and penetrating, his gestures of exceptional vigour and flawless distinction.'[34]

Malatesta presented another persona on the stump. He had a natural gravitas in his facial expression but was also remembered for a subtle irony and a sly smile that broke out on his face when he was in full flow. His lively eyes caught the listener at rallies in an address that appeared as a conversation between friends. He avoided the pseudoscientific phraseology, violent and paradoxical turns of phrase or verbal abuse that were the stock-in-trade of so many of his fellow anarchists and socialists. Reflecting the dialogic style of his very successful pamphlets, he avoided 'difficult' words, scientific or Latinate jargon, with which the socialist and syndicalist professors loved to indulge their readers or audience. Thus as Luigi Fabbri recalled, his audience could express disappointment because they had expected more and were used to the flashy and passionate performances of other orators.[35]

The Revolutionary Moment: Malatesta and the *Biennio Rosso* (1919–1920)[36]

In the years before 1919–1920, the myth surrounding Malatesta was constructed through the mass media and the local anarchist and socialist popular cultures of Italy and the Italian diaspora. The making of the Malatesta myth would require a similar study to that of Lucy Riall's of Garibaldi, albeit I do not believe that Malatesta himself had such an investment in the process as Garibaldi clearly did. But like Garibaldi and Mazzini, his reputation within his own circles was not always solid and assured. There were many antiorganizationalist anarchists and murky groups involved in terrorism, which shunned him or worse. He was denounced as the 'dictator' of anarchism and the *camorrista* of anarchism (perhaps harking back to his Neapolitan origins, as he certainly spoke with a noticeable Neapolitan accent). During exile in London, paranoia amongst the anarchist colony was rife: thus in the aftermath of the so-called Rubino affair of 1902–1903 Malatesta was shunned by a goodly number of comrades and retired from the scene in a depressive mood for several months.[37] He refused to get involved in projects for a national anarchist newspaper in Italy before *Umanità Nova* was founded in 1920 because he felt he did not possess the moral suasion over his fellow anarchists to create the sort of newspaper he would want to see emerge. That is why although Malatesta was involved in many national and international projects (the First International, an Italian 'anarchist party' in the early 1890s, the international committee to defend anarchists and libertarians at the London Congress of the Second International of 1896, the International Anarchist Conference of 1907, or the varieties of attempts at a national anarchist organization in Italy before and after the First World War), he preferred a small group of acolytes, collaborators and family members (exemplified in his London host family, the Defendis) rather than larger organizations to do his most effective political organizing, such as those associates involved in the newspaper *L'Agitazione* (Ancona) in 1897–1898 or *Volontà* (Ancona) in 1913–1915.[38] Within these restricted circles he possessed a quiet and assured form of personal charisma as numerous testimonies of first encounters with him attest (see the portraits by Armando Borghi, Luigi Fabbri, Max Nettlau or the British journalist George Slocombe).[39]

By 1919 the Garibaldi and Lenin legends preceded his final return to his homeland, filtered through the grapevine of the popular, 'subversive' culture.[40] But there was also an image constructed by the mass-circulation press. First, Malatesta was pictured as a tribune of the people, but also as one of the princely Malatestas, who, along with Kropotkin and Bakunin, were related to the highest levels of European aristocracy. This fantastic invention invoked unexpected connections in the most unlikely places, so that the press lapped up the presumed friendly alliance with Queen Sophia the widow of the last Bourbon ruler of the Kingdom of Naples. Even Giovanni Giolitti, prime minister of Italy, was firmly convinced that Malatesta and the queen lay behind Gaetano Bresci's assassination of the Savoyard King Umberto in 1900.[41] Malatesta was also pictured as an Italian *narodnik*, who had been declassed and gone to the people in the 1870s, abandoning his medical studies to become an electrician and gas fitter. Rather than a man of mysterious aristocratic origins, scheming with anarchist assassins and deposed queens, he was known as a selfless, quiet man living in London's Islington, behaving as a latter-day Mazzinian improver, who would never apply violent methods in his abode of exile, and in any case disapproved of terrorism on principle. When Malatesta was nearly deported from London in 1912, the British Liberal and Conservative press defended him, directly recalling Gladstone' broadsides against 'Re Bomba'. In Islington a local reputation for probity mobilized the neighbourhood and fed into monster demonstrations in favour of this latter-day 'hero of two worlds'.

Indeed if the English knew their part in this remembered ritual of the Risorgimento, Malatesta's peregrinations around the globe, as anar-

chist and trade union organizer (in Argentina, 1885–1889, and the USA
and Cuba, 1899–1900) and as fighter supporting oppressed peoples (in
Bosnia in 1876 and Egypt in 1882), also had resonances in the lives of
Garibaldi and Mazzini. Furthermore, his flight from a prison island recalled the escape of Kropotkin from the Peter and Paul Fortress in Moscow or Bakunin's from Siberia.[42]

Thus the charismatic persona was ready to be activated when he arrived suddenly and mysteriously in Italy at Christmas, 1919.[43] He arrived
in an Italy in which a series of charismatic moments were unfolding.[44]
Mass mobilization was occurring on the Right and Left. Woodrow Wilson drew delirious crowds in Rome for his vision of new world order,
but so too did D'Annunzio at Fiume in a quest to subvert that order,
after Italy did not get all it wanted at Versailles: Italian socialism had
its demagogic barnstormers such as Nicola Bombacci and a dozen other
imitators.[45] The eruption of mass democracy, land and factory occupa-
tions, army mutinies and cost of living riots threatened the very fabric of
the old order, or at least frightened its rulers. And although Mussolini
was still largely sidelined, he too was perfecting his charismatic politics in
the shadow of D'Annunzio. The socialist, syndicalist and anarchist Left
grew with mushroom-like rapidity. And one of the organizing themes
was the return of Malatesta from London. Speeches recalled the exiles
of Garibaldi and Mazzini abroad, and also the jailing of the 'warrior'
anarchist Amilcare Cipriani in the 1880s and the campaign to free him
from incarceration. As Max Nettlau remembered, many hoped that in the
person of Malatesta they had found a leader, a saviour or a liberator. The
old legend of Garibaldi and the recent cult of Lenin had been fused in
Malatesta's persona with the notion of Malatesta as a socialist Garibaldi or
the Italian Lenin.[46] Songs circulated in which Lenin and Malatesta arrive
to liberate a war-weary populace.[47]

So what was the effect of Malatesta on this fever-pitch Italy? Malatesta
was arrested in October 1920 and jailed until July 1921. During his period of freedom from December 1919 to October 1920 he rode the wave
of enthusiasm set off by his arrival home. However, in retrospect he probably lost valuable time in his constant barnstorming, something he grew
to realize during the process itself.[48] His presence helped the anarchists
achieve their greatest popularity since the decline of the First International forty years previously and indeed the Malatestan *Umanità nova* briefly
challenged the dominance of the all-powerful *Avanti!* in its Milanese
heartland during the summer of 1920.[49] But the anarchists were divided
amongst themselves and the maximalist socialists never came to an agreement with them. Meanwhile the reformist leadership of the trade unions
retained control and outmanoeuvred the maximalist, anarchist and syndi-

calist Lefts during the occupation of the factories in September 1920. The reformist and maximalist socialists (except for pockets of the Po Valley and Apulia where anarchists and syndicalists predominated) harnessed the militancy of the landless labourers in the countryside. Perhaps there was a slight chance that a bizarre alliance of Gabriele D'Annunzio and Malatesta could have marched on Rome in early 1920 and overthrown the government of Francesco Nitti, but clearly the nationalist middle classes and rank and file leftists were too busy killing each other to sink their difference to attack the government in Rome. Thus the limitations of pure charismatic politics are demonstrated in these stillborn negotiations.[50]

In any case, Malatesta was carried forward in a whirlwind of enthusiasm throughout northern and central Italy. His arrival had been courtesy of Captain Giulietti, the charismatic boss of the seafarers' union, friend to the unorthodox Right and Left, parliamentary maverick and 'social' war interventionist who supported D'Annunizio in Fiume and opposed the Allied intervention in Russia and demonstrated this by ordering the hijacking of a shipload of armaments destined for the Whites and sending it to Fiume.[51]

After landing at Taranto on Christmas Eve 1919, Malatesta arrived in Genoa the next day and was met by tens of thousands of workers from its industrial hinterlands; and then on 29 December he reached Turin, where the reaction was even more hysterical. He was virtually 'kidnapped' to the *Casa del popolo*, but as Armando Borghi recalls, those poor devils who has a similar goatee to Malatesta were hoisted on shoulders with shouts of 'Long Live Lenin!', 'Long Live Malatesta!'[52] Between February and June 1920, the situation was more precarious for Malatesta. Although still drawing great crowds he was arrested briefly in Tuscany in February 1920 and shot at by the police and civilians at Piacenza in April and Milan in June. His eventual arrest followed the death of two policemen at a rally in Bologna in October.

What did Malatesta make of all of this? First it should be recalled that the arrest of Malatesta following the events in October is rather ironic, since he was the most rational speaker on the platform in Bologna and tried to calm the crowd.[53] Malatesta did not relish the charismatic situations in which he found himself. He disapproved the idolatry of his person by the crowds or the anarchist movement and criticized Pisan anarchists who acclaimed him the Spartacus or Lenin of Italy. Indeed he devoted an entire article to it: '*Grazie, ma basta*' (Thanks, but that's enough).[54] He was disturbed by the cult of the 'Italian Lenin' and felt it inappropriate, morally degrading and politically dangerous to exalt a dead or living human being. He quickly drew parallels between the Jacobins in the French Revolution and the Bolsheviks in the Russian Revolution. Unlike Gramsci who believed that the charismatic dictatorship of Lenin guaranteed the safety of a libertarian regime of workers' and peasants' councils, Malatesta felt that the Bolsheviks, like the Jacobins, would devour the revolution and in turn be devoured by a new Robespierre and a new Napoleon.[55]

Earlier, Malatesta's critique of terrorism during the 1890s was linked to the pernicious effects of hero worship. While he was ambiguous about the role of assassinations in anarchist strategy, nevertheless he felt that such politics were not conducive to the creation of a libertarian personality or an anarchist society. 'One thing is certain', Malatesta explained in a newspaper article written in 1894, 'that with a number of bombs and a number of blows of the knife a society like bourgeois society cannot be overthrown, being built, at it is, on an enormous mass of private interests and prejudices and sustained, more than it by force of arms, by the inertia of the masses and their habits of submission'. Heroic sacrifice, paradoxically, would deepen craven hero worship in the masses.[56]

Malatesta's political project was based on different first principles. Thus to recall Robert Michels, he anticipated the German's iron law of oligarchy and his critique of the bureaucratization of radical organizations and trade unions, including anarchist-friendly syndicalist trade unions. Malatesta was wary of an uncritical form of syndicalism, because for him the natural tendency for revolutionary trade union leadership was towards oligarchy and deradicalization. He felt that anarchist trade unionists should act as libertarian ginger groups in whatever type of trade union they found themselves, remaining a vigilant voice against corporatism, corruption and trade union tribunes and bosses.[57] Thus Malatesta favoured the politics of the Socratic dialogue, not the charismatic harangue. If he possessed a charisma it was the charisma of the young Gramsci or William Morris. He believed in making anarchists one by one, not swaying oceanic crowds: in creating those generations of cadres who were, as I have said, the heart and soul of the Italian anarchist movement before fascism and the rise of communism ripped apart and replaced its previously resilient networks.

Malatesta was in any case very sanguine about his impact on crowds in 1920. He contrasted the close and friendly relationships he had developed in Ancona in 1897–1898 and 1913–1914 with the fleeting effects of the social hurricane of 1920 when his arrival in a town was an occasion, 'a pretext, if you will, to give vent to popular feeling'.[58] So as I have suggested on several occasions, Malatesta was just one of a series of individuals who were catapulted into massive if brief popularity by a number of charismatic moments, which punctuated the *biennio rosso*. Whereas in February 1920 Malatesta was imprisoned after the incident at Tombolo in Tuscany and released after eighteen hours for fear of social unrest, his arrest in October 1920, following the anticlimax of the occupation of the factories, failed to raise significant protest. Perhaps the last time the Left could mobilize around Malatesta was in the spring of 1921 when the old coalition, including elements of the social interventionist Left, came out to protest in solidarity with Malatesta and his fellow imprisoned anarchists' hunger strike, demanding a speedy trial for the imprisoned hunger strikers. But this was cut short when a group of antiorganizationalist anarchists misplaced a bomb intended for the police chief of Milan and killed twenty-one men, women and children enjoying a performance of Franz Lehar's light opera *The Blue Waltz*.[59]

After Malatesta's release from prison in July 1921 the tide had turned, the Left was on the run and Mussolini's movement, which had made a breakthrough in the Po Valley in the spring, was on the ascent. Whereas in Malatesta's case the charismatic moment had no solid organizational base in which to root itself, fascism in the provinces in the Po Valley and the Italo-Slavic frontier of Trieste existed autonomously and in tension with Mussolini in Milan, who established a party in order to tame his own movement.[60] So in this case the charismatic personality, the charismatic moment and an institutional structure fused with fateful consequences.

Conclusion

Let us return to Weber's models. Malatesta was not a charismatic Caesar. His politics stood against this. Nor was he a barnstorming speaker who could easily take advantage of the charismatic moments presented to him during the *biennio rosso*. But he did establish a charismatic linkage with smaller extended family and exile networks, a variation on the theme of countercultural leader Weber describes in *Economy and Society*, which allowed Malatesta to exercise influence in Italy despite being hardly present for decades. But if Weber had Otto Gross in mind, the unstable guru of a sexual utopia, Malatesta was a far more sober and less exploitative charismatic chief. Indeed part of his charisma relied precisely on the consistency of a life dominated by mundane physical labour, interspersed with bouts of revolutionary journalism. Fascist goons destroyed the printing presses of *Umanità nova* after the March on Rome. With the installation of the Mussolini government in Rome, the Left was initially suppressed, albeit it revived in 1924 and survived through to 1926. A bronchial Malatesta was forced to return to labouring and so at the age of seventy he was found doing gas fitting and electrical jobs in damp attics during a dismal Roman winter.

Malatesta was a practical politician: he understood like Weber that society abhors a vacuum and that organization and technology had to be kept running after the revolution. Unlike Kropotkin who believed the basis of anarchism could be found in the superiority of mutual aid present in nature and human society, Malatesta detached human politics, political science and sociology from biological analogies. Anarchism was not scientific, it was a form of human politics which involved will and carefully thought out programmes – thus two of his most famous newspapers or journals were entitled *Volontà* (Will, 1913–1915) and *Pensiero e Volontà* (Thought and Will, 1924–1926).

Malatesta wanted anarchism to be viable in the modern industrial city and therefore he felt Kropotkin's spontaneity, reinforced by his biological determinism, made light of the complex problems of keeping an industrial city alive in the wake of a revolution: he criticized the cult of the general strike since a city would starve within a few days and the solidarity of the strikers would fragment. Thus Malatesta argued against the Italian advocates of Kropotkinite anarchocommunist spontaneity, reminding them that organization was a seamless web in which one merely replaced authoritarian varieties with increasingly antistatist and consensual forms of organization.[61] Similarly, Weber criticized Michels for a naïve and pessimistic determinism, which underwrote his 'Iron Law of Oligarchy'. 'Democracy as such', Weber explains, 'is opposed to the "rule of bureaucracy", in spite and perhaps because of its unavoidable yet unintentional promotion of bureaucratization. Under certain conditions, democracy creates breaks in the bureaucratic pattern and impediments to bureaucratic organization.'[62] Thus like Malatesta's libertarian ginger groups in the trade unions it was possible to work against the trends of bureaucratization and oligarchicalization. In this regard Malatesta shared Weber's and indeed Gramsci's antideterminism.

Malatesta knew that the anarchists were a minority and one gets the impression that he wanted them to be the gadflies of the revolution: the libertarian, loyal opposition, after the united fronts he promoted (the Red Week is the supreme exemplar), had overthrown the old order. An anarchist society could only be realized through moral suasion, education and personal example. Publicly Weber had no time for anarchist utopias but he was tempted by the anarchist vision as demonstrated by this remark he made to Michels after the younger man had published in the *Archiv* the famous article on the oligarchical tendencies of modern society, which foreshadowed his monograph on political parties.

> There are two possibilities: either (1) 'my kingdom is not this world' Tolstoy, or syndicalism thought to its conclusion, which is nothing more than the sentence 'the goal means nothing to me, the movement everything' translated in a revolutionary-political personal statement, but one that you too

have certainly not thought through to its conclusion. (I shall probably write something about this sometime) or (2) affirmation of culture (that is objective culture) expressing itself in sociological conditions of all technique .... In the second case all talk of revolution is farce; any thought of replacing the domination of man over man by any kind of socialist society or ingeniously devised form of democracy is utopia.[63]

Weber did not write about Malatesta, but an ethically consistent if naïve anarchist such as Ernst Toller was not too dissimilar. And though he would have dismissed Malatesta's quest, Malatesta shared with Toller that ethical personalism which was the foundation stone for Weber's modern charismatic politician and/or leader of countercultural movements. We have seen how in the 1890s terrorist violence was linked in Malatesta's mind with hero worship and the potentiality of authoritarianism in the masses. Although he was appalled by the violence unleashed by the Great War, embodied in fascism and Bolshevism, the painful conundrum posed by the use of violence (for he remained convinced of the need for a violent revolution until his death) and the authoritarian nature of violence itself was never resolved in his thought. Nevertheless, Malatesta was a political animal invested with *Persönlichkeit*, who was keenly aware of the gap between the ethic of ultimate ends (*Gesinnungsethik*) and the ethic of responsibility (*Verantwortungsethik*).

Notes

1. I would like to thank the Institute for Advanced Study, Princeton for a visiting fellowship between September 2006 and April 2007 where research for this paper was carried out. I would also like to thank Professor Diego Gambetta and Fellows of Nuffield College, Oxford for hosting me as a Jemolo Fellow during the Michelmas term in 2008, when the final version of this chapter was written.
2. For the history of Italian anarchism to 1945 (in chronological order) see N. Pernicone. 1992. *Italian Anarchism 1864–1892*, Princeton: Princeton University Press; P.C. Masini. 1981. *Storia degli anarchici italiani nell'epoca degli attentati*, Milan: Rizzoli; C. Levy. 1989. 'Italian Anarchism, 1870–1926', in D. Goodway (ed.), *For Anarchism, History, Theory, Practice*, London: Routledge, 25–78; L. Di Lembo. 2001. *Guerra di classe e lotta umana. L'anarchismo in Italia dal biennio rosso alla guerra di Spagna (1919–1939)*, Pisa: BFS; F. Giulietti. 2004. *Il movimento anarchico italiano nella lotta contro il fascismo*, Manduria, Bari and Rome: Lacaita; and A. Aruffo. 2005. *Breve storia degli anarchici italiani 1870–1970*, Rome: Datanews.
3. Excellent recent summaries of Weber's thought are found in S. Whimster. 2007. *Understanding Weber*, London: Routledge; and J. Radkau. 2009. *Max Weber, a Biography*, Cambridge: Polity.
4. For Max Weber's politics see W.J. Mommsen. 1985. *Max Weber and German Politics 1890–1920*, Chicago: University of Chicago. I review the arguments about his attraction to anarchism and the complex agenda which lay behind it in C. Levy. 1999. 'Max Weber, Anarchism and Libertarian Culture: Personality and Power Politics', in S. Whimster (ed.),

Max Weber and the Culture of Anarchy, Basingstoke: Macmillan, 83–109. Also see K.-L. Ay. 1999. 'Max Weber: A German Intellectual and the Question of War Guilt after the Great War', in Whimster, *Max Weber and the Culture of Anarchy*, 110–28.

5. D. Beetham, 1985. *Max Weber and the Theory of Modern Bourgeois Politics*, Cambridge: Polity, 1985; F. Tuccari. 1993. *I dilemmi della democrazia moderna. Max Weber e Robert Michels*, Bari: Laterza.

6. W. Hennis. 1988. *Max Weber: Essays in Reconstruction*, London: Allen & Unwin, 150; R. Schroeder. 1991. '"Personality" and "Inner Distance": The Conceptions of the Individual in Max Weber's Sociology', *History of Human Sciences* 4(1), 61–78; R. Bologh. 1995. *Love or Greatness: Max Weber and Masculine Thinking – A Feminist Enquiry*, London: Unwin Hyman, 106; P. Lassman and R. Speirs (eds). 1995. *Weber: Political Writings*, Cambridge: Cambridge University Press, xxii; S. Whimster and S. Lash (eds). 1987. *Max Weber: Rationality and Modernity*, London: Allen & Unwin, 266.

7. É. Karádi. 1987. 'Ernst Bloch and Georg Lukács in Max Weber's Heidelberg', in W.J. Mommsen and J. Osterhammel (eds), *Max Weber and His Contemporaries*, London: Allen & Unwin, 500; W.J. Mommsen. 1987. 'Robert Michels and Max Weber: Moral Conviction versus the Politics of Responsibility', in Mommsen and Osterhammel, *Max Weber and His Contemporaries*, 121–38.

8. For his libertarian and countercultural encounters and influences, see contributions in Whimster, *Understanding Weber*. For the last writings and speeches and fears of German collapse, see G. Roth. 1988–89. 'Weber's Political Failure', *Telos* 78(Winter), 136–49; and W. Schluchter. 1996. *Paradoxes of Modernity: Culture and Conduct in the Theory of Max Weber*, Stanford: Stanford University Press, 7–41.

9. For the Weber–Michels' relationship, see A. Mitzman. 1973. *Sociology and Estrangement: Three Sociologists in Imperial Germany*, New York: Knopf; Mommsen, 'Robert Michels and Max Weber'; Tuccari, *I dilemmi della democrazia moderna*.

10. M. Ridolfi. 1992. *Il PSI e la nascita del partito di massa, 1892–1922*, Bari: Laterza, 150; Tuccari, *I dilemmi della democrazia moderna*.

11. D. Beetham. 1977. 'From Socialism to Fascism: The Relation between Theory and Practice in the Work of Robert Michels', *Political Studies* 25(1), 3–24, and 25(2), 161–81.

12. C. Levy. 1987. 'Max Weber and Antonio Gramsci', in Mommsen and Osterhammel, *Max Weber and His Contemporaries*, 392–93.

13. Mommsen, 'Robert Michels and Max Weber'.

14. D. Chalcraft. 1993. 'Weber, Wagner and Thoughts of Death', *Sociology* 27(3), 433–39; W. Schwentker. 1987. 'Passion as a Model of Life: Max Weber, the Otto Gross Circle and Eroticism', in Mommsen and Osterhammel, *Max Weber and His Contemporaries*, 483–98; Levy, 'Max Weber, Anarchism and Libertarian Culture'; U. Linse. 1999. 'Sexual Revolution and Anarchism: Erich Mühsam', in Whimster, *Max Weber and the Culture of Anarchy*, 110–28.

15. C. Levy. 2001. 'The People and the Professors: Socialism and the Educated Middle Classes in Italy, 1870–1915', *Journal of Modern Italian Studies* 6(2), 195–208.

16. Ridolfi, *Il PSI e la nascita del partito di massa*, 154–79.

17. S. Falasca-Zamponi. 1997. *Fascist Spectacle: The Aesthetics of Power in Mussolini's Italy*, Berkeley: University of California Press, 43; A. Luparini. 2001. *Anarchici di Mussolini: dalla sinistra al fascismo tra rivoluzione e revisionismo*, Montespertoli: MIR Edizioni; S.P. Whitaker. 2002. *The Anarcho-individualist Origins of Italian Fascism*, New York: Peter Lang.

18. For *sovversivismo*, see C. Levy. 2007. '"*Sovversivismo*": The Radical Political Culture of Otherness in Liberal Italy', *Journal of Political Ideologies* 12(2), 147–61. For the creation of the Garibaldi myth, see Lucy Riall's wonderful book: L. Riall. 2007. *Garibaldi: Invention of a Hero*, New Haven: Yale University Press.

19. A. Gramsci. 1975. *Quaderni del carcere*, ed. V. Gerratana, vol. 1, Turin: Einaudi, 223.

20. C. Levy. 1999. *Gramsci and the Anarchists*, Oxford: Berg.

21. Levy, '"*Sovversivismo*"', 149–50; 155–58; C. Levy. 2011. *Antonio Gramsci: Marxism, Modernity and Machiavelli*, Cambridge: Polity.
22. See my remarks in: C. Levy. forthcoming. *The Rooted Cosmopolitan: Errico Malatesta, the Life and Times of an Italian Anarchist in Exile*.
23. Levy, 'Italian Anarchism, 1870–1926'.
24. C. Levy. 2000.'Currents of Italian Syndicalism before 1926', *International Review of Social History* 45(2), 209–50.
25. The best account of the Red Week is still L. Lotti. 1965. *La Settimana Rossa*, Florence: Le Monnier.
26. For a thorough biography, see G. Berti. 2003. *Errico Malatesta e il movimento anarchico italiano e internazionale*, Milan: Francoangeli.
27. For the exile network and Malatesta, see C. Levy. 1981. 'Malatesta in Exile', *Annali della Fondazione Einaudi* 15, 245–70; P. Brunello and P. DiPaola (eds). 2003. *Errico Malatesta. Autobiografia mai scritta: Ricordi (1853–1932)*, Caserta: Spartaco.
28. Levy, 'Malatesta in Exile', 11.
29. Pernicone, *Italian Anarchism*, 144.
30. L. Fabbri. 1951. *Malatesta, l'uomo e il pensiero*, Naples: Edizioni RL, 34.
31. E. Malatesta. 1975 (1935). 'Dichiarazioni Autodifesa alla Assise di Milano. Un Ricordo di Ancona', *Errico Malatesta Pagine di lotta quotidiana e scritti vari, 1919/1923, Scritti volume 2*, Carrara: Tipografica Cooperativa, 312.
32. V. Richards. 1965. *Malatesta: Life and Ideas*, London: Freedom Press, 217.
33. See the various treatments of Galleani: P.C. Masini. 1974. *Storia degli anarchici dal Bakunin a Malatesta (1862–1892)*, Milan: Rizzoli; Masini, *Storia degli anarchici italiani nell'epoca degli attentati*; P. Avrich. 1991. *Sacco and Vanzetti: The Anarchist Background*, Princeton: Princeton University Press; Pernicone, *Italian Anarchism*; N. Pernicone. 1993. 'Luigi Galleani and Italian Anarchist Terrorism in the United States', *Studi Emigrazione* 30, 469–88; N. Whelehan. 2005. 'Luigi Galleani and Peter Kropotkin in Comparative Perspective', *Anarchist Studies* 13(2), 147–68; N. Pernicone. 2005. *Carlo Tresca: Portrait of a Rebel*, New York: Palgrave Macmillan; B. Gage. 2009. *The Day Wall Street Exploded: A Story of America in its First Age of Terror*, Oxford: Oxford University Press.
34. Quoted in Avrich, *Sacco and Vanzetti*, 47.
35. Fabbri, *Malatesta*, 29–30. For a prime example of maximalist socialist rhetoric at its most demagogic, see S. Noiret. 1991. *Massimalismo e crisi dello stato liberale. Nicola Bombacci (1879–1924)*, Milan: FrancoAngeli.
36. I also discuss this in C. Levy. 1998.'Charisma and Social Movements: Errico Malatesta and Italian Anarchism', *Modern Italy* 3(2), 205–17.
37. For the Rubino affair and Malatesta's uneven relationship with other Italian anarchist exiles in London, see P. Di Paola. 2007. 'The Spies who Came in from the Heat: the International Surveillance of the Anarchists in London', *European History Quarterly* 37(3), 189–215.
38. Levy, 'Errico Malatesta in Exile'.
39. This is a major theme of Levy, 'Errico Malatesta in Exile'.
40. R. Vivarelli. 1991. *Storia delle origini del fascismo. L'Italia dalla grande guerra alla Marcia su Roma*, 2 vols, vol. 2, Bologna: Il Mulino, 766; C. Petracchi. 1990. 'Il mito della rivoluzione sovietica in Italia, 1917–1920', *Storia contemporanea* 13, 1107–30.
41. C. Levy. 2007. 'The Anarchist Assassin in Italian History 1870s to 1930s', in S. Gundle and L. Rinaldi (eds), *Assassination and Murder in Modern Italy: Transformations in Society and Culture*, New York and London: Palgrave Macmillan, 207–32.
42. For these aspects of his life, see Berti, *Errico Malatesta* and Levy, *The Rooted Cosmopolitan*.
43. For Malatesta during the *biennio rosso*, see P. Finzi. 1990. *La nota persona. Errico Malatesta in Italia Dicembre 1919–Luglio 1920*, Ragusa: La Fiaccola.
44. For a general account of the *biennio rosso*, see Vivarelli, *Storia delle origini del fascismo*. I summarize the role of the anarchists and syndicalists during the *biennio rosso* in Levy, 'Italian Anarchism', 61–75 and Levy, *Gramsci and the Anarchists*.

45. For Wilson in Italy, see D. Rossini. 2008. *Woodrow Wilson and the American Myth in Italy: Culture, Diplomacy and War Propaganda*, Cambridge: Harvard University Press.
46. M. Nettlau. 1922. *Errico Malatesta*, New York: Il Martello, 261.
47. See the discussion in S. Pivato. 2005. *Bella ciao. Canto e politica nella storia d'Italia*, Rome and Bari: Laterza.
48. In general see Finzi, *La nota persona*.
49. For a vivid description of the role of the anarchists in Milan in 1919–1920, see V. Mantovani. 1979. *Mazurka blu. La strage del Diana*, Milan: Rusconi.
50. Vivarelli summarizes the events in *Storia delle origini del fascismo* and I cover it in Levy, 'Currents of Italian Syndicalism', 224.
51. For Giulietti, see G. Salotti. 1982. *Giuseppe Giulietti*, Rome: Bonacci. The most recent account of the subversive and countercultural activities at Fiume is in C. Salaris. 2002. *Alla festa della rivoluzione. Artisti e libertari con D'Annunzio a Fiume*, Bologna: Il Mulino.
52. Quoted in Mantovani, *Mazurka Blu*, 156.
53. Fabbri, *Malatesta*, 31.
54. *Il Libertario*, La Spezia, 8 January 1920; *Volontà*, 16 January 1920.
55. Levy, 'Italian Anarchism', 73; P. Nursey-Bray. 1995. 'Malatesta and the Anarchist Revolution', *Anarchist Studies* 3(1), 25–44; Finzi, *La nota persona*, 81. For general overviews of the relationship between the anarchists, the communists and the Russian Revolution, see S. Fedele. 1996. *Una breve illusione. Gli anarchici italiani e la Russia Sovietica 1917–1939*, Milan: FrancoAngeli; Levy, *Gramsci and the Anarchists*, 1999; F. Giuletti. 2007. 'Anarchici contro comunisti. Movimento anarchico italiano e bolschevichi', *Italia contemporanea* 247(June), 165–93.
56. E. Malatesta. 1894. 'The Duties of the Present Hour', *Liberty*, August, 61–62; C. Levy. 1993. 'Malatesta in London: the Era of Dynamite', in L. Sponza and A. Tosi (eds), *A Century of Italian Emigration to Britain 1880s to 1980s: Five Essays*, Supplement to *The Italianist*, 13, 5–42.
57. Levy, 'Malatesta in Exile'.
58. Quoted in Finzi, *La nota persona*, 81.
59. In general see Mantovani, *Mazurka blu*.
60. E. Gentile. 1989. *Storia del Partito Fascista 1919–1922. Movimento e milizia*, Bari: Laterza.
61. See Paul Nursey-Brays' treatment of Malatesta's thought, 'Malatesta and the Anarchist Revolution'. And for Kropotkin and his Italian antiorganizationalist anarchocommunists, see Whelehan, 'Luigi Galleani and Peter Kropotkin'.
62. M. Weber. 1978. *Economy and Society: An Outline of Interpretive Sociology*, 4 vols, ed. G. Roth and C. Wittich, vol. 2, Berkeley: University of California Press, 991.
63. Quoted in Levy, 'Max Weber, Anarchism and Libertarian Culture', 97.

CHAPTER 5

PASIONARIA

A Case of Charisma
through Representation

Juan Avilés

In May 1944, a group of leaders held a meeting in Moscow to appoint a new general secretary of the Spanish Communist Party (*Partido Comunista de España*, PCE). The Bulgarian Stepan Stepanov, who acted as an intermediary between the PCE and the international communist movement, was the first to speak and his words showed the extraordinary prestige that Dolores Ibárruri, known all over the world as Pasionaria, had achieved as a result of her role in the Spanish Civil War. Stepanov stated that, apart from the Soviet Communist Party, the PCE was the only one which could rely on such a personality as Dolores Ibárruri. He felt like a dwarf in the shade of such a giant, he declared.[1] This homage to Pasionaria was in part a result of the revolutionary glory the Spanish people had achieved through their resistance to fascism during the three-year Civil War. However, it also showed that the international communist leaders assumed that Ibárruri was a leader worthy of her people in her revolutionary strength. Should we conclude that she was regarded as a charismatic leader in the sense that Max Weber gave to this expression? Did she become a leader because people recognized extraordinary qualities in her?[2]

Preliminary Remarks

The answers are not simple, given that the specific characteristics of charismatic leadership are difficult to define and the word *charisma* is usually

---

Notes for this chapter begin on page 115.

employed in such a vague manner that it leads to confusion, to the extent that William Spinrad has proposed avoiding the term altogether in the analysis of political phenomena.[3] However, the concept of charisma may be useful if the sense in which it is used is adequately explained. Some preliminary remarks are therefore needed.

In the case of Pasionaria, needless to say, her leadership was not considered to be in any way charged with supernatural meaning; it was purely human, as is the case with other past and current revolutionary leaders expressly mentioned by Weber as examples of charismatic leaders.[4] According to Weber, charismatic domination is based on a special interaction between leaders and followers, so that the validity of a leader's charisma is demonstrated by his followers' recognition. However, that recognition does not determine the legitimacy of the leader but must be seen as the fulfilment of a duty: the followers must recognize their leader's charisma.[5] In this sense the meeting during which Pasionaria was elected general secretary was revealing: Stepanov did not put it to the vote but made reference to the exceptional personality of the woman who was going to lead the party from that moment on.

Charismatic leadership has both a personal, psychological dimension: the leader's qualities; and a sociological dimension: the circumstances which make his or her recognition possible. According to Martin Spencer, 'the person may possess gifts, the situation may generate tensions, the charisma itself is the *historical product* of the interaction between the two' (emphasis in original).[6] We must therefore keep in mind the specific qualities that endowed Dolores Ibárruri with her charisma as well as the specific circumstances of the Spanish Civil War in which that charisma was recognized.

As for the situations which foster charismatic leadership, two observations made by Liah Greenfeld are worthy of consideration. First, people are more usually attracted by a charismatic leader during a crisis in which a situation of anomy emerges: 'a condition of acute inconsistency between different values, norms and cognitions, including the perception of reality, which, as a result of this inconsistency, neutralize each other and lose their authority'.[7] These anomic situations foster revolutionary change. Weber called attention to the revolutionary potential of charismatic authority that breaks the existing rules in order to impose new values.[8]

Greenfeld also emphasizes that some value systems foster charismatic leadership in particular. Those societies that place a high value on individual freedom and demonstrate a high regard for rationality are less likely to nurture charismatic leadership. On the other hand the tendency to submit to the values of the group – be it a nation, a religious community or a social class – at the expense of the individual free will fosters charismatic authority.[9] Therefore the communist movement with its revolutionary vocation, its contempt for the individual and its class-based ethos was particularly suitable for charismatic authority.

In order to analyse the kind of charismatic leadership represented by Pasionaria the typologies coined by Greenfeld and Spencer to clarify Weber's insight may be of help. Greenfeld distinguishes between personal charisma and institutional charisma. Genuine charisma is personal and it is characterized by the capacity to create a contagious excitement, as in the case of prophets, whereas institutional charisma represents a type of authority characterized by its embodiment of the fundamental values and principles of the group.[10] Genuine charisma leads to a break with existing norms driven by a leader, but this does not happen in the case of institutional charisma. Revolutionary leaders like Pasionaria may be considered examples of institutional charisma when they follow the steps of previous leaders. Some of her speeches were charismatic in the sense that they were able to generate enthusiasm, but they did not carry a personal message. Her strength was her ability to embody collective values, such as revolutionary faith or popular heroism.

Martin Spencer distinguishes two kinds of charismatic leadership, one that is based on mastery and one based on representation. The savant, the general or the ruler may have charismatic mastery, that is to say, a capacity to control events and therefore to arrange the future. In the case of revolutionary leaders their ability to control events is limited, but history is full of instances in which they were able to maintain and even to increase their forces despite successive defeats. The revolutionary leader creates charisma 'by convincing his followers that *his vision of the future will come to pass*' (emphasis in original). The successful politician, general or revolutionary leader who despite defeats is able to convey to his followers his unshakable faith in triumph reveals a charismatic mastery which gives rise to awe. On the other hand the charisma practised through representation generates enthusiasm because it offers an order that satisfies fundamental needs and desires of the followers. Of course a charismatic leader may combine mastery with representation but there are also leaders who have charisma based on representation but do not achieve real mastery: for instance a king who reigns but does not govern.[11] I think this was Pasionaria's case during most of her political career.

Spencer also distinguishes three styles of representation: the innovator, who creates values suitable for satisfying unknown needs of the followers; the articulator, capable of expressing in words what his or her followers wish to hear; and the symbolizer, who does not create new values but simply stands for them. As we shall see, Pasionaria was never an innovator, she sometimes acted as articulator, and she was mostly and for a long time the symbolizer of communist values.

A Singular Personality

Dolores Ibárruri was internationally noticed for the first time during the seventeenth Congress of the Soviet Communist Party, which she addressed in February 1934 as the representative of the PCE. She was very pleased with having attracted the attention of the congress, as she explained in a letter to her Spanish comrades: 'You should be proud; a wife of a poor miner from Somorrostro, but one who represents the Communist Party, of a country where the rise of revolution leads to the urgent task of conquering power, received the overwhelming ovations of the Congress; every conversation revolved around the Spanish delegate's intervention.'[12] Before she went back to Spain she had the courage to criticize the line of her party on trade unions in the presence of one of the main leaders of the Communist International, Dimitri Manuilski, who invited her to stay in Moscow a few more days and participate in the debate on the new trade-union line.

The particular situation of Spain, a country in which the Communist Party was very weak but which had a strong working-class movement controlled by socialists and anarchosyndicalists and where the proclamation of the Republic three years earlier had created great revolutionary expectations, contributed to the interest people had in Pasionaria. Her personality was, however, also an important factor. Her oratorical strength, which stemmed both from her voice and her gestures, drew the attention of the audience despite the fact that most delegates could only follow her speech in translation. During her conversation with Manuilski she showed an independent character. She was a woman and that could have been a liability in a candidate for leadership, but in an overwhelmingly masculine gathering it made her energy more remarkable. The fact that she was the wife of a poor miner was by no means an inconvenience because it demonstrated that she belonged to the working class, which represented humanity's future. Therefore she really had the right qualities to become a symbol of the Communist International, and the International played a very important role in her promotion. If Pasionaria became a charismatic leader she was certainly one of the institutional kind. The values she fostered were radically opposed to traditional Spanish ones, but she did not create or articulate them; they were the values of international communism.

Her natural intelligence, her absolute loyalty to the PCE, her strong character, her aggressiveness against the enemies of her party, her mastery as a speaker able to provoke both hate and pity were key factors paving her way to leadership. All these personal qualities gave her prestige among the Spanish militants and in the International, but if in the years of civil war she became the international symbol of working women, of the Spanish people and of the revolution which would someday succeed, it was mainly through the propaganda effort of the Communist International, which considered her the most appropriate representative of the Spanish people fighting against fascism.

Dolores Ibárruri was born in 1895 in the Basque mining region of Somorrostro, one of the most rebellious strongholds of the Spanish working class. Her father was a Basque miner and her mother was a Castilian who had worked in the mine until she got married. Hers was a Catholic and right-wing family which had attained its modest comfort with great efforts. Dolores attended school until she was fifteen and she wanted to become a teacher but her family could not afford to pay for her schooling. She married a miner who, unlike her father, was a socialist. With him she experienced poverty, especially during his spells in prison as a result of his revolutionary activities, and he introduced her to socialist militancy. She abandoned Catholicism, redirected her faith to the revolutionary ideal and began reading socialist doctrine, acquiring an articulate revolutionary vision unusual in her rustic environment. She explained this in a sketch of her life which she wrote for the Communist International twenty years later.

> When I got married and broke with my family as a consequence of marrying a socialist, which meant an apostasy for them, a completely new perspective opened before me when my husband, who was not educated but had a formidable revolutionary spirit, started to introduce me to the socialist ideals. Despite doing so in an unsophisticated manner, as he was a non-literate miner, I understood that there was something magnificent in those ideas and I begged him to borrow socialist literature from the socialist library.[13]

She joined the Socialist Party in 1918.

In 1919 she published her first article in a socialist paper under the pseudonym of Pasionaria (passionflower), a pen name with obvious Christian origins, because it refers to the Passion of Christ and His Mother's suffering. Dolores herself was named after Mater Dolorosa and was very devoted to her as a child. This pseudonym, which accompanied her all her life and became famous all over the world, suited her not only because she was always passionate, but because she took upon herself the representation of the suffering of the Spanish mothers during the Civil War.

When the Communist Party was founded the whole socialist group of Somorrostro, where Dolores and her husband were militants, joined it and she was elected a member of its first Vizcaya provincial committee. This was at the beginning of two years of serious conflicts in the mining region, during which there were even armed clashes between socialists and communists. Then, in 1923, the PCE was banned by the newly established dictatorship of Primo de Rivera. During the seven years of dictatorship, when her husband was arrested several times and some of their daughters died as children, Pasionaria showed her courage, participating in several protests. Her comrades recognized her value and she was elected a member of the Central Committee of the PCE in 1930.

During the first years of the Republic the PCE adopted a very hostile stance towards the new regime, which it condemned as reactionary despite the fact that the Socialist Party was part of the governing coalition. This political line resulted in very few votes for the Communists and led to the imprisonment of some of them. Pasionaria herself was imprisoned three times but those years also witnessed her rising to the leadership of the party. In 1931 she moved to Madrid and separated from her husband. She became an editor of the party's newspaper and in 1932 she was appointed secretary for women's affairs of the Central Committee. She was very concerned by the scant interest her party showed in proselytizing among women. 'Our own comrades are opposed to the participation of women in political and social life', she wrote in an essay published in the party's newspaper.[14] She also became a leader of the Women's National Committee against War and Fascism, which held its first congress in Madrid in July 1934. It was one of the front organizations open to people of different ideologies which communists began to foster as part of their new antifascist strategy. The Asturias uprising took place soon after that, and was supported by socialists, communists and anarchosyndicalists in an attempt to put an end to the right-wing electoral advantage and to establish a revolutionary regime. Its defeat led to a repression which Pasionaria denounced vehemently. It was then that she began to dress in black. She was forty years old and the black clothes bestowed on her a certain dignity; besides, they contributed to the image she would adopt, of a woman who represented the people's suffering.

The Birth of a Charismatic Figure

Pasionaria's charisma emerged at the beginning of the Civil War, when she delivered highly emotive speeches in which the watchwords of that moment were expressed in effective although not very original phrases which would become memorable and enhance her public image. In Madrid, just at the beginning of the war, she spoke the words which would become the motto of republican fighters, 'They shall not pass!' At a meeting in Paris two months later she made a declaration of patriotic dignity: 'The Spanish people would rather die on their feet than live on their knees'. Then during a multitudinous meeting held in Madrid in October she made a vigorous, womanly appeal to manly courage: 'It is better to be the widow of a hero than the wife of a coward'. These sentences may seem trivial when read now, but one must imagine the tense atmosphere and the energetic yet feminine voice that pronounced them in order to understand the strength of their appeal.

Her speech in Paris was delivered when she was visiting France as a member of the Spanish People's Front delegation with the aim of obtaining a more favourable attitude on the part of Léon Blum's government towards the republican cause. Invited by the French communists, who played a fundamental role in the international propaganda campaign for the Spanish Republic, Pasionaria had the opportunity to intervene at a multitudinous meeting held in a big stadium, the winter cycle track. Her short speech was along the lines of the Communist International, whose propaganda did not represent the fight in Spain as a socialist revolution but as a defence of freedom against the fascist threat. She pointed out that parties with different ideologies fought together against reactionary aggression supported by foreign fascist powers, and fought also for the freedom of all countries. They needed armaments for that: 'We need weapons to defend freedom and peace!' She spoke in Spanish, so the impact of her speech on the audience was mainly due to her appearance, her voice and her gestures, but her message was immediately spread by the French press, multiplying the effect of this oratorical masterpiece. In a country like France, shocked by the tragic experience of the Great War and willing to avoid a new war at all cost, Pasionaria combined two apparently contradictory ideas: the shipment of weapons to a country at war and the fight for international peace.[15]

In Spain Pasionaria had already become popular during the tense months before the outbreak of the Civil War. She had been elected as a member of parliament in February and although the PCE was part of the People's Front coalition that supported republican government she did not hide her contempt for republican rule of law. In two parliamentary speeches which helped to make her one of the most important figures on the political scene, she asked for the imprisonment of the right-wing leaders because of their responsibility for the repression of the left-wing uprising which took place in Asturias in October 1934. She accused José María Gil Robles, chief of the main right-wing party, of being responsible for the 'most terrible torture and repression in Spanish proletarian history' and she stated that she had witnessed the suffering of those mothers whose sons had been tortured. The mothers' suffering constituted the principal emotional content of her speech, which served to launch an unusual proposal before the parliament: the imprisonment of the main opposition party's leader and all those who had governed in the period when the repression of the Asturian uprising took place.[16] The socialist press acclaimed this 'vibrant and emotive speech of comrade Pasionaria'.[17] Later, during the last great debate of the republican parliament, one month before the outbreak of the Civil War, when the right-wing leaders accused the government of tolerating the revolutionary violence of socialists and communists, Pasionaria gave them the most aggressive reply. She said that in order to avoid disturbances it was necessary to send to prison those employers who did not accept the government's decisions, those landowners who condemned the peasants to starvation, those right-wing deputies who were responsible for the 1934 repression and who now dared to accuse the government.[18] Her speech was highly acclaimed. She was congratulated by many republican, socialist and communist members and the left-wing press praised her. A socialist newspaper said she had the face of a Mater Dolorosa and a clear, emphatic and resolute voice, while a republican paper noted her severe and dramatic figure, like that of a heroine.[19]

During the Civil War Pasionaria not only evoked the suffering of mothers and that of the working people but also presented herself as the representative of all that suffering. She said as much in a widely reported response that she wrote to a Soviet working woman who had sent her a letter of admiration.

> I represent the millenarian suffering of the exploited masses, scoffed, deprived of all joy, all happiness, all rights; my voice expresses the rebellious spirit of a people who do not want to be slaves, who wish and yearn for freedom, culture, well-being, progress. My voice vibrates with the tears of those mothers who cannot laugh or feel joy, who can only feel pain and suffering.[20]

The other main topic of her speeches was the exaltation of the revolutionary resolve of the Communist Party, which she contrasted with the weakness of the other left-wing parties. In her speeches the people and the communists were the ones who fought, and although the communists were represented in a coalition government of all the left-wing parties, she supported no future for any other party. When in June 1937 Pasionaria presented a report on the unification of the Communist and Socialist Parties she stated that the socialists would have to adhere fully to Leninist and Stalinist principles. Her report concluded with a profession of faith in the world revolutionary leader:

> We are Stalinists because the great theory of Marx, Engels and Lenin has been enriched by Stalin, who has taught the Communists to maintain an unshakable Stalinist determination, even in the worst situations, whether fighting or at work, and to defend the principle of irreconcilability with the class enemy and with the renegades of the revolutionary cause.

Among these renegades the Trotskyites stood out because they were 'a poisonous plant' which had grown in the bosom of the proletariat, had also infiltrated the Socialist Party, and had to be eradicated.[21]

In the years of the Civil War those vibrant speeches and writings gave Pasionaria charisma but it was of the representational type. She was the best symbol of the Communist Party's values but she was not a decisive force in the formulation of its policy. The Communist leader Santiago Carrillo recognized this in his memoirs, stating that Dolores Ibárruri was prominent among the leaders of the party, thanks to her unique personal qualities, such as her beautiful voice, her geniality and her ability to forge sentences that moved the audience, but that she 'was politically criticized on some occasions', particularly 'for carrying her criticism of the other parties too far'.[22] For instance she was against the participation of her party in the coalition formed in September 1936 by the socialist leader Francisco Largo Caballero, but nevertheless it joined that government. Of course it was not Ibárruri who was general secretary at the time, but José Díaz. On the other hand the party's direction was heavily influenced by the Communist International's delegates, particularly Victorio Codovilla at the beginning of the war and later Palmiro Togliatti. The Soviet ambassador Marcel Rosenberg informed Moscow in September 1936 that, with the exception of Pasionaria, the PCE lacked leaders who had national authority and that Codovilla had profited from the situation and assumed leadership improperly.[23] The French communist André Marty was of a similar opinion; he informed them that General Secretary José Díaz was the only person capable of assuming leadership but that this was not possible due to his illness and all the decisions were taken by Codovilla, whereas the rest of Spanish leaders only followed orders or performed specific tasks, which in the case of Pasionaria were those related to women and propaganda.[24]

Mastery and Representation

For fifteen years, from 1944 to 1959, Pasionaria was general secretary of the PCE. Her prestige in the international communist movement was immense and her party duly promoted a cult of personality around her, but does that mean that she exerted a charismatic authority over her party? There are some reasons to doubt it. The circumstances were not appropriate for such a development because the party had experienced total defeat during the Civil War; it survived in the interior of Spain in a clandestine state and faced brutal repression, while its main leaders lived in exile. The effective leadership of Pasionaria was also hindered because during the greatest part of that period she was not in France, which was the fundamental base for the control of the party. And finally Dolores Ibárruri seems always to have had more ability for propaganda than for political management. Nevertheless it was not until 1959 that she was relegated to the symbolic function of president of the PCE.

As general secretary she had enjoyed the kind of cult of personality which was due to the most revered communist leaders of the Stalinist age. Her case was quite exceptional, as unlike Mao Zedong or Kim Il-sung she was not the leader of her country but a party leader exiled after defeat. On the other hand the cult of personality was not characteristic of Spanish political culture and therefore her cult should be traced to the Soviet example. After the Russian Revolution Lenin had been exalted by the Bolsheviks as an outstanding leader, but the real beginning of the personality cult in the Soviet Union should be dated around 1931, when both Lenin and Stalin, as the new incarnation of the dead leader, became infallible oracles of a new faith.[25] From that moment until his death Stalin was regarded as 'the source of all initiative in Soviet society, the fount of all wisdom and the reason for all successes'.[26] Certainly Pasionaria did not reach such an extraordinary status but nevertheless it is puzzling that Stepanov could have considered her the greatest leader of world communism after Stalin himself. Possibly that was not due to her personal charisma but to her useful role as an icon of antifascism. There is no doubt that during the Spanish Civil War she had been promoted by the Comintern as the symbol of the Spanish people's fight against fascism and that was the origin of her extraordinary status among world communist leaders. Moreover she was a great asset for the PCE in the hard years of its persecution by Franco's regime.

An example of the cult of her personality is an article published in 1950 by the theoretical journal of the party, *Nuestra Bandera*, according to which the name of Pasionaria was 'admired by all the peoples of the world'; her life was 'studied with admiration by the communists from various countries'; she was respected as a mother who had known how to educate her children, making heroes of them at the service of the sacred cause of communism; in India, women used to kiss her portrait and in China, they called her 'our beloved Pasionaria'; in the cities and towns of Spain, thousands of working families considered her a 'saint woman', the only one who could 'save Spain'; in the cold and damp prisons, she kept up the hope of prisoners, and tens of heroes had died speaking her name. Worker and daughter of workers, comrade of José Díaz, educated according to the immortal principles of Marxism-Leninism-Stalinism, she was 'the chief of the Communist Party and of the Spanish people, for her unshakable fidelity towards Lenin and Stalin, for her immense faith in working class power, for her proletarian internationalism, for her infinite love of the Soviet Union and its glorious chief, the great Stalin'.[27]

Nowadays these sentences may sound bogus but it would be a mistake to think that they were empty words. Probably the trust in superhuman leaders helped many communists to continue their fight in extremely hard circumstances. You can hardly doubt the sincerity of a communist militant condemned to death when he addressed a clandestine letter to Ibárruri in which he presented her as an 'incarnation of our heroic people'.[28] And a perfect instance of what Martin Spencer designated charisma based on representation is a passage from a poem written by Rafael Alberti for her sixtieth birthday: 'She is something else: the working class,/ mother of the morning sun,/ compass of our victory,/ sure saving star,/ Pasionaria, the new dawn, is the Communist Party.'[29]

When Alberti produced this outstanding expression of a personality cult Stalin was already dead and the international communist movement was on the eve of great changes that would also affect the PCE. In December 1955 Spain was admitted to the United Nations, reinforcing in this way the growing international acceptance obtained by Franco's regime. The PCE published a communiqué, approved by Dolores Ibárruri, which condemned this event as a new offence of imperialism against Spanish democracy. Nothing was indeed new except for the fact that the Soviet delegation had voted in favour of the entry of Spain. The party's veteran leaders preferred to ignore this but Santiago Carrillo appreciated its meaning: it was a symptom of the new atmosphere of peaceful coexistence with the West fostered by Khrushchev. Therefore Carrillo wrote a long article about this question for the theoretical journal of the party arguing that the entry of new countries into the UN represented the triumph of the policy of peaceful coexistence supported by the Soviet Union and that the end of Spain's isolation would contribute to its democratic transformation.[30]

Pasionaria realized that Carrillo and his comrades in Paris had initiated a change in the party's policy without her participation and she prepared an adequate response which began with a debate in the delegation of the PCE at the twentieth Congress of the Soviet Union Communist Party. The crisis probably would have ended with Carrillo's defeat if a formidable event had not taken place: the secret session of the congress held on 24 February, during which Khrushchev presented the famous report in which he denounced the cult of Stalin's personality and revealed some of his crimes. This represented a great blow for many communists, including Pasionaria: the most important communist leader after Lenin, he whose words had been received as articles of faith, was now denounced by his successor.

After the congress of the Soviet Union Communist Party the political debate continued in the Spanish delegation. Dolores accused Carrillo, who was absent, and his collaborator Fernando Claudín, who attended the meeting, of leading the activity of the party in Spain without the other leaders' participation. She pointed out that she had not been informed about what was happening in the party and in the country. Claudín repeated the ideas presented by Khrushchev's report and reminded the delegation that a cult of personality had also been promoted for Dolores Ibárruri.[31] However the main object of his attack was her collaborator, Vicente Uribe, whom Claudín and Carrillo were determined to present as the supreme Spanish instance of the cult of personality that communists should now condemn. The Paris group defended very optimistic ideas about the possibilities for change in Spain and in contrast Uribe's realism seemed spineless. Finally Pasionaria concluded that Carrillo and Claudín's position was more appropriate to the new times and she accepted Uribe's ejection from the leadership. On the other hand her support was fundamental for Carrillo, because he feared that if she fought with all her prestige the political change he intended to bring about, most of the party would be very reluctant to follow his line. Therefore it was Dolores Ibárruri who presented the new communist strategy before the plenary meeting of the Executive Committee. This strategy would soon be known as one of national reconciliation, based on an agreement which would lead to Franco's fall by entirely peaceful means. On the other hand, Carrillo exempted Dolores Ibárruri of any responsibility regarding the cult of personality and he presented her as the constant supporter of the party's renovation.[32]

The assertion of the new political line was consolidated that summer at the meeting of the Central Committee of the PCE, which took place in the German Democratic Republic. In her report Dolores Ibárruri offered a political commitment 'to all the civil and military forces' opposed to Franco to fight for basic democratic freedoms, 'as the first step towards the reconciliation of the Spaniards'. The obvious contradiction in this proposal is that these basic democratic freedoms did not exist in the Soviet Union and in the so-called popular democracies like the German Democratic Republic. And in the paragraphs that Dolores Ibárruri dedicated to Stalin in her report, she did not mention any of his crimes and presented so many alleviating circumstances that she seemed to excuse his excesses. She concluded that Stalin had been one of the most consistent Marxists and had led the party's fight against Trotskyites, the right-wing opportunists, the middle-class nationalists and the intrigues caused by the agents of capitalism.[33] It would not be an exaggeration to say that, while she exhorted the Spanish people to come to terms with the Civil War and to support national reconciliation, she was attempting to justify Stalinist terror. She was not able to foster a real change of perspective and with hindsight there is no doubt that Carrillo was the real winner and she was the great loser that summer of 1956, although she maintained her position as general secretary.

Carrillo proposed that she move to Paris in order to effectively lead the executive committee. However, she thought that life would be hard for her in France as she would have to keep out of sight because the PCE was illegal there and she was too well known. Besides, according to the memoirs of her collaborator Irene Falcón, she was worried and tense, probably hurt by Khrushchev's revelations and inwardly convinced that she was not able to perform the role of supreme leader of the party any more.[34] In any case, from 1956 on she was relegated to the background. This was evident during preparations for the unsuccessful national political strike of June 1959: it was planned by Carrillo and she was informed when it had already been prepared. Despite the efforts made by clandestine propaganda the call to strike was scarcely honoured and there were many arrests. This failure, which Carrillo and his collaborators tried to present as a success, prompted Dolores Ibárruri to resign soon after. She did not have the energy to contend for leadership against her rival or to impose a strategy to follow but she was not willing to continue assuming a false role. After her resignation in July 1959, Carrillo assumed the position of general secretary and reserved for her a new position, the presidency of the PCE.[35]

For more than twenty years, until Carrillo's resignation in 1982, the cooperation between the president and the general secretary proceeded smoothly. In his memoirs, Carrillo is very proud of the decisive support Ibárruri gave to all his political initiatives during those years.[36] This is unquestionable but it does not seem to have been accompanied by a mutual understanding. According to Claudín: 'Her relationship with Carrillo was always distant, in contrast to what happened with Uribe, but she never confronted him. She considered the party's unity paramount. Moreover, she felt old and tired.'[37]

During the last stage of her life Ibárruri's charisma was only of the representational type; she became a queen who did not reign. Carrillo was in charge of the party's management and she was more and more isolated in Moscow, but she continued to represent the historical traditions of the party. The Soviet Union granted her the highest distinctions: she received a Ph.D. *honoris causa* in 1961, the Lenin Peace Prize in 1962 and the Order of Lenin in 1965. She visited several communist countries, including Cuba in 1963 and Yugoslavia in 1965. As in former times she played the role of censor against dissidents: now they were Fernando Claudín and

Jorge Semprún, whose actions were condemned during a meeting of the Executive Committee which was held in Prague and not in Paris in order to facilitate her attendance. She accused them of being intellectuals, aloof from the working class, and of having returned to the social-democratic reformism of the years of her youth: 'Have we fought during almost half a century against reformism and anti-Marxist revisionism to get this result?' Some years later Semprún remembered the speech in which Pasionaria had denounced them 'with her splendid, metallic, coarse, harmonious voice'.[38] However, her most important intervention in those years was her support of Santiago Carrillo's condemnation of the invasion of Czechoslovakia in 1968. Despite her long years of identification with the Soviet Union, her loyalty was mostly directed towards the PCE and she closed ranks with its leaders, depriving in this way the pro-Soviet group of significant support.[39]

During the last years of Franco's regime, the party asked her to intervene in two multitudinous meetings aimed at reinforcing the adherence of militants and sympathizers abroad to the new party's orientation, the first near Paris in 1971 and the second in Geneva in 1974. Three years later, just before the first free elections since 1936, her dream of coming back to Spain came true. She was again elected a member of parliament but it was too late for her, because by then she was eighty-one years old. She was a historic figure but had no political influence and she resigned soon after being elected, in order to leave the way open to younger militants. Moreover, the Communist Party itself would not play in the new Spanish democracy the hegemonic role on the Left that its militants had expected. Again, as in 1931, that role belonged to the Socialist Party. When she died in 1989 the Berlin Wall had just fallen and communism was on the point of becoming no more than a historical memory. Thousands of people attended her funeral in the last display of her charisma but twenty-three years later she is almost forgotten. This is not surprising because her image is too exclusively linked to the PCE for her to become an icon of the Spanish Left, nowadays mainly represented by the socialists, who promote a remembrance of the Civil War centred on Franco's victims not on the revolutionary leaders of bygone days, much less on such a fierce foe of their party as Dolores Ibárruri had always been.

Conclusion

What could be concluded in answer to the questions posed at the beginning of this chapter? Was she a charismatic leader in the sense that Max Weber gave to this expression? Did her leadership depend on the recognition of her extraordinary qualities? Probably the right answer to both questions is yes, but only if we accept the concepts of institutional charisma and charisma based on representation. Pasionaria had gifts of her own that were well suited to the situation of her country in the 1930s. She was a courageous woman inspired by an unbreakable faith in communism, a fierce debater and a great speaker, able to inspire commitment through her effective oratory and her strong yet feminine voice. For the Comintern propaganda aimed at presenting the Spanish Civil War not as a great revolutionary insurrection but as the heroic struggle of a people against foreign fascists and their Spanish servants, this brave woman, always modestly dressed in black, was a perfect icon. And in fact she won in Spain the hearts of many fighters and sufferers. But she did not have any vision of the future of her own to transmit to her followers; she had only the communist vision coined by others. She did not innovate, she only symbolized, but for some time she was a truly charismatic symbol. But then, charisma of either the genuine or the representational type is always unstable and as communist faith faded so did her charisma and finally her own image, which probably means nothing to most young Spaniards today.

Notes

1. G. Morán. 1986. *Miseria y grandeza del Partido Comunista de España, 1939–1985*, Barcelona: Planeta, 74–77.
2. M. Weber. 1983. *Economía y sociedad: esbozo de sociología comprensiva*, Mexico: FCE, 193.
3. W. Spinrad. 1991. 'Charisma: A Blighted Concept and an Alternative Formula', *Political Science Quarterly* 106(2), 310.
4. Weber, *Economía y sociedad*, 215.
5. Weber, *Economía y sociedad*, 194.
6. M. Spencer. 1973. 'What Is Charisma?', *The British Journal of Sociology* 24(3), 352.
7. L. Greenfeld. 1989. 'Reflections on Two Charismas', *The British Journal of Sociology* 36(1), 124.
8. Weber, *Economía y sociedad*, 851.
9. Greenfeld, 'Reflections on Two Charismas', 129.
10. Greenfeld, 'Reflections on Two Charismas', 118–20.
11. Spencer, 'What Is Charisma?', 345–51.
12. Archivo del Partido Comunista de España, Madrid (hereafter AHPCE). Microfilm VI–101.
13. AHPCE, 13. D. Ibárruri, 'Autobiografía', Moscow, 18 July 1935.
14. *Mundo Obrero*, 16 April 1933.
15. D. Ibárruri. 1968. *En la lucha: palabras y hechos, 1936–1939*, Moscow: Progreso, 43–46.
16. *Diario de las Sesiones de Cortes*, 2 April 1936.
17. *El Socialista*, 3 April 1936.
18. *Diario de las Sesiones de Cortes*, 16 June 1936.
19. *Claridad* and *La Libertad*, 17 June 1936.

20. Letter to Xenia Sukovskaya, *Euzkadi Roja*, 31 December 1936.
21. AHPCE. D. Ibárruri, 'Informe pronunciado ante el Pleno del C.C. del Partido Comunista, celebrado en Valencia, en los días del 18 al 20 de junio de 1937'.
22. S. Carrillo. 1993. *Memorias*, Barcelona: Planeta, 261–62.
23. M. Rosenberg, 25 September 1936, quoted in R. Radosh, M. Habeck and G. Sevostianov (eds). 2001. *Spain Betrayed: The Soviet Union in the Spanish Civil War.* New Haven, CT: Yale University Press, 31.
24. A. Marty, 14 October 1936, quoted in Radosh, Habeck and Sevostianov, *Spain Betrayed*, 38–39.
25. R.C. Tucker. 1979. 'The Rise of Stalin's Personality Cult', *The American Historical Review* 84(2), 347–66.
26. G. Gill. 1980. 'The Soviet Leader Cult: Reflections on the Structure of Leadership in the Soviet Union', *British Journal of Political Science* 10(2), 171.
27. *Nuestra Bandera*, March 1950, 245–65.
28. AHPCE 18/4, J. Rodríguez, 22 June 1951.
29. AHPCE 19/1, R. Alberti, 'Una Pasionaria para Dolores'.
30. Morán, *Miseria y grandeza*, 253–57. Carrillo, *Memorias*, 442–44.
31. Morán, *Miseria y grandeza*, 258–64.
32. Carrillo, *Memorias*, 447–53. Morán, *Miseria y grandeza*, 268.
33. AHPCE 20/3, 'Por la reconciliación de los españoles hacia la democratización de España: informe presentado ante el Pleno del Comité Central del Partido Comunista de España, reunido en los últimos días de agosto de 1956'.
34. Carrillo, *Memorias*, 454. Ibárruri, 'Por la reconciliación', 153. I. Falcón. 1996. *Asalto a los cielos: mi vida junto a Pasionaria*, Madrid: Temas de Hoy, 315–16.
35. AHPCE 16/4, D. Ibárruri, 1 May 1959. Morán, *Miseria y grandeza*, 324–33.
36. Carrillo, *Memorias*, 476.
37. F. Claudín. 1983. *Carrillo: crónica de un secretario general*, Barcelona: Planeta, 145.
38. J. Semprún. 1977. *Autobiografía de Federico Sánchez*, Barcelona: Planeta, 342.
39. Falcón, *Asalto a los cielos*, 348–55; S. Sánchez Montero. 1997. *Camino de libertad: memorias*, Madrid: Temas de Hoy, 285–86; Claudín, *Carrillo*, 197–200; Carrillo, *Memorias*, 503; Morán, *Miseria y grandeza*, 445.

CHAPTER 6

MAO ZEDONG

Charismatic Leadership and the Contradictions
of Socialist Revolution

Arif Dirlik

It seems fairly safe to observe that while not all charismatic leaders are
radicals or revolutionaries, all successful revolutionary leaders are charismatic.[1] As James Downton wrote in his book *Rebel Leadership*:

> Only a few rebel leaders succeed in making revolutions. These are the men
> and women who, by the very nature of their successes beyond the pattern of
> everyday life, assume a mythical stature and join history's collection of heroic
> figures. Such persons as these are enshrined by nations and loved by the masses
> because they seemed able to change the course of history by the power of their
> social vision, through their cunning, and by the force of their will.[2]

Any individual capable of convincing many of the possibility of realizing
an entirely new order that exists only in his/her imagination needs all the
'gift of grace' s/he can get. The particular mode of persuasion may differ
from case to case, but whatever the mode, the very audacity of the vision
seems to wrap the charismatic leader in a transcendental aura similar to
that which attends magicians, seers and prophets.

It is important, nevertheless, to be attentive to the workings of charisma and its various dimensions (individual or collective, psychological,
social-structural or cultural) within different revolutionary contexts. Eric
Hobsbawm concluded from his many historical studies of insurgent behaviour that modern revolutionaries – most importantly socialist revolutionaries – were distinguished from the rebels of earlier times by a theoretically

and socially informed vision of the future, and of how to get there from the present.[3] This is not very surprising because modern revolutionaries were shaped by the assumptions of the very order they sought to overthrow. This is the legal-rationalistic order of capitalism and the modern bureaucratic state founded on the impersonal principles of an abstract rationalism. Bourgeois society discovered in the rational pursuit of interest a means to overcome the irrationality of the passions, a characteristic also associated, we may note, with charismatic politics.[4] Socialist opponents of capitalism were to go even further in their denial of the passions and their commitment to the possibility of rational social organization, even if they were divided on how this rationality might be instituted – from the anarchists who lodged rationality in the individual moral faculty to the state socialists who identified the state as the guarantor of a rational order. Socialists in existing socialist societies were to go farthest in expanding the scope of the bureaucratic organization of society in efforts to overcome what was deemed to be the 'anarchic' capitalist market.

I suggest in this discussion that in the context of socialist revolutions such as the Chinese, the question of charisma may not be disassociated from the question of rationality, because the two were equally important in empowering revolutionary leadership. They were also at the source of fundamental contradictions of a divisive nature. In the case of a revolutionary leader such as Mao Zedong, unquestionably a charismatic leader, the charisma came at least in part from demonstrated ability to read the social situation, which had been crucial to the success of the Communist Revolution of which Mao had been the leader. One could find an analogy here to the soothsayers of old, reading leaves and shells, but they nevertheless belong to two different intellectual universes. Mao's charisma, which had multiple sources, also endowed with prestige his readings and interpretations. When the two clashed, however, and the charisma took over at the expense of the rationality, the consequences could be disastrous, as they were during the Cultural Revolution. That event itself could be viewed as a grand effort to overcome the contradictions between the revolutionary necessity of charismatic vision and authority, and the equally necessary theoretical and analytical confrontation of revolution in a postrevolutionary society, which was ignored the more it seemed like an obstacle to the realization of charismatic promise: charisma set against its routinization. Reason and charisma, the contrast between which was crucial to Max Weber's analysis of authority, may nevertheless be deeply entangled in revolutionary situations, capable of mutual reinforcement, but also potentially at odds with one another. Their contradictory relationship may best be grasped in Mao's favourite law of the dialectic: 'the unity of opposites', understood in both their mutual determination and their mutual negation.

A Note on Charismatic Leadership

Weber's concept of charisma presents obvious problems that have led some scholars to question its analytical utility. Charisma in Weber's presentation is at once an attribute of the personal qualities of the leader and a product of a social and political – if not entirely sociopsychological – relationship between the leader and the led. He wrote:

> The term 'charisma' will be applied to a certain quality of an individual personality by virtue of which he is set apart from ordinary men and treated as endowed with supernatural, superhuman, or at least specifically exceptional powers or qualities .... How the quality in question would be judged from any ethical, esthetic or other such points of view is naturally entirely indifferent for purposes of definition. What is alone important is how the individual is actually regarded by those subject to charismatic authority, by his 'followers' or 'disciples' .... It is recognition on the part of those subject to authority which is decisive for the validity of charisma .... Psychologically this 'recognition' is a matter of complete personal devotion to the possessor of the quality, arising out of enthusiasm, or of despair and hope .... If proof of his charismatic qualification fails him for long, the leader endowed with charisma tends to think his god or magical or heroic powers have deserted him ...[. A]bove all if his leadership fails to benefit his followers, it is likely that his charismatic authority will disappear.[5]

Weber used the concept of 'charismatic authority' to explain what could not be accommodated within the other two types of authority he identified in political systems: 'legal authority', characteristic of modern society, based on performance within an impersonal legal order, and 'traditional authority', which, while personal, operated within 'the area of accustomed obligations'.[6] Charismatic authority, by contrast, referred to highly personalized authority which also enabled, based on the prestige of the leader, innovation and radical transformation, as against routinized performance which characterized the other two types of authority. By its very nature, however, this type of authority was unstable, and must be transformed in the course of events – 'routinized' – into one of the other types of authority.

'Charisma' as a concept is intended to provide a sociological understanding of radical change as against systemic conservatism, as well as the ubiquitous historical presence of so-called heroes or great men (and less often, women) in bringing about such change.[7] The endowment of the individual leader is very much entangled here with the interaction between the leader and the led within specific social and political contexts. As Lindholm has put it, 'charisma is, above all, *a relationship*, a mutual mingling of the inner selves of leader and follower' (emphasis in the original).[8]

And yet, it appears to me that it is this mutual entanglement of the personal and the social that gives rise to an unresolved circularity in Weber's presentation of the concept which is evident in the quotation above: charisma, the 'gift of grace', is an individual endowment that is the source of attraction to the individual leader, and yet its recognition by those subject to the authority of the leader is 'decisive' for its validity. William Friedland, who noted the uneasy tension (or contradiction) between the psychological and the sociological in Weber's notion of charisma, observed commonsensically that, 'while there are plenty of people with messages, these must be relevant to social groups before they begin to be received and become the basis for action'.[9] Friedland's observation points to another question. While Weber's distinction of charismatic from other types of authority depended in some measure on the obliviousness of the charismatic to questions of interest, especially economic interest, Weber himself noted that charismatic authority depended for its sustenance on the ability of the leader to bring benefits to the followers. The statement blurs the distinction between the charismatic and the rational, the basis for legal authority. Likewise, Weber wrote in several places that traditional authority, itself highly personalized, was not always distinguishable from the charismatic, which has led at least one observer to note that the concept is residual, to explain what cannot be explained by the other two types of authority, but quite fuzzy in terms of its own internal consistency.[10]

The concept of charisma thus suffers from a boundary problem. In its unfolding, it also has gone through an inflation to the point of 'conceptual triviality'.[11] Weber's effort to distance the concept from its original grounding in religion has opened it up to application in all kinds of unlikely areas. A simple catalogue search of books with 'charisma' in their titles shows, interspersed with the works of Max Weber, an overwhelming number of titles on management, personal magnetism, and dating. The concept has even been applied to computers.[12] This conceptual inflation has led Philip Smith to call for a restoration of the original, religious sense of charisma, and especially the emphasis in charismatic movements on the 'we' and the 'they', on the binarism of good and evil, which would also foreground once again the importance and autonomy of the cultural.[13]

This is an important intervention, and yet it suffers from the age-old problem of the identification of the charismatic with the irrational or the prerational, which, recalling what I observed above, precludes the possibility of the rational in the charismatic, especially in modern social movements which base their claims not on access to the transcendental or the supernatural but on the demands of social theory and rational analysis.[14] To accommodate such movements, it may be useful to broaden the concept while keeping in mind the boundaries necessary to guard against its inflation. Translated into secular terms, 'charisma' may be restricted to those individuals who display unusual acuity in leadership, as suggested for example by the idea of 'genius', at once secular and transcendent, being beyond the reach of ordinary people. In order to set limits on the inflation of the concept, it may be necessary to retain as its basic condition a stipulation that it is indeed a 'gift of grace', whether in a transcendental sense of a sacred endowment, or in the more mundane sense of a quality not accessible to all, such as genius, which, while secular, retains nevertheless the mystery suggested by 'the gift of grace' (as in the adjective *gifted*, for instance). As such, charisma is a 'gift' that may not be learned or taught but is a natural endowment of sorts that distinguishes the charismatic from the run of the mill religious, ideological or intellectual leader.[15] Similarly, the good/evil distinction may be reconceptualized usefully as an inside/outside distinction that retains a sense of the exclusive nature of charismatic movements without reducing the concept to the strictly religious manifestations of such a distinction. Such may be the case, for instance, with an exclusive political party that draws its boundaries in keeping with faith in the ideological guidance of a charismatic leader, much in the fashion of a 'community of believers'.

This revision of Weber's concept of charisma still leaves open the question of the context of charisma, which would seem to be another indispensable condition of the concept's particularity. At the very least, it seems necessary to draw a distinction between charisma as a product of face-to-face relationships (personal magnetism, so to speak) and charisma as a product of public interactions, which is the real underlying intention in the formulation of the concept. The relationship between a charismatic leader and his/her public following is of necessity a remote one, and yet it is also premised on a sense of unity between the leader and the led, which raises the fundamental question of the transmission of charisma, rendering charisma into a problem in communication ranging from rhetorical persuasion to spectacular participation in group activity. Not the least of the questions raised by this recognition is the constructedness of charisma which, while it is almost a condition of a charismatic social movement, inevitably raises the contradictory issue of authenticity. This problem gains in urgency when we recognize that charisma may be a quality not just of an individual leader but also of an organization, such as a political party that claims legitimacy on the basis of claims to truth or ideological acuity, what Antonio Gramsci famously described as 'the modern prince'. Indeed, as we shall see below, in the case of the Communist Party of China, while the party and the leader may each benefit from the claims to charismatic leadership of the other, they may also collide on occasion if the leader turns against the organization (or vice versa), which may be more of a problem of charismatic social movements than is generally recognized.

These considerations point to two further questions of significance, one pertaining to the charismatic leader, the other to those led by charisma. It is possible to argue on the basis of the evidence of charismatic movements historically that whatever the endowments of the charismatic leader, those endowments are enriched by the construction of symbolisms and situations intended to enhance charisma, which raises questions about the relationship between charisma and conscious political activity and design, not to say theatre. As far as I am aware, Weber's analysis has surprisingly little to say on the ritualization of charisma. As the medium for the transmission of charisma between leader and led, rituals may not only be an essential component of the establishment of charismatic claims, but may be equally important to the sustenance or routinization of charisma – no less for legal-rational than for traditional authority. Similarly, analysis must account for questions concerning the followers of the charismatic leader, who are not to be reduced to a homogeneous mass. The relationship of the followers to the leader and, therefore, to the appeals of charisma may vary greatly, once again demanding attention to questions of political position and social, economic and cultural interest.[16]

There are two other questions of somewhat different import that are of particular interest in the present context: the relationship of charisma to routinized activity, and the question of cultural or, more precisely, historical context. Prominent sociologists from Edward Shils to S.N. Eisenstadt have sought to modify Weber's original formulations to render charisma into not a deviation from but an integral part of routinized activity, a source of innovation within the system but also, for the same reason, a necessity of order.[17] Eisenstadt is especially persuasive on the question of charisma and innovation, which is a staple of much of the work on charisma in management and the training of chief executive officers. The emphasis here is once again on the rationality of the concept. But it raises a further question that Eisenstadt does not go into: is it also possible to extend the same rationality into a break with the existing institution, in other words, radical transformation? What is the relationship between 'routine' innovation and radical change? The question also enables a more historical approach to charismatic leadership which may move back and forth between the two types of change depending on historical circumstances, which may be quite pertinent to understanding the historical trajectory of a leader such as Mao Zedong.

The other question is cultural and historical, beyond the sociology of charisma. There has been considerable attention in studies of charisma to the question of context: the context in which populations may be drawn or lured into the magnetism of charisma. What is less often asked is whether there may be a variation in this attraction in different historical circumstances, especially when they involve different cultural contexts.[18] Without being drawn into a culturalist particularism, it is important to ask nevertheless what part 'culture' may play in the operation and practices of charisma, especially since the question of charisma seems to be intimately entangled in questions of symbolism and communication. If such is the case, moreover, do the differences refer primarily to differences in the social and psychological dynamics of charisma, or to particularities in its construction, which are not merely cultural but also historical.

Given these various problems, it seems best not only to eschew any precise definition of the content and boundaries of charisma as concept, but also to view it in its relationship to other types of legitimization which may differ from context to context, and endow it with changing historical meaning and significance. The alternative may be to deny to it any significance at all, which may deprive analysis of an heuristic tool which, however fuzzy, seeks to account for an important dimension of politics that eludes rational or customary expectations of political behaviour.

Mao as Charismatic Leader

Whether we take charisma to be a personal attribute, or the product of the relationship between the leader and the led, there is much to suggest that Mao Zedong was a charismatic leader. It is more difficult to say why, or whether this was always the case in the course of the half-century and more that he was involved in politics – most of that time as the unquestioned if not always totally or universally respected leader of the Communist Revolution.

In his celebrated book that introduced Mao (and the Communist Party) to the attention of the English-language world, *Red Star over China*, Edgar Snow wrote:

> Do not suppose, first of all, that Mao Tse-tung could be the 'saviour' of China. Nonsense. There will never be any one 'saviour' of China. Yet undeniably you feel a certain force of destiny in him. It is nothing quick or flashy, but a kind of solid elemental vitality. You feel that whatever there is extraordinary in this man grows out of the uncanny degree to which he synthesizes and expresses the urgent demands of millions of Chinese, and especially the peasantry – those impoverished, underfed, exploited, illiterate, but kind, generous, courageous and just now rather rebellious human beings who are the vast majority of the Chinese people. If these demands and the movement that is pressing them forward can regenerate China, then in this deeply historical sense Mao Tse-tung may possibly become a very great man.[19]

Mao Zedong did become a 'great man' after Snow wrote these lines, even if his greatness has become a matter of dispute since then as much for its sources as for its consequences. If anything, he would gain in stature over the years as a leader endowed with extraordinary characteristics. Visiting Mao once again nearly three decades later, Snow expressed the opinions of many in China and abroad when he wrote that what made Mao 'formidable was that he was not just a party boss but by many millions of Chinese was quite genuinely regarded as a teacher, statesman, strategist, philosopher, poet laureate, national hero, head of the family, and greatest liberator in history. He was to them Confucius plus Lao-tzu plus Rousseau plus Marx plus Buddha.'[20]

Edgar Snow was, for some, excessively sympathetic to Mao. More importantly, his commentaries on Mao, especially in *Red Star over China*, hold a special place because of the enormous influence they exerted in and outside China on subsequent commentators. Some Chinese writers have suggested that what he had to say in that book about Mao, who was little known at the time outside of party circles, contributed significantly to the first wave of 'Mao fever' in China, and even in the communist base in Yan'an, in the 1940s after it had been translated into Chinese.[21]

Mao was able to awe even those known for their cynicism by his political acumen, commitment to the revolution, and ability to voice the deepest aspirations of the Chinese revolution. President Richard Nixon, who met Mao in the 1970s, was very much impressed that 'although Mao spoke with some difficulty, it was clear that his mind was moving like lightening'.[22] Nixon's national security advisor Henry Kissinger, no slouch when it came to diplomatic realpolitik, was even more deeply impressed in his several meetings with the Chairman. Quite aware that 'one usually cannot tell when meeting a famous and powerful leader to what extent one is impressed by his personality or awed by his status and repute', Kissinger continued:

> In Mao's case there could be no doubt. Except for the suddenness of the summons there was no ceremony. The interior appointments were as modest as the exterior. Mao just stood there, surrounded by books, tall and powerfully built for a Chinese. He fixed the visitor with a smile both penetrating and slightly mocking, warning by his bearing that there was no point in seeking to deceive this specialist in the foibles and duplicity of man. I have met no one, with the possible exception of Charles de Gaulle, who so distilled raw, concentrated willpower. He was planted there with a female attendant close by to help steady him (and on my last visits to hold him up); he dominated the room – not by the pomp that in most states confers a degree of majesty on the leaders, but by exuding in almost intangible form the overwhelming drive to prevail.[23]

The impression that Mao left on Kissinger is further evident in the adjectives scattered through his descriptions of their meetings: colossal, great, demonic, overwhelming etc.[24] It is an impression that was shared by many, foreign and Chinese, who came into contact with Mao.[25] Even André Malraux, possibly the most reflective among Mao's European and American visitors, and the most measured with his adjectives, saw in the ailing Mao not 'a sick man, but a bronze emperor', if only to conclude his visit with a sense of a revolution doomed to failure, and Mao as a lonely 'old man' watching time go by: 'He reminded me of the emperors, and now he reminds me, standing there, of the rust-covered shields of the army chiefs which belonged to the funerary avenues of the emperors, and are to be found abandoned in the sorghum fields.'[26] The sense of tragedy, too, may be read as a tribute to Mao's charisma.

Mao appeared larger than life even to his would-be detractors. Dr Li Zhisui, one of Mao's personal physicians whose memoirs would provide much fodder for Mao-bashers in the United States, throughout his memoirs described Mao in superlative terms, whether positively or negatively.[27] He himself confessed to an adulation of Mao long before he had been assigned his duties as one of the Chairman's physicians. Li's description of his initial encounter with Mao, which portrays him lying naked under a towel, his flesh pink and his belly bulging, may seem disrespectful to those who are unwilling to recognize the Chairman's humanity. Li also made many an allegation about Mao's sexual activity and his callousness towards human life which are contradicted by many who were close to Mao. I am not concerned here with what may or may not be accurate in accounts such as Li's.[28] And as Weber observed, whether a leader is charismatic is a question that is not to be answered on ethical or aesthetic grounds.

What emerges from Li's descriptions confirms the impressions of most witnesses to Mao's qualifications as a leader. Mao's ruthlessness, a major point of the memoirs, is neither particularly fresh news nor very surprising for the leader of a protracted revolution. Indeed, the difference between an account such as Li's and those more sympathetic to Mao, including the likes of Nixon and Kissinger, lies not so much in the characteristics attributed to Mao as in the evaluation of those characteristics. The same may be said of other characteristics that emerge out of Li's account: Mao's tremendous energy, his self-confidence and sense of mission, his identification with great figures from the past, especially an emperor such as Qin Shi Huangdi, his devotion to reading, but above all his unpredictability and distaste for routine, which was revealing of an urge to define his context rather than be defined by it. Li's allegations about Mao's appetite for young sex partners, which invited undue attention and much self-righteous condemnation from reviewers of the book, may have contributed to his charismatic appeal among his followers.[29]

It is quite possible that the question of Mao as a charismatic leader would not have arisen had it not been for the Cultural Revolution of the 1960s. It is possible to suggest that the characteristics identified by those who came into contact with Mao may be applicable to any outstanding leader, and do not necessarily point to charismatic appeal unless we use an inflated definition of charisma. As I have discussed above, serious theorists of charisma beginning with Max Weber have long known that charisma is not just an individual endowment but a product of interaction between the individual leader and his/her followers, observers and interlocutors. The charismatic qualities of a controversial figure such as Mao Zedong may be in the eyes of the beholder more than is the case for most people. Not everyone who came into contact with Mao found him to be charismatic. One companion of his youthful days, writing about the same time as Snow, but from a different political perspective, wrote of Mao as a young man in his twenties.

> Mao was not unusual in appearance, as some people have maintained, with his hair growing low on his forehead, like the devils pictured by old-time artists, nor did he have any especially striking features. In fact I have never observed anything unusual in his appearance. To me he always seemed quite an ordinary, normal-looking person. His face was rather large, but his eyes were neither large nor penetrating, nor had they the sly, cunning look sometimes attributed to them. His nose was flattish and of a typical Chinese shape. His ears were well proportioned; his mouth, quite small; his teeth very white and even. These good white teeth helped to make his smile quite charming, so that no one would imagine that he was not genuinely sincere. He walked rather slowly, with his legs somewhat separated. In a way that reminded one of a duck waddling. His movements in sitting or standing were very slow. Also, he spoke very slowly and he was by no means a gifted speaker.[30]

Mao's 'ordinariness', noted by many in later years, even after he became the leader of the People's Republic of China, interestingly may account for the appeal he held for those who came into contact with him, as well as the Chinese population at large, especially the rural population. There is a curious twist in Siao-yu's account of the young Mao, who works his way from a peasant boy educated on popular novels of heroism to becoming one of the founders and movers of the Communist Party in 1921, who integrates in his person, however uneasily, the 'primitive rebels' of *Shuihu zhuan* (Outlaws of the Marsh) and the Marxist revolutionary of the twentieth century. The combination would prove to be powerful in generating Mao's charisma, which would draw upon his ability to bring a native perspective into Marxism and translate Marxism into a popular idiom in the pursuit of revolution.

Still, whatever Mao's personal charm or magnetism, it was not until the Cultural Revolution and after that this magnetism generated a social movement, which is an indispensable condition of charismatic leadership. Some analysts of charisma, such as Ann Willner, have questioned Mao's qualifications as a charismatic leader on the grounds that 'sympathetic visitors during the Yunan [*sic*] period, such as Edgar Snow, did not observe or at least write about any charismatically oriented follower perceptions. These seem to have emerged and flowered after the institution of the cult of Mao and the onset of a repressive regime.'[31] Willner places Mao under the heading of 'marginals and misnomers', which she contrasts not only with 'charismatics' but with 'probable charismatics' as well.

It is not clear why 'the institution of the cult of Mao and the onset of a repressive regime' should disqualify Mao as a charismatic leader, and the Cultural Revolution[32] as a charismatic movement. The constructedness of charisma does not render a charismatic leader or movement inauthentic or 'counterfeit', as Willner herself concedes, and it is possible to suggest that there is a historical link in many cases between charismatic movements and 'repressive regimes', as arbitrariness is built into the very nature of personalized charismatic leadership as Weber conceived it.[33] Zhang Zhanbin and Sun Yifu identify two periods of 'Mao Fever' prior to the Cultural Revolution: one in Yan'an, the other following the establishment of the People's Republic in 1949.[34] It is not clear in these cases whether the Mao cult was a cult of Mao the leader, or of the party. Raymond Wylie has demonstrated that the emergence of Mao as leader during the Yan'an Period was accompanied by the apotheosizing of 'Mao Zedong Thought' which was a collective product, and was viewed as such by the party.[35] The Mao fever of the 1950s was called forth by Zhou Enlai. In either case, the Mao cult was indistinguishable from the cult of Mao Zedong Thought, which was intimately linked with the power and prestige of the Communist Party itself, which contrasts sharply with the Mao cult of the Cultural Revolution which would set Mao the leader against the party itself.[36]

It was also with the Cultural Revolution that the promotion of Mao assumed a religious or near-religious dimension, loyalty to Mao or an abstractly conceived Mao Zedong Thought (now set apart from and against the party) became the ultimate test of political correctness, and the interpretation of Mao Zedong Thought provided an outlet for conflicting social and political interests, creating fecund grounds for political arbitrariness. Beginning with the People's Liberation Army under the command of Marshall Lin Biao in the early 1960s, the cult of Mao infused all aspects of Chinese society. The manufacturing of the cult was accompanied by the literal production of Mao images in popular art forms (busts, posters, badges etc.) and the publication of *Quotations from Chairman Mao Tse-Tung* ('The Little Red Book') in millions of copies, not just in Chinese but in many languages, including Esperanto. Devotion to Mao was promoted not only through exemplary popular heroes, mostly People's Liberation Army soldiers, such as Lei Feng, but also through revolutionary operas such as *The East Is Red* (1965), which offered in spectacular form an account of the Chinese Revolution based around the figure of Mao, the action presided over by the portrait of Mao in various shades of bright sunlight ('the red sun in our hearts'), to which revolutionary women offered their supine bodies. While 'The Little Red Book' reduced Mao's thinking to easily remembered and recitable slogans, it also served (along with a number of brief essays by Mao) as an inspirational text that promoted service to society as well as a kind of constitution for revolutionary change, as a sympathetic Chinese scholar has observed.[37] The effect of the cult, however we might wish to interpret it, was to equate loyalty to Mao with loyalty to the revolution, and loyalty to the revolution with selfless service to society and revolutionary change. In the process, the Communist Party itself became an emblem of corruption and a vehicle with the potential to slide back from socialism to the restoration of bourgeois rule.

What distinguished the Cultural Revolution from previous episodes of Mao fever, however, was most importantly the mass mobilization it set in motion for the revitalization of the revolution. The situation in the PRC in the early 1960s was typical of circumstances that breed charismatic movements. The political crisis created by tendencies towards the routinization of the revolution, quite evident in the increased bureaucratization of not only the state but also the Communist Party, was exacerbated by challenges to the leadership of Mao, who already enjoyed cultic status within the party and society at large. The political crisis itself came in the midst of a social and cultural crisis as the promise of socialism lagged behind its achievements, and conflict between the new and the old elites created status inconsistencies and uncertainties, raising the level of anxiety in society especially among the first postrevolutionary generation coming of political age.[38] It was this generation that was to make the revolution against a party showing signs of bureaucratic ossification, and in the process revolutionize itself. Mao's call for a 'revolution within the revolution' fell on receptive ears. It was this new youth that ultimately brought into everyday life and culture the message that had originated in the People's Liberation Army, hanging on to every pronouncement that Mao made, rendering him not just a leader but a sacred guide to everyday life.[39] Many a rosy-cheeked Red Guard swooned and broke into tears of joy at a distant glimpse, or even the thought of Mao – much like teenagers in the U.S. fainting at the mere sight of their musical idols.[40]

In his study of the Cultural Revolution, *The Failure of Charisma*, Wang Shaoguang has argued that participants in the Cultural Revolution behaved quite 'rationally', interpreting Mao in accordance with their particular interests. Wang's argument is in some ways motivated by disciplinary considerations: to prove to the 'rational choice' advocates that revolutionary choices, too, could be rational. It is not to be ignored, nevertheless, that even such interest was articulated through a devotional language which was derivative of Mao's pronouncements; in other words, that rationality had a situational character – not far from Weber's notion of 'instrumental rationality'.[41] If this raises questions about the authenticity of mass devotion to Mao, it needs to be remembered that conflict over authenticity was itself a factor in deepening the devotional aspects of the movement until the pursuit of authenticity became its own end, overshadowing the call to revolutionary service with which the movement had originated, and sharpening battle lines not around the class divisions that the revolution was supposed to address but around claims to representation of and devotion to Mao the leader.[42]

This may indeed be a feature of charismatic movements that deserves closer attention. It is apparent in presecular charismatic movements which, motivated by resort to transcendental authority beyond the reach of human reason, had little need for social analysis, including class analysis. But it may also be important in understanding charisma in modern political movements, where the resort to religious sanction serves as a substitute for social analysis, and sanctions the erasure of the social by faith in individualized leadership – at its extreme, the *Führer* principle.

In an immediate sense, for all the rhetoric of class, the Cultural Revolution failed to formulate a plausible theoretical analysis of class in postrevolutionary, postsocialist society. In hindsight, the rhetoric of class and class struggle during these years appears to be more an expression of revolutionary nostalgia than a theoretical guide for moving society further into socialism. On the eve of launching the Cultural Revolution, Mao imparted to André Malraux a strong sense that the revolution had been a failure, even if he was prepared to give its success one last shot, when he quietly confided, 'I am alone with the masses. Waiting.'[43] The confession contrasts deeply with the evangelical exuberance that Cultural Revolution rhetoric conveyed. In the end, he was to gamble his charisma against the inertia of history. The social analysis to which he owed much of his legitimacy as leader of the revolution was overtaken in the process by the personalization of revolution which, were it not tragic, would be material for farce.

Contrary to the contemporary demonization of Mao and the Cultural Revolution, from a perspective that takes seriously the Chinese Revolution, and the pursuit of socialism, there were good historical and ideological reasons for launching the Cultural Revolution.[44] And arguably, given the party's resistance to further pursuit of the revolution, Mao had no choice but to put his own person and prestige on the line. Whether or not Mao was personally responsible for his deification, he did condone it, at least for a while. Any serious evaluation of the Cultural Revolution, especially from left-wing perspectives, demands a critical evaluation of what the consequences were of rendering Mao's charisma into the central principle of revolution, and surrender to the will of the leader a requirement of his followers.

The deification of Mao that the Cultural Revolution produced was officially rejected following Mao's death in 1976, but the ideological legacy of the Cultural Revolution is by no means dead as far as Mao is concerned. Mao fever gripped the People's Republic of China once again in the 1990s around the hundredth anniversary of Mao's birth in 1993, shortly after the Tiananmen Square massacre of 1989. This time around there was no movement in the sense of a political movement, or even a celebration of Mao Zedong Thought as in the pre-Cultural Revolution episodes. In keeping with the times, the Mao fever of the 1990s took the form of consumption, with a proliferation of Mao memorabilia for different walks of life (from charms for taxis, to lighters playing *The East Is Red*, to highly priced golden Mao coins), different-sized pocketbooks, Mao songs (now intended for flourishing karaoke establishments), Mao restaurants, and gossipy literature on Mao. Mao was now a national hero, a folk hero, who could be celebrated so long as his politics remained forgotten. But the politics could not be suppressed altogether. Party corruption had been an issue in the Tiananmen demonstration of 1989, as had the evidence of increasing inequalities in society. Mao appeared once again as an emblem of personal integrity and commitment to revolutionary equality. Those who were unhappy with the rapid opening to the outside world could recall Mao for his insistence on national autonomy. There were rumours of those who committed suicide to visit Mao in the underworld, and report to him all the things that had gone wrong since his departure. And peasants around China built temples to Mao, literally making him into a deity, if only a silent one. Evidence of such activity is hard to come by as it was suppressed by the government, but there is some evidence nevertheless.[45]

Concluding Observations:
Mao, Charisma, Reason and Revolution

If Mao Zedong may indeed be described as a charismatic leader, we need to ask not only what the concept of charisma explains about Mao as a leader, but also what the elements that went into the making of Mao's charisma may tell us about charisma as a concept. Throughout his life, Mao impressed those who came into contact with him for his sense of mission, his commitment to China's dignity and the welfare of the common people, and his determination to see his goals through to their conclusion. This was not just the case with admirers such as Edgar Snow, Anna Louise Strong and Agnes Smedley, not to mention his loyal Chinese followers. It was also true of Siao-yu who, though not impressed with Mao personally, nevertheless portrayed him as a combination of Marxist theorist and tactician and a heroic figure out of *Shuihu zhuan*. It was true of Li Zhisui who, for all his negative portrayals of Mao, was quite taken by Mao's commitment and his will to power.

Not the least of the characteristics that these observers noted of Mao was his ability to communicate with ordinary people, and the effectiveness with which he articulated their aspirations and needs, which, judging by available evidence, has earned him their lasting trust and devotion. This characteristic also calls into question the frequent depiction of Mao as an emperor, or a reincarnation of an imperial figure, at least in the sense ordinarily intended; by his detractors who would make him into a twentieth-century oriental despot, or by André Malraux, who nostalgically saw in him a dying emperor, 'alone with the masses', determined to give one last shot to the rejuvenation of his receding vision. It is possible that many in China, especially in rural China, endowed Mao with extraordinary powers simply because he was a powerful ruler. We may recall here that while Weber viewed charismatic authority as a negation of 'traditional authority', he also recognized that traditional authority had derived legitimacy in part from claims of access to powers beyond the reach of ordinary people, drawing for evidence on the example of Chinese emperors who had been viewed by their subjects as intermediaries between heaven and earth, and whose activities were crucial to the proper working of the cosmic order.

If Mao benefited from association with the legacies of imperial charisma in Chinese political theory and culture, however, it was in the profoundly ambiguous sense suggested by Weber's ambivalence toward charismatic and traditional authority: that his charismatic leadership at once fed off past legacies and challenged those legacies in the name of powers that transcended tradition – in this case, 'the people' – in whose name the revolution was conducted. This is suggested also by his association with the heroes of *Shuihu zhuan*, bandit rebels against traditional authority, who were invoked frequently enough by twentieth-century Chinese popular revolutionaries.[46] On the other hand, if Mao has been viewed by many in rural China (if not just in rural China) as a ruler-in-waiting, as most peasant rebel leaders were, it was in a twentieth-century guise of

Marxist theoretician, gifted at translating Marxism into the language of the peasantry, and aspirations of that peasantry into Marxist theoretical categories.

Mao was made into a cult figure after his rise to the position of party leader in the 1940s, reaching a crescendo during the Cultural Revolution when his charisma was set against the party itself. His charisma, in other words, was constructed, which would appear to be the case with most charismatic leadership, modern or premodern, Left, liberal or Right, Chinese or otherwise. Nevertheless, this should not blind us to the important part played by his leadership, theoretically and in practice, in the victory of the Communist Party, and the success of the revolutionary movement. The importance of this aspect of Mao's leadership does not get much attention these days, when the urge to 'forget' memories of the revolution has come to shape interpretations of Mao and his part in the Chinese Revolution. The importance of theory and social analysis in the making of socialist revolutionary leadership, to which I referred above with reference to the work of Eric Hobsbawm, nevertheless remains a crucial analytic difference in evaluating Mao.

This difference is readily apparent in a comparison of Mao to his rebel predecessors in modern China, of which leaders of the Taiping Heavenly Kingdom of the mid-nineteenth century are exemplary. Taiping leaders such as Hong Xiuquan, who derived their legitimacy from claims to communication with the supreme deity, may be viewed as classical cases of charismatic leadership in the divine sanction they claimed, in their insistence on an uncompromising distinction between good and evil (friends and enemy), in the irreconcilability of the faithful and their enemies, and their millenarian promises of collective salvation. Whatever the powers attributed to Mao at the height of the Cultural Revolution, when his charisma overshadowed the more rational aspects of his leadership, the persistence of the language of social analysis remains as evidence of the theoretical distance that the Chinese revolution traversed over the century between the two events.[47]

In a stringent sense of Weber's notion of charismatic leadership, which is distinguished by claims to divine and magical powers by or for the leader, it is only during the Cultural Revolution and its transmutations in subsequent years that Mao may be described as a charismatic leader. Over his long career, Mao's charisma in a broader sense derived more from his tenacity, his theoretical perspicacity and his grasp of the problems of the Chinese revolution than from such 'irrational' claims as those that came forward during the Cultural Revolution. It is arguable that the Cultural Revolution, in spite of plausible historical reasons for its launching, nevertheless represented a betrayal of an earlier commitment to sound theoretical reasoning in the making of revolution. Indeed, the Cultural Revolution's deification of Mao, and the concomitant privileging of unthinking passion over reasoned activity, brought into Chinese socialism the aestheticized politics that has been associated with fascism.[48]

That charisma need not be set against reason, or that it may be associated with rational but innovative leadership, is implicit in the interpretation of charisma by commentators on Mao such as Eisenstadt. If Mao continues to be remembered with awe by most Chinese citizens in spite of negative memories of the Cultural Revolution, as well as conscious efforts to discredit it, it is for these other contributions to the success of the revolution in China. This is the case, one might argue, even for the postrevolutionary deification of Mao in rural China. There is obviously a long tradition in Chinese popular religion of turning historical and fictional figures into deities, and it is this pantheon that Mao has joined – at least in some sectors of Chinese society. But this, too, is not to be attributed to the irrationality or the backwardness of the Chinese peasant, because Mao, deified, serves as a witness to popular protest against corruption and the betrayal of socialist promises of justice and equality – not justice and equality in an abstract sense but in terms of the needs and aspirations of the people, especially the rural people.

It is here that we possibly have another culturally specific manifestation of charismatic leadership.[49] To reiterate a point that I have made above, Mao had a widely acknowledged ability to bring the needs and aspirations of the rural people into the pursuit of socialism, as well as to translate Marxism and the socialist vision into the language of the people – for which he himself was frequently dismissed by intellectuals as just another peasant. He owed much of his charisma to his ability to voice the needs of the people, in their language. The people may be returning the favour by deifying him. It is a different deification than during the Cultural Revolution: not in the service of power but as a protest against its corruption.

Notes

1. I am grateful for their comments and encouragement to Roxann Prazniak, Li Guannan, Xie Shaobo and participants in the conference, 'Charisma and Emergent Social Movements', Institute of Biography, University of Groningen, 6–7 November 2008.
2. J.V. Downton. 1973. *Rebel Leadership: Commitment and Charisma in the Revolutionary Process*, New York: The Free Press, 1.
3. For this distinction, see, E.J. Hobsbawm. 1965. *Primitive Rebels: Archaic Forms of Social Movement in the 19th and 20th Centuries*, New York: W.W. Norton, 58–59.
4. A. Hirschman. 1977. *The Passions and the Interests: Political Arguments for Capitalism before Its Triumph*, Princeton: Princeton University Press.

5. M. Weber. 1968. *Max Weber on Charisma and Institution Building*, ed. S.N. Eisenstadt, Chicago: University of Chicago Press, 48–51.
6. Weber, *Max Weber on Charisma*, 46.
7. R. Bendix. 1960. *Max Weber: An Intellectual Portrait*, Garden City: Doubleday and Co., 272–93.
8. C. Lindholm. 1990. *Charisma*, Cambridge: Basil Blackwell, 7. For further elaborations of 'charisma', see also, M. Weber. 1947. 'Charismatic Authority', in M. Weber, *The Theory of Social and Economic Organization*, ed. T. Parsons, tr. A.M. Henderson and T. Parsons, New York: Oxford University Press, 358–63; Bendix, *Max Weber*, 393–94; A.R. Willner. 1968. *Charismatic Political Leadership: A Theory*, Princeton: Woodrow Wilson School of Public and International Affairs Research Monographs, no. 32, 4; and R. Eatwell. 2007. 'The Concept and Theory of Charismatic Leadership', in A.C. Pinto, R. Eatwell and S.U. Larsen (eds), *Charisma and Fascism in Interwar Europe*, London: Routledge, 3–18.
9. W.H. Friedland. 1964. 'For a Sociological Concept of Charisma', *Social Forces* 43(1), 21.
10. Friedland, 'For a Sociological Concept of Charisma'. Weber refers to 'benefits' to followers in the citation above. For his discussion of the charismatic and the economic, see Weber, *The Theory of Social and Economic Organization*, 358–63.
11. P. Smith. 2000. 'Culture and Charisma: Outline of a Theory', *Acta Sociologica* 43, 101–11.
12. B.J. Fogg. 1997. 'Charismatic Computers: Creating More Likable and Persuasive Interactive Technologies by Leveraging Principles from Social Psychology'. This Stanford Communications Ph.D. dissertation project is informed, according to the author, by the 'computers are social actors (CASA) paradigm'. http://virtual.inesc.pt/rct/show.php?id=73
13. Fogg, 'Charismatic Computers', 102–5.
14. For a defence of the concept as an explanation in political mobilization, with reference to the Cultural Revolution in the People's Republic of China, see J. Andreas. 2007. 'The Structure of Charismatic Mobilization: A Case Study of Rebellion during the Cultural Revolution', *American Sociological Review* 72(3), 434–58.
15. The terminology of charisma is usually laden with these simultaneous senses of the secular and the sacred. The Chinese term for charisma, *meili*, translated also as 'charming', literally means 'demon-force'. *Charming* itself, a commonplace word in secular usage, also bears the mysteries of its etymological origins.
16. This question has been raised eloquently in S.G. Wang. 1995. *The Failure of Charisma: The Cultural Revolution in Wuhan*, New York: Oxford University Press.
17. E. Shils. 1965. 'Charisma, Order, and Status', *American Sociological Review* 30(2), 199–213, and S.N. Eisenstadt, 'Introduction', in Weber, *Max Weber on Charisma and Nation Building*, ix-lvi.
18. One scholar who has given close attention to the question is A.R. Willner. 1968. *Charismatic Political Leadership: a Theory*, Princeton: Woodrow Wilson School of Public and International Affairs Research Monographs, no. 32.
19. E. Snow. 1944. *Red Star over China*, 2nd ed., New York: Grove Press, 71.
20. E. Snow. 1971. *Red China Today: on the Other Side of the River*, New York: Vintage Books, 170.
21. Z.B. Zhang and Y.F.Sun. 1991. *Zhongguo: Mao Zedong re* (China: Mao Zedong Fever), Xiangtan: Beiyue wenyi chuban she, 134–54.
22. R.M. Nixon. 1978. *The Memoirs of Richard Nixon*, London: Sigwick and Jackson, 561.
23. H. Kissinger. 1979. *The White House Years*, Boston: Little, Brown and Co., 1058.
24. Kissinger, *The White House Years*, 1058–66, passim.
25. For an extensive selection of impressions of Mao by Chinese and foreigners from different walks of life, see L.Q. Deng (ed.). 2004. *Zhongwai Mingren Pingshuo Mao Zedong* (Famous Chinese and Non-Chinese on Mao Zedong), Beijing: Zhongyang minzu chuban she.
26. A. Malraux. 1967. *Anti-Memoirs*, tr. T. Kilmartin, Middlesex: Penguin Books, 428. See p. 213 for the 'bronze emperor'. Mao's concerns about his mortality and the future of the

revolution provided the basis for Robert Jay Lifton's psychoanalytical exploration of the Cultural Revolution in R.J. Lifton. 1968. *Revolutionary Immortality: Mao Tse-tung and the Chinese Cultural Revolution*, New York: Vintage Books.

27. Z.S. Li. 1994. *The Private Life of Chairman Mao: The Memoirs of Mao's Personal Physician*, trans. H.C. Tai, New York: Random House.

28. For a thorough evaluation of such accounts, see M.B. Gao. 2008. *The Battle for China's Past: Mao and the Cultural Revolution*, London: Pluto Press. See pp. 97–116 for Gao's discussion of Li Zhisui's memoirs.

29. The characteristics I have singled out are scattered repeatedly throughout Li's book, and do not call for documentation here. The interested reader will spot them without any difficulty. For sexuality in charismatic appeal, with reference to the Indonesian leader Sukarno, see A.R. Willner. 1984. *The Spellbinders: Charismatic Political Leadership*, New Haven: Yale University Press, 131–33.

30. Siao-yu. 1973. *Mao Tse-tung and I Were Beggars: The True Adventures of Young Mao and His Friend on a 'Begging Trip' through Central China*, New York: Collier Books, 36–37.

31. Willner, *The Spellbinders*, 39.

32. The Cultural Revolution officially lasted for three years, from 1966 to 1969, and is recalled presently as 'ten years of disaster' (1966–1976), but is best viewed over a period of two decades, beginning in 1956 and ending with Mao's death in 1976, in order to grasp not just its consequences but also the problems that provoked it.

33. Willner, *The Spellbinders*, 12–14.

34. Zhang and Sun, *Zhongguo*, 131–81.

35. R.F. Wylie. 1980. *The Emergence of Maoism: Mao Tse-tung, Chen Po-ta, and the Search for Chinese Theory, 1935–1945*, Stanford: Stanford University Press.

36. A study that explicitly explores the issue of charisma in the years following the victory of the Communist Party is L. Dittmer. 1987. *China's Continuous Revolution: The Post-Liberation Epoch, 1949–1981*, Berkeley: University of California Press.

37. Han Dongping, Talk on the Thirtieth Anniversary of the Cultural Revolution, New School for Social Research, New York (1996). I may add here that like all constitutions, this 'constitution', too, was open to interpretation, and served as a site for conflict over different social and political interests. At its height, some of the Red Guards were to attack Mao himself for not being sufficiently Maoist. A humorous collection of the creativity and good deeds inspired by Mao Zedong Thought is available in G. Urban (ed.). 1971. *The Miracles of Chairman Mao: A Compendium of Devotional Literature, 1966–1970*, Los Angeles: Nash Publishing. In addition to the little *Red Book*, Cultural Revolution ideals of service were promoted through the so-called 'three most widely read essays': 'Serve the People', 'In Memory of Dr. Norman Bethune', and Mao's reading of a traditional parable, 'The Foolish Old Man Who Removed the Mountain'. A representative selection of Mao posters is readily available on the internet in a collection put together by Stefan Landsberger of Leiden University. S. Landsberger. 2008. *The Mao Cult*, retrieved from http://chineseposters.net/themes/mao-cult.php

38. These anxieties have been analysed in A. Chan. 1985. *Children of Mao: Personality Development and Political Activism in the Red Guard Generation*, Seattle: University of Washington Press.

39. There are many memoirs of the Cultural Revolution that discuss everyday practices of Mao-worship. For an analysis, see L. Xing. 2004. *Rhetoric of the Cultural Revolution: The Impact on Chinese Thought, Culture and Communication*, Columbia: University of South Carolina Press, especially the discussion of everyday rituals, pp. 132–42. Cultural Revolution practices surrounding the deification of Mao had antecedents in earlier party history, but they arguably reached an unprecedented intensity during the Cultural Revolution, and were intended not to consolidate a revolutionary 'community of discourse', but to restore an evangelical fervour to revolutionary faith by surrendering unconditionally to the prom-

ise of an idolized leader. For the role of 'discourse' in the Chinese Revolution, see D.E. Apter and T. Saich. 1994. *Revolutionary Discourse in Mao's Republic*, Cambridge: Harvard University Press. For 'communities of discourse', see R. Wuthnow. 1989. *Communities of Discourse: Ideology and Social Structure in the Reformation, the Enlightenment and European Socialism*, Cambridge: Harvard University Press.

40. See, for an example, the recollections of Liang Heng, who would become a leader in the Democracy Movement in the 1980s: H. Liang and J. Shapiro. 1983. *Son of the Revolution*, New York: Vintage Books, 124–25.

41. H.Y. Lee. 1978. *Politics of the Chinese Cultural Revolution: A Case Study*, Berkeley: University of California Press; W. Hinton. 1972. *Hundred Day War: The Cultural Revolution at Tsinghua University*, New York: Monthly Review Press; Wang, *The Failure of Charisma*.

42. These battles led to the devolution of charisma to those at the ground level who served as unofficial proxies for and representatives of Mao, serving as charismatic leaders in their own right. For a discussion of Tsinghua University from this angle, see Andreas, 'The Structure of Charismatic Mobilization', fn. 13. For issues of class, the 'biologization' of class, and social versus ideological forces in class identification, see R.C. Kraus. 1981. *Class Conflict in Chinese Socialism*, New York: Columbia University Press.

43. Malraux, *Anti-memoirs*, 426.

44. A. Dirlik. 2003. 'The Politics of the Cultural Revolution in Historical Perspective', in K.Y. Law (ed.), *The Chinese Cultural Revolution Reconsidered: Beyond Purge and Holocaust*, Basingstoke and New York: Palgrave, 158–83.

45. For a discussion of this most recent Mao fever, see Zhang and Sun, *Zhongguo*, especially chapters 6–7. See the appendix for a picture of a Mao temple in Zhejiang, where Mao is placed in the seat assigned to the Buddha in Buddhist temples, flanked by Zhou Enlai and Mao's first wife, Yang Kaihui (who was assassinated by the Guomindang), placed in the positions assigned to Boddhisatvas. I am grateful to Dr Yu Keping for this photograph which he took while travelling around his home province of Zhejiang.

46. See, for an example, R. Prazniak. 1999. *Of Camel Kings and Other Things: Rural Rebels against Modernity in Late Imperial China*, Lanham: Rowman & Littlefield.

47. For discussions of the religion in the Taiping Heavenly Kingdom and its revolutionary implications, see R.P. Weller. 1994. *Resistance, Chaos and Control in China: Taiping Rebels, Taiwanese Ghosts, and Tiananmen*, Basingstoke: Macmillan; and R.G. Wagner. 1982. *Reenacting the Heavenly Vision: The Role of Religion in the Taiping Rebellion*, Berkeley: Institute of Asian Studies.

48. For a discussion, see B.R. Wheeler. 2001. 'Modernist Reenchantments I: From Liberalism to Aestheticized Politics', *German Quarterly* 74(3), 223–37; and B.R. Wheeler. 2002. 'Modernist Reenchantments II: From Aestheticized Politics to the Artwork', *German Quarterly* 75(2), 113–26. For a recent work celebrating the Cultural Revolution politics of passion, see M.R. Dutton. 2005. *Policing Chinese Politics: A History*, Durham: Duke University Press. It is not surprising that Dutton's work is premised upon an equivalence between Mao and the Nazi theoretician Carl Schmitt, who has recently gained popularity among frustrated leftists in search of an alibi against liberalism. Schmitt's uncompromising friend/enemy distinction, the point of departure for his idea of the political, does indeed find a parallel in Mao's 1926 questions, 'Who are our friends? Who are our enemies?' Dutton conveniently overlooks the fact that during the years of the revolution, Mao followed these questions with concrete analyses that complicated the constitution of both friend and enemy. It was during the Cultural Revolution that the binarism took on the overtones of uncompromising religious antagonism between good and evil that Philip Smith has observed to be typical of 'genuinely' charismatic moments (Smith, 'Culture and Charisma', fn. 10). At its worst – as with the rendering of class into a biological category (so-called 'bloodline theory') – the Cultural Revolution rendered Maoism into a variant of fascist politics – hardly anything to be celebrated for its passion.

49. Mao's image among the people at large differs radically from his image among urban intellectuals, especially among those intellectuals, former participants in the Cultural Revolution, who now seek to redeem themselves by blaming him for all the misdeeds of the Cultural Revolution, down to the street level. Unfortunately, it is these intellectuals (the likes of Jung Chang) who receive the most enthusiastic reception among readers abroad as they speak the same language as their foreign readers. For alternative views, see D.P. Han. 2000. *The Unknown Cultural Revolution: Educational Reforms and Their Impact on China's Rural Development*, New York: Garland Publishers; and, M.B. Gao. 1999. *Gao Village: A Portrait of Rural Life in Modern China*, Hong Kong: Hong Kong University Press. For a comprehensive discussion of the problems in Mao's portrayal and reception, see Gao, *The Battle for China's Past*, fn. 27.

II. Charismatic Observations

CHAPTER 7

CHARISMATIC LEADERS, POLITICAL RELIGION AND SOCIAL MOVEMENTS

Western Europe at the End of the Nineteenth Century

Henk te Velde

When Max Weber discovered a new type of leadership in the politics of the late nineteenth century, he tried to make sense of it by borrowing the word and the concept of charisma from religious studies. This is no coincidence. Descriptions of charismatic leadership virtually always use religious words in order to characterize the experience of the followers or the alleged qualities of the leader. On the other hand, it could also be argued that so-called 'political religions' could hardly do without charismatic leaders. This calls into question the democratic nature of charismatic leadership, since political religions have often been seen as undemocratic. In general, the use of religious words in politics has often been regarded as an indication that democracy was in danger. I will use the charismatic leaders of the late nineteenth century as a case study to investigate the ambiguous relationship between charisma, political religion and democracy in connection with the emergence of new social movements and political parties.

Charisma as a Product of Its Time

It could be argued that different times call for different leaders. Winston Churchill could never have become such a successful leader if there had not been a war; when the war was over he was voted out by a large majority and replaced by the much more ordinary Labour leader Clement

Attlee. This was a change of politics from the Conservatives to Labour, but it was also a choice for another type of leader. According to the historian Martin Conway, the postwar period was a time of nationally and ideologically almost indistinguishable grey men in grey suits.[1] Leadership is a product of its age.

At the same time, however, certain qualities of the charismatic type of leader seem to be almost timeless, or at least the way people tend to describe those qualities is. One will almost invariably find religious language. This was even true for the seemingly unprecedented case of the Dutch politician Pim Fortuyn in 2002, who compared his political quest with the journey of Moses to the promised land, almost a cliché in self-descriptions of charismatic leaders.[2] There are no clues that Fortuyn consciously copied charismatic predecessors; he seems to have thought up the clichés all by himself. His adherents also pictured their devotion in religious terms, comparing their emotions for instance to the experience of the followers of 'Jomanda', a somewhat melodramatic Dutch faith healer. They certainly did not follow historical examples. In this case the religious language was all the more surprising given the fact that Dutch society is currently one of the most secularized societies in the world. Dutch politics have also tended to be rather sober, or to use another word, rather boring; and it had been a very long time since a leader of this type had appeared on the national political scene. However, the moment a truly charismatic leader appeared, his performance was immediately couched in religious terms.[3]

On the other hand, Fortuyn is also a good case in point if one wanted to argue that leaders have to wait for their moment. He had dreamt his dream of a more than ordinary political 'mission' for many years, had literally tried to acquire a position in virtually every available political party, but had failed miserably. Then, suddenly, at the end of 2001, after a period of rather quiet and uninspiring domestic politics and after the dramatic shock of 9/11, his time had come. It could be argued that this situation provided him with the crisis the charismatic leader needs, according to Weber. In addition, he succeeded in dramatizing the sociopolitical situation of the Netherlands by famously writing and speaking about the 'mess' (*puinhoop*) the established parties had created.[4] However, for the purposes of this chapter the religious language he used is the most interesting element. This contribution will concentrate on the (quasi)religious elements of charismatic leadership and try to relate those to their political functions.

Charisma and Political Religion

The combination of political leadership and a religious mission has often been explosive, and the 'political religion' involved in this type of transforming and highly ambiguous leadership has often been associated with totalitarianism. The most (in)famous examples are of course the fascist leaders of the 1930s, and the concept of charisma first became widely known as an expression used to describe the magical power of these leaders. Hermann Rauschning's *Die Revolution des Nihilismus* (1938) was an important factor in spreading the use of the word. In order to explain or exemplify Hitler's charismatic appeal Rauschning quotes words such as *faith* and *religion* that the followers used to express their fascination by the leader; it was, he explains, a kind of 'religious ecstasy'.[5] Almost at the same time the concept of 'political religion' was applied to totalitarian regimes and acquired its current meaning of exclusive and fundamentalist sacralization of politics. Crucial in this respect was the work of the Austrian philosopher Eric Voegelin, who responded to the challenge of national socialism, too.[6] Although the study of charismatic leadership is not necessarily part of the study of political religion, in practice the two are closely linked: the cult of the leader is often considered to be one of the most important parts or even the single most important part of a political religion.[7] The connection between charisma and political religion has, on the other hand, contributed to the awareness of the risks of charismatic leadership. It has seemed to be a dark power, a power that bewitches people and makes them do terrible things; it has also become a byword for totalitarian dictatorship.

This was virtually the opposite of the story most historians tell about what happened in the period of democratization of European politics of the late nineteenth century. This period was also full of charismatic leaders, but they are seen as great emancipators, who mobilized people who until then had not taken part in organized politics. Weber's most conspicuous example of charismatic leadership was William Gladstone, 'the people's William' and famous British Liberal leader. He championed extension of suffrage and succeeded, according to Colin Matthew, perhaps his most prominent biographer, in reconciling dramatic performance and rational debate. According to contemporary comments, he 'found the people who live in cottages hostile to political parties, and succeeded in uniting them with the rest of his countrymen'.[8] Many of the great early socialist leaders could also be described as charismatic leaders, such as the German socialist Ferdinand Lassalle, the Dutch socialist Ferdinand Domela Nieuwenhuis or the British socialist James Keir Hardie.[9] In all of these cases religious language abounded. They were called 'prophets', 'apostles', 'Messiahs' and so on, and they were 'martyrs' for the good cause, so it would make sense to speak of 'political religion' in their case, too, but no one would call them totalitarian leaders.

This suggests that the connection between political religion and totalitarianism is less simple than has sometimes been assumed. Charismatic leaders could endanger the cause of democracy, but they could also promote it. The religious words show the unusual aspect of the charismatic experience, and they demonstrate that the relationship between charismatic leadership and democracy is a complex matter. It is not a question of democracy *or* charismatic leaders. This has not always been acknowledged. In his last book on social movements the historical sociologist Charles Tilly mentions the relation in passing when he says that social movements are 'not necessarily democratic, since ethnic, religious, and nationalist movements sometimes invest their powers in charismatic leaders rather than democratic deliberation yet still insist that those leaders embody the will of the people at large'.[10] Apparently, Tilly is arguing that social movements are not 'democratic' if they prefer charismatic leaders to 'democratic deliberation'.

This raises the issue of what democracy really is. This is one of the most interesting questions in the study of charismatic leadership. It is clearly not a solution simply to set charisma against democracy, but it is not very convincing either just to cheer the democratic power of charisma. Democracy has many faces, and charisma can tell us something about those faces. For instance, socialist historiography has not praised leaders such as Domela Nieuwenhuis or Lassalle unconditionally, and one of the reasons for this is that these leaders did not really fit in with the conditions of modern party machines. This is a crucial question that could explain the problematic relationship between charismatic leadership and democracy.

Charisma and Populism

In order to get an understanding of this matter a good starting point is to underline the affinity between charisma and populism. This affinity is so obvious that 'populist charisma' sometimes almost seems to be a pleonasm. It is not so easy to imagine charisma without some sort of populism. Arguably, this is a matter of definitions. Populism should not be seen as a term of abuse, but as a neutral term denoting an aspect of democratic, albeit demagogic, politics. On the other hand, charisma in the strongest sense of the word implies a symbiotic relationship between the leader and his followers, which is apparent in the cases mentioned above, but is not so obvious in Caesarist leaders, such as Charles de Gaulle. Like charisma, populism has an ambiguous relationship with democracy. Populism opposes the 'people' to the elite and it does not like institutions. Like charismatic politics, populist politics is, according to political theorist Margaret Canovan,

> not ordinary, routine politics. It has the revivalist flavour of a movement, pow-
> ered by the enthusiasm that draws normally unpolitical people into the politi-
> cal arena [also something it has in common with charisma – *HtV*]. This extra
> emotional ingredient can turn politics into a campaign to save the country or
> to bring about a great renewal. Associated with this mood is the tendency for
> heightened emotions to be focused on a charismatic leader. Personalized lead-
> ership is a natural corollary of the reaction against politics-as-usual. Rejecting
> ossified institutional structures, including bureaucratic layers of organization,
> populists celebrate both spontaneous action at the grassroots and a close per-
> sonal tie between leader and followers.[11]

This type of politics has existed for a long time, but normally the term *populism* has been reserved for (and acquired its current meaning in) movements that emerged from the end of the nineteenth century. The American People's Party and populist movement of the late nineteenth century are often quoted as early examples of populism.[12] The late nine-teenth century also saw the emergence of the modern charismatic leader and in Europe this was also the period of the emergence of modern politi-cal parties, which soon became important scapegoats for populists. This has been the case from the moment political parties became dominant forces in politics in the early twentieth century.

Modern populism and modern political parties both offered a form of 'democratization' of politics and from that perspective they could at first seem to be allies. Both advocated a role for the 'masses' in politics, and both argued that the politics of the notables had to make way for a politics of 'the people'. In this early stage of resistance against established politics populism and modern parties went hand in hand and charismatic leaders such as Gladstone, Domela Nieuwenhuis or Lassalle could serve as symbols or even leaders of new political movements and parties. Glad-stone addressed the National Liberal Federation at its founding meeting[13] and Domela and Lassalle were the leaders of socialist parties.

Soon, however, the tension between charismatic leadership and par-ties started to grow. Abraham Kuyper, for example, was and remained the charismatic leader of the Neo-Calvinist Antirevolutionaire Partij, the first modern political party in the Netherlands (founded in 1879). He operated on the assumption that Robert Michels attributed to some socialist lead-ers: 'Le Parti, c'est moi'.[14] At first this assumption was tacitly accepted, but increasingly it caused tension. After 1900 the party elite started to criticize his leadership and it was only thanks to his unassailable position as the prophet-founder of the party that he remained in place. He could also hold on to his position because he was a formidable organizer and manager, who directed his party as an army. In that respect he could be compared to Joseph Chamberlain in England, who was a party manager with charismatic qualities, though Kuyper was a more emotional character.[15]

Oratory and the Autonomy of the Followers

Charismatic leaders of the late nineteenth century were popular leaders. Weber saw in charismatic leaders a potential antidote to the disruptive changes that the advent of the masses spelled for the political system in states with a representative government. These leaders should domesticate the masses, as it were, and perhaps popular Caesarist leaders such as Bismarck to a certain extent, in fact, did.[16] However, the charismatic leader in the pure Weberian sense of the who had a 'religious', symbiotic bond with his followers, often had another, almost opposite effect. He 'woke up' the masses, as an often recurring rhetorical phrase would have it. He demonstrated (or at least declared) to people outside established politics that he was 'one of them' – 'I am one of yourselves', Gladstone said to his audience[17] – and took their ideas seriously and was looking for companions instead of slaves. The effect a charismatic leader could have by presenting himself in this way was most visible at mass meetings.

It could be argued that the 'true' charismatic leader is first and foremost a man or woman of the spoken word, an orator. The capacity to spellbind an audience united leaders as diverse as the liberal Gladstone and the socialist/anarchist Domela Nieuwenhuis. They both were prolific writers, but their written style was mediocre, and not very effective in producing the commitment and attachment their speeches were famous for. How are we to judge their oratorical achievements? Were they not just bewitching their audience with oratorical fireworks in a theatrical setting? Ever since Rauschning and similar theorists, the concept of the charismatic speaker has conjured up the images of Hitler rehearsing his speeches in front of a mirror and of the artificial setting of Leni Riefenstahl's famous documentary film *Triumph of the Will*. It is also clear that not only were the performances of the fascist dictators rehearsed, but late nineteenth-century performances by charismatic leaders were often carefully staged, too: banners and large portraits decorating the halls, and singing of battle songs by a massive audience.[18] In this sense it seems obvious that charismatic leadership is the very opposite of 'democratic deliberation' (Tilly), which entails open debate instead of a mechanical show.

On the other hand, there are clear indications that the success of the late nineteenth-century charismatic leaders in fact depended on their ability to *boost* democratic deliberation. Colin Matthew does not deny the theatrical side of Gladstone's performances, but he argues that people read the content of his speech in the newspapers the next day. His charismatic appearance made his speeches the news of the day and even the journals of his conservative opponents had to print them, if only for commercial reasons.[19] Thus, he did not need an organization to spread his gospel, and there was no bureaucracy that would prevent outsiders from participating in the political debates his campaigns stimulated. Even though many people practically worshipped Gladstone, his political presence doubtlessly stimulated political debates. *Mutatis mutandis*, something comparable seems to have happened in early German socialism. Charismatic leaders – besides Lassalle, who is not the best example, the German historian Welskopp mentions a number of other cases – were the centre of noisy public meetings with literally a great deal of 'democratic deliberation'; perhaps not a debate with formal rules and everyone having their say, but certainly with a lot of interaction between the orator and his audience, and a lot of *Wortmeldungen*. In the emotional atmosphere of oratorical duels in public meetings speakers could rise to a greater height than in formal parliamentary assemblies, which some early socialists considered as a puppet theatre anyway.[20]

It all comes down to the question of what 'democratic deliberation' is. If this is defined as a quiet and sober exchange of formal arguments, then the well organized, stable, institutional context of parliament and established political parties is clearly what is needed in order to have a proper democratic debate. But if the 'democratic' element is valued more highly, in the sense of free, open access and the participation of a large public, then the conclusion might be different. The same ambiguity goes for these charismatic leaders, too. The vehemence of their presentation often interrupted normal and formal settings of debate, but could, on the other hand, create space for popular participation and involvement. This second, positive effect applied at the end of the nineteenth century in particular. For many people the new participation in politics was exciting, even entertaining, and an intellectual stimulus. This was an important experience, even if this probably happened mainly during a short period when political parties were being invented but did not yet dominate the political scene. Charismatic politics are inherently unstable, because they depend on the popularity of a person instead of a stable institutional setting. In the agitated transitional period of the end of the nineteenth century they flourished. This is, of course, not to say that they only developed at the end of the nineteenth century, but that they have mainly occurred intermittently during periods of important changes in political life, or at least only sometimes dominated politics.

This is another argument that charismatic leadership will be more successful in some periods and situations than in others. Weber stresses the social aspect of charisma. It is not (only) a particular quality of an individual; it is crucial that his or her supporters will attribute charismatic authority to an individual. In this sense the followers do not passively receive a charismatic aura, but they really, actively, create charisma themselves. This is illustrated by the fact that many social movements of the nineteenth century were not founded by a charismatic leader, but that the charismatic leader was 'found' by the movement. Many famous charismatic leaders of the late nineteenth century did not really start a social movement, but were in fact drawn into it. For instance, William Gladstone jumped onto a moving train. He had resigned from the leadership of the Liberal Party and had almost retired from politics when the Bulgarian Agitation of the late 1870s offered him the opportunity to make a comeback as the charismatic Grand Old Man.[21] The starting point of the charismatic career of Ferdinand Lassalle was a letter written by workers in order to persuade him to take over the leadership. Ferdinand Domela Nieuwenhuis wrote in his autobiography that he was drawn into the socialist movement before he knew it. In this sense charismatic leaders of the late nineteenth century should not be considered as founders but as catalysts. Their presence often gave public respectability to a popular movement – gentlemen participating in a workers' movement – and made it easier to operate on a national scale, instead of mainly locally. In general, they facilitated the connection with national politics.

Charismatic leadership in the late nineteenth century reinforced the impression that a new era had come. This was not business as usual, but 'politics in a new key' (Carl Schorschke)[22] that took into account the concerns and dreams of ordinary people. In the words of Canovan, this was the populist or 'redemptive' side of politics – as opposed to ordinary, pragmatic politics. She has carefully chosen this religious word, which is more or less an equivalent of words such as 'a politics of faith', used by Michael Oakeshott, whom she is quoting.[23] Politics as usual is about piecemeal engineering and muddling through instead of redemption. Literature on populism tells us that there is a link between populism and a religious form of politics. Populism promises a radical change, a radical and simple solution to problems, a conversion of politics and society, and this type of radicalism often expresses itself in a religious guise. *Redemption, conversion*: resounding religious words that characterize the radical, though sometimes short-lived experience that participants in populist and charismatic movements go through.

In fact, their common 'religious' nature has been advanced as one of the important (perhaps pleonastic) links between populism and charismatic leadership.[24] It is no coincidence that *democracy* and *populism* both contain the word *people* (*demos, populus*). Populism and its companion, charismatic leadership, are at least 'democratic' in the sense of a large audience, but they often neglect democracy in the sense of careful procedures of interaction and decision making, to say the least. Religious devotion to the leader does not seem to be very promising from the point of view of independent democratic deliberation. All too clearly, it seems to confirm the classical mistrust of the lazy or misled common people with their 'lack of interest in organizations which have a long-range perspective, and a readiness to follow leaders who offer a demonological interpretation of the evil forces (either religious or political) which are conspiring against [them]', according to the political scientist Seymour Martin Lipset.[25]

However, the political energy released by charismatic leaders could also stimulate early socialists or Gladstonian petty bourgeois to participate in public debate. In Britain the peak of Gladstone's popularity around 1880 coincided with the short-lived flourishing of so-called mock parliaments where people from all walks of life engaged in passionate debates.[26] The advance of the well organized political parties from the end of the nineteenth century spelled the end of the Gladstonian period in politics and of the popularity of the local parliaments. Something comparable happened in socialist Germany when the SPD began to dominate the political scene and the world of passionate debates in public meetings began to disappear,[27] or in the Netherlands when the SDAP (the Dutch equivalent of the SPD and its sister party) became the most important socialist party and a disciplined body. In all of these cases the charismatic experience had not been tantamount to servile obedience, but a catalyst for democratic participation, though not the origin of participation. Charismatic leadership was not more than a catalyst, and one of the difficult dilemmas of modern democracies has been how to organize mass participation without destroying it.

Organization of Democracy

How we value the role of charismatic leaders will depend on our evaluation of the interplay of social movements, parties and democracy. According to Tilly a crucial element in the development of social movements was the emergence of what he calls 'WUNC displays': Worthiness, Unity, Numbers, Commitment.[28] In order to gain political influence and achieve their aims modern social movements have advocated disciplined, homogeneous, massive public action by dedicated followers. In short, the social movement Tilly pictures is a sort of ideal army. Perhaps without realizing it, or at least without paying much attention to it, Tilly has thus painted the struggle for power of the modern political party from the late nineteenth century on. Besides religious metaphors, many army metaphors were used to describe the modern democratic party as a 'kriegführende Partei' (a war party).[29] It was a means to reach the end that was democracy, and in order to reach that end internal democracy was less important than the strength of discipline. Should one value commitment and (democratic) numbers most highly, then the 'religious' charismatic experience was crucial. But if worthiness and unity, in short, discipline, were more important, then the organization of the war party, the organization for battle, the army fit for political struggles, was what counted the most.[30] Seen from this latter perspective, charismatic leaders were rather inconvenient. Although leaders such as August Bebel, the leader of the German socialist party, or Abraham Kuyper were usually described as 'generals', and were very good at disciplining their parties, the typical element of charismatic leadership is its disturbing rather than its disciplining effect. Of course, this does not mean that charismatic leaders in the late nineteenth century did not like to be obeyed, on the contrary, but most of them had difficulty accepting the ordered and bureaucratic structures of the modern political party. In their case, authority could only mean their own authority, not the authority of rules and regulations. This type of leader is very good at promoting commitment rather than producing unity and worthiness, although the latter qualities could be by-products of the former. It is no coincidence that, for instance, social-democratic criticism of Domela Nieuwenhuis, besides focusing on the 'sectarian' aspects of his leadership, was also directed at his 'individualism'.[31]

At first glance it makes perfect sense that an army – or machine, another word that was being used – is needed in order to realize the dream the charismatic prophet is holding out to his faithful disciples. However, late nineteenth-century charismatic leadership was often more about emotional and ideological power than about the power to get things done or the power to realize things against the will of others. Of course, Gladstone was prime minister for a long time, but he spellbound and moved the mass of the population by his moral oratory, not by a party organization. He reached the peak of his charismatic power over the masses when he engaged in the moral-populist 'Bulgarian agitation' against the massacres of Christian Bulgarians by the Turks in the 1870s. This was just a few years before his famous Midlothian election tour in 1880. He was in opposition then, and had even retired as a leader of the parliamentary Liberal Party. Also, many early socialist leaders were rather apostles or prophets than party managers, let alone strategic administrators. It could thus be argued that the power, or perhaps it is better to say authority, that was inherent in their charismatic position was of another kind than the power of pragmatic politicians.

For a moment at the end of the nineteenth century it seemed that democratization would almost bring heaven on earth, but then it turned out that democracy had several faces. The tension between the promise of political change and participation in politics, and the 'army' that was needed to bring these about, is the central question of what has remained the most famous analysis of the modern mass party, by Robert Michels (1911).[32] It has not always been noticed that Michels' book about the German socialist party is as much about leadership as it is about the party machine. For example, the titles of all but the last part of the book refer to leadership. Michels is interested in charismatic leadership, and the book abounds with religious metaphors referring to apostles, prophets, martyrs, sects, Christ, evangelism. It is a book by someone who first believed in the redemptive power of democracy, but then lost that belief, because he came to think that the 'kriegführende Partei', the army that was needed to bring about democracy, destroyed the very thing it was meant to achieve.

Michels did not see a solution, because he thought that every organization would produce a certain oligarchy and that a pure democracy would remain an illusion. He was probably right; we will indeed not get a heaven on earth. However, one of the reasons for his gloomy analysis was that he considered the effects of leadership only in the framework of organization. According to him, the growth of the power of leaders was directly proportional to the growth of the organization.[33] And the growth of the organization was equal to the loss of democracy. If one sees it that way the conclusion is obvious: (charismatic) leadership is detrimental to democracy. But if we realize that political parties and charismatic leaders both responded to the need for popular participation in politics, but that they each showed just one of 'the two faces of democracy', then the picture looks a bit different. The party as organization or even as 'army' belonged to the practical side of democracy; it was a means to an end in the struggle for power. The charismatic leaders, on the other hand, belonged to the redemptive side of democracy: they held out the dream of an ideal world and the promise of a pure democracy, where the people really mattered.

Where the two sides of democracy are mixed, resulting in a party-like organization and structure *and* an all-embracing charismatic leadership, the distance to totalitarian politics is small – as the practices of national socialism and also Michels' later sympathy for fascism show. But if the two are separated, then it becomes clear what the promises and dangers of both sides are. An organization calls for bureaucratic routine, including clear rules and procedures, and periodic supervision by the members. Hardly any space for charismatic leaders there. Charismatic leaders are impossible to control; they inspire, get things on the move for better or for worse, give a glimpse of another world. They are popular leaders, but should not have absolute power. They are better at criticizing power than at exercising it.

Conclusion

With good reason, the Annales school and the Marxist historians of the postwar period did not have the previous predilection of historians for 'Great Men'. However, the Weberian, sociological approach to leadership avoids the pitfall of placing Great Men or Women outside of history. Leadership is a product of its age, and the political religion charismatic leaders preached at the end of the nineteenth century was useful as moral criticism of an establishment that needed to change and to democratize. Their success could also be interpreted as a sign of the success of the social movements that had already developed before they entered the stage, and as a sign that these movements needed a spectacular centre but were still 'movements' in the sense that they preferred an emotional appeal as a means of mobilization to organizational management as such.

In that respect the charismatic leaders were more important than the new organizations they inspired, but subsequently often abhorred or at least did not really like. Had the new political parties started as bureaucratic organizations which advocated piecemeal engineering, they would not have succeeded in the way they did. It is hard to imagine their success without the initial populist politics of redemption that accompanied them. They needed a political religion, and in particular apostles, martyrs and Messiahs. It is hard to imagine the political religion of the end of the nineteenth century without the charismatic leaders that embodied it. In retrospect it could be argued that these leaders played a crucial role in the emergence of the new political parties. They could do so precisely because the early political parties started as flexible social movements, still largely without 'WUNC displays', rather than bureaucratic parts of the established state. When the parties 'solidified' into fixed organizations, the charismatic leader either had to leave or more or less turn into an autocrat. In the more fluid situation of the early social movement, charismatic leaders had played the role of supporting the development of political activity by workers and petty bourgeois. The religious aspect of their politics resembled the totalitarian political religion of the 1930s in some or even many of its massive and theatrical elements, and in the promise of a new world, but their politics did not have to resemble totalitarianism in what it did to individual participants. The audience could also interpret the leaders' message as a moral exhortation to think for themselves. These leaders took them seriously and put into words what they had only vaguely intuited! It could be the starting point for slavish adoration, but also for independent political activity, in particular if the movement already existed before the leader appeared.

It seems to me that precisely this ambiguous element – does charismatic politics encourage adoration or independence? – explains the complicated relationship of charismatic leadership and democracy. Be that as it may, the occurrence of charismatic leadership was a sign of commotion and a stimulus for commotion. The periodic appearance of charismatic leaders in democratic regimes shows the periodic need for 'redemptive' politics. This is a discomforting message, because in the long run politics cannot offer redemption. On the other hand, politics is more than administration alone. Sometimes charismatic leaders remind us of the tensions inherent to parliamentary democracy.

Notes

1. M. Conway. 2004. 'The Rise and Fall of Western Europe's Democratic Age, 1945–1973', *Contemporary European History* 13, 71; idem. 2002. 'Democracy in Postwar Western Europe: The Triumph of a Political Model', *European History Quarterly* 32, 60.
2. P. Fortuyn in the conclusion of his 1995 *De verweesde samenleving: een religieus-sociologisch traktaat*, Utrecht: Bruna. Other examples: H.C.G. Matthew. 1995. *Gladstone 1875–1898*, Oxford: Clarendon Press, 298; H. te Velde. 1996. 'Ervaring en zingeving in de politiek. Het politieke charisma in de tijd van Abraham Kuyper', *Theoretische Geschiedenis* 23(4), 524.
3. J.E. Ellemers. 2002. 'Pim Fortuyn: een zuiver geval van charismatisch gezag', *Facta. Sociaal-wetenschappelijk magazine*, November, 2–5. Cf. H. te Velde. 2002. 'Drees und Fortuyn. Der Stil politischer Führerschaft in den Niederlanden seit 1945', *Jahrbuch Zentrum für Niederlande-Studien*, 11–25; P.J. Margry. 2003. 'The Murder of Pim Fortuyn and Collective Emotions: Hype, Hysteria and Holiness in the Netherlands?', *Etnofoor. Antropologisch tijdschrift* 16, 102–27. Arguably, the short-lived Fortuyn-mania fits the classic form of charisma better than the cases analysed by R. Eatwell. 2002. 'The Rebirth of Rightwing Charisma? The Cases of Jean-Marie Le Pen and Vladimir Zhirinovsky', *Totalitarian Movements and Political Religions* 3, 1–23.
4. P. Fortuyn. 2002. *De puinhopen van acht jaar Paars*, Rotterdam: Speakers Academy Uitgeverij.
5. H. Rauschning. 1938. *Die Revolution des Nihilismus. Kulisse und Wirklichkeit im Dritten Reich*, Zürich and New York: Europa Verlag, 58–61 ('Das Charisma der Führergestalt').
6. E. Gentile. 2006. *Politics as Religion*, Princeton: Princeton University Press, 4 and 140 (definition). See also H. Maier. 2007. 'Political Religion: A Concept and Its Limitations', *Totalitarian Movements and Political Religions* 8, 5–16; E. Gentile. 2005. 'Political Religion: A Concept and Its Critics – a Critical Survey', *Totalitarian Movements and Political Religions* 6(1), 19–32.

7. Cf. the most thorough introduction to political religion, Gentile, *Politics as Religion*, chapter 5; it is no coincidence that the review *Totalitarian Movements and Political Religions* contains a lot of articles about charismatic leadership.
8. H.C.G. Matthew. 1998. 'Gladstone, Rhetoric and Politics', in P.J. Jagger (ed.), *Gladstone*, London and Rio Grande: The Hambledon Press, 213–34, 278–80; *Newcastle Weekly Chronicle* (1880), quoted by E. Biagini. 1992. *Liberty, Retrenchment and Reform: Popular Liberalism in the Age of Gladstone, 1860–1880*, Cambridge: Cambridge University Press, 369.
9. H. te Velde. 2005. 'Charismatic Leadership, c. 1870–1914: A Comparative European Perspective', in R. Toye and J. Gottlieb (eds), *Making Reputations: Power, Persuasion and the Individual in Modern British Politics*, London and New York: I.B. Tauris.
10. C. Tilly. 2004. *Social Movements, 1768–2004*, Boulder and London: Paradigm Publishers, 13.
11. M. Canovan. 1999. 'Trust the People! Populism and the Two Faces of Democracy', *Political Studies* 47, 6. I thank Flip Kramer (University of Groningen) for discussing this article with me.
12. E.g., P. Taggart. 2000. *Populism*, Buckingham and Philadelphia: Open University Press, chapter 3.
13. In the famous M. Ostrogorski. 1902, reprint 1922. *Democracy and the Organization of Political Parties*, New York and London: MacMillan, vol. 1, 178 ff., the author actually associates Gladstone too closely with the Federation; after this initial meeting Gladstone had nothing more to do with it.
14. R. Michels. 1911/1925, reprint 1989. *Zur Soziologie des Parteiwesens in der modernen Demokratie*, Stuttgart: Kröner Verlag, chapter III–3, 216. Cf. H. te Velde. 2002. *Stijlen van leiderschap. Persoon en politiek van Thorbecke tot Den Uyl*, Amsterdam: Wereldbibliotheek, 84; J. Koch. 2006. *Abraham Kuyper. Een biografie*, Amsterdam: Boom.
15. P.T. Marsh. 1994. *Joseph Chamberlain: Entrepreneur in Politics*, New Haven: Yale University Press.
16. H.-U. Wehler. 1995. *Deutsche Gesellschaftsgeschichte (1849–1914)*, Munich: Beck, 368–77, 849–54.
17. Biagini, *Liberty, Retrenchment and Reform*, 417.
18. Biagini, *Liberty, Retrenchment and Reform*, 418–22, draws a parallel between Gladstone and Lassalle in this respect; cf. Te Velde, *Stijlen van leiderschap*, 99.
19. Matthew, *Gladstone*.
20. T. Welskopp. 2000. *Das Banner der Brüderlichkeit. Die deutsche Sozialdemokratie vom Vormärz bis zum Sozialistengesetz*, Bonn: Dietz, 395 (in a chapter about charisma).
21. The classic analysis is by R. Shannon. 1963. *Gladstone and the Bulgarian Agitation 1876*, London: Thomas Nelson.
22. C. Schorschke. 1980. *Fin de Siècle Vienna: Politics and Culture*, New York: Knopf.
23. Canovan, 'Trust the People'.
24. E.g., Taggart, *Populism*, 101.
25. S.M. Lipset. 1960. *Political Man: The Social Bases of Politic*, Garden City: Anchor Books, 115, quoted by I. de Haan. 2002. 'From Moses to Maggie: Popular Political Wisdom and the Republican Tradition in Political Thought', *The Public* 2, 34.
26. J. van Rijn. 2010. *De eeuw van het debat. De ontwikkeling van het publieke debat in Nederland en Engeland, 1800–1920*, Amsterdam: Wereldbibliotheek (with a summary in English), about these British mock parliaments, compared to Dutch and British debating societies.
27. Welskopp, *Das Banner der Brüderlichkeit*.
28. Tilly, *Social Movements*, 4 and passim.
29. Cf. e.g., Michels, *Zur Soziologie des Parteiwesens*, chapter I A 3: 'Die moderne demokratische Partei als kriegführende Partei; der Militantismus'.
30. Cf. Te Velde, 'Charismatic Leadership', 46–47.
31. See e.g. the classical biographical essay about Domela in J. Romein and A. Romein. 1938–1940, reprint 1977. *Erflaters van onze beschaving*, Amsterdam: Querido.
32. Michels, *Zur Soziologie des Parteiwesens*.
33. Michels, *Zur Soziologie des Parteiwesens*, 26.

CHAPTER 8

'*JE NE SAIS QUOI*'
Some Reflections on the Study of Charisma

Marc Reynebeau

Throughout history extraordinary personal qualities have always been attributed to leaders and rulers. They were usually derived from some kind of largely hereditary metaphysical blessing and were underscored by rituals, propaganda and image building of religious, artistic and other kinds. Thus rulers could command obedience, respect, reverence, admiration and even veneration. Divine authority not only provided premodern sovereigns with mere formal legitimacy, by which they could proclaim themselves *imperator in regno suo*;[1] it also endowed them with an elaborate array of exceptional human qualities deemed necessary for the responsibilities of ruling, such as wisdom, courage, foresight, perseverance, military insight, ethical sensibility and sometimes even artistic talent or healing powers.[2]

By coining the word *charisma* to describe a sociological phenomenon Max Weber created a useful and much needed terminological tool for the study of those personal qualities and their political consequences in other contexts than premodern sovereignty.[3] Although Weber's ideas on charisma date from the early twentieth century, they still are the main reference for most studies on the subject. This indicates that no new major theoretical framework on the issue has been developed or, if it has been, that it has not been able to impose itself on scholars.

This is odd as history since Weber's death in 1920 does not lack examples of charismatic leadership, sometimes benign and sometimes disastrous, ranging from Nelson Mandela to Adolf Hitler. The recent perception that even in long-established democracies the practice of political power is increasingly becoming more personalized adds to the relevance of the subject to contemporary political science.[4]

A Conceptual Problem

The lack of new paradigms in scholarship on charisma suggests an apparent uneasiness on the part of the social sciences with the subject. This probably reflects the very nature of the phenomenon itself: it often seems fuzzy, difficult to grasp or based on contradictory arguments. In the entertainment business charisma is called the X-factor, which is never detectable as such, but only shows itself by phenotypic traits. In colloquial French, charisma is often referred to as someone's *je ne sais quoi* – which literally means 'I don't know what', and can be translated merely into 'something'. Writing about the Soviet regime, François Furet could only describe the role of Stalin's personality in it as 'quelque chose qui lui était essentiel', as 'something' which was essential to that regime, admitting tacitly to not being able to elaborate on the nature of that implied 'essence'.[5]

It is easy to imagine the reasons for the social sciences' apparent discomfort with the very idea of charisma. It does not sit well with liberal political thought, the dominant ideological framework amongst scholars, which is based on rational conviction, not on transcendental imposition or emotional seduction, as is often implied in charisma. In a parallel evolution historians have gradually enlarged the notion of political agency by shaking off the idea that history was little more than the collected biographies of kings, generals, popes and other dead white males. Moreover the magnetic influence of a single person seems contradictory to the very core of democracy, in which final authority and legitimacy lie with large groups of people, the constituency, not with individuals. This is particularly the case in most social and labour movements, which are often based on egalitarianism, collective action, mass emancipation and solidarity among 'the wretched of the earth'.

These apparent contradictions explain why Weber tackled the subject in the first place: the obvious role of charismatic leaders seemed to be a striking anomaly in the early twentieth century context of emerging mass democracy.[6] The enigma inspired Weber's colleague Robert Michels to study an analogous subject, oligarchic leadership in political parties. In the same period Gaetano Mosca and Vilfredo Pareto developed the early sociological theories on elite formation.

Apparently a world that had changed drastically and become more complex than ever before needed new ways of political management, even if this implied a modernization of premodern 'personal rule' – or a re-phrasing of traditional hierarchy. This feeling is not dissimilar to the one expressed by the narrator of Saul Bellow's novel *Humboldt's Gift* (1975) that 'apparently, life lost the ability to arrange itself. It had to *be* arranged …[. T]he human enterprise, so grand and infinitely varied, had now to be managed by exceptional persons. He was an exceptional person, therefore he was an eligible candidate for power.'[7]

Not only are the contradictions that inspired Weber or Michels puzzling in themselves; the conceptual vagueness of the notion of charisma itself also entails some dangers. It explains for instance why it often risks being overstretched. As it is not easily defined, it tends to be broadened to the extent that it even ceases to be meaningful, by confusing charisma with populism, dictatorship, messianism or mere popularity. When a word can mean everything, in the end it does not mean anything at all.

A Metaphorical Problem

A more fundamental hazard resides in the metaphorical origin of the word itself. By describing charismatic *Herrschaft* with reference to the Greek word for 'gift of grace' or 'divine favour' (χάρισμα), Weber stuck to the religious terminology. No doubt religion offers an apt, interesting and versatile array of metaphors for the study of charisma. But however useful and necessary it is as a vehicle of thought, a metaphor is only a comparative device and should never take on a life of its own. Eventually the metaphor ends up as one of those *nomina nuda* Umberto Eco wrote about in the final sentence of his novel *The Name of the Rose* (1980). A metaphor should certainly not be confused with 'the thing' itself. Hence scholars ought to be cautious in transposing automatically any aspect or characteristic of religious charisma to its secular counterpart.

This is not merely a problem of vocabulary. Religious and secular charisma differ structurally, which make analogies precarious and conditional. For instance, the exceptional personal qualities of the sovereign were part of and inherently linked to the divine blessing of which they were a result. In a modern, secular context, it seems to work the other way around: charisma only comes in a second phase, as a result of perceived exceptional features of the individual which are 'discovered' first and by which the charismatic effect is engendered. Nevertheless, in premodern times public perception was important as well: religious crowning *ordines* were intended to confirm divine blessing *in conspectu populi*.[8]

Furthermore, it should be kept in mind that premodern charisma came as a whole. The ruler had received divine blessing, with all that this entails, or he had not. Today it can be observed that politicians and other leaders show some but not necessarily all of the traits associated with charisma. Hence they are only charismatic to a certain degree. Some are more charismatic than others, some stay charismatic for a longer stretch of time than others. These differences in degree should be taken into account, more specifically to avoid the terminological overstretch mentioned above. The question then arises at which point an exceptional personality turns into a charismatic one and whether the characteristics necessary for such a personality vary with time and place.

Moreover, religious charisma suggests in an individual the presence of magical or supernatural elements that convey a certain attraction to large groups of people and convince them that this individual is a fit and legitimate ruler. However, by sticking to expressions like 'blessed', 'spell', 'magic' or 'enchanting', as often happens, nothing is explained yet. It does not go beyond a tautological rephrasing of the religious metaphor. The same goes for the qualification of someone's personality as 'magnetic', which only repeats a metaphor derived from physics, without exploring the factual nature of the phenomenon as such. Thus the metaphorical analogy with religious charisma risks inducing intellectual paralysis and creating a false certainty of insight.

A Methodological Problem

A comprehensive study of charisma should necessarily avoid the essentialist approach. It can do so by developing a proper language which treats the occurrence as what it is: an historical and hence contingent phenomenon. Here a parallel can be drawn with the study of nationalism, in which the idea of nation poses similar conceptual problems to that of charisma, especially since for nationalists the nation is basically the core of a belief system.[9] Nevertheless it can be studied pragmatically as an 'imagined community'.[10] Whatever someone's personal convictions on the subject are, it should be taken seriously because it is there, and 'the problem is not how best and most elegantly to deplore it, but how to work with it so that it can be politicized'.[11] Or, one might add, so that it can be historicized.

Contingency even goes for scholars. For them, charisma is only there when they, for whichever reason, are inclined to notice it. Indeed it is perfectly possible to write a history of the Soviet Union – as has been done numerous times – without elaborating on the influence of Stalin's personality, by treating him not as a charismatic leader but simply as a dictator who ruled by repression and fear or as the 'face' of a system and an ideology.

The French historian François Furet went further. But then he had been a member of the French Communist Party. So he knew by personal experience how 'essential' Stalin's charisma had been, even on an individual emotional level. Indeed, it has been noticed that many communists experienced Stalin's death as a personal loss, indicating the presence of a definite emotional bond.[12] It is even thinkable that the weeping North Koreans shown on television at the funeral of Kim Il-sung in 1994 and of Kim Jong-il in 2011 were expressing genuine grief.

So the charismatic effect does exist. But it fits into a broader picture. On the one hand, even a leader who is considered by the outside world or by history to be a ruthless dictator or worse, can in his own time and within his own constituency mobilize a loyal and sometimes even loving following that was 'seduced' by his charisma. On the other hand, as is often the case with loyalty and love, submission to charisma is not necessarily unconditional. It must be beneficial for the followers as well. Many Germans remained loyal to Hitler even in the final years of World War II because most of them benefited considerably from public services provided for by the Third Reich, despite the hardships of war.[13] Once the authorities lost the ability to provide those services, including protection from Allied bombings, the support for the regime dwindled rapidly, in spite of the charisma of its *Führer*. Contrary to what happened in almost every country that was occupied by the Nazis, no significant resistance movement emerged in Allied-occupied Germany. As the Dutch historian E.H. Kossmann put it: 'It is fair to suppose that for the masses of the population in any period of history the form of government under which they live matters only in so far as they experience its material consequences'.[14]

A Modest Proposal

In this volume Henk te Velde points out that the phenomenon of charisma 'raises the issue of what democracy really is, and it seems to me that one of the most interesting things about the study of charismatic leadership is exactly this question'. This remark – in which the reference to democracy might even be extended to politics in general – is interesting as it illustrates the need for a specific approach which contextualizes the issue.

Charisma is indeed particularly difficult to tackle when it is studied separately, as a set of an individual's unusual skills and characteristics. Explanations then risk being self-referring or ending up in the logical fallacy of *post hoc ergo propter hoc*, especially since one usually knows in advance that a particular leader is charismatic. Sometimes it seems too easy to suppose a causal relationship between an individual's assumed charisma and his political success. When one goes out looking for charismatic traits, it is probably not difficult to qualify some as such. Whether they really played a political role and how they did so still remains to be examined. Furthermore, even if one can catalogue all traits which might have produced the charismatic effect, comparisons and generalizations remain difficult.

Therefore it might seem more productive not to focus an investigation on someone's charismatic traits as such, but on the charismatic effect, which implies an examination of the interaction between the leader and his following, as is done in most contributions in this volume. There charisma becomes relevant because then it can be seen at work. This pragmatic approach does not limit itself to a speculative description or tautological contemplation of a leader's presumed extraordinary qualities. It highlights charisma's contingency and makes its function within a specific historical or political context the focal point of the investigation. And most important of all, it takes into account a very basic prerequisite of the phenomenon: it must be experienced in order to have an effect. A hermit can be charismatic, but there is nobody out there who can be influenced by it.

One might even wonder whether charisma really exists without interaction. Charisma is irrelevant when it is not perceived and acknowledged by contemporaries, when it is not at work. And it is even possible to organize and provoke a charismatic effect, as is often done by propaganda in personality cults, perhaps endowing the leader with some kind of bogus charisma. But that does not matter very much, as long as this leader is perceived as truly charismatic.

How does charisma really work then? Critics of elite theories have pointed out that leadership is not necessarily founded on an individual's superior endowments, but is the outcome of a social advantage in acquiring power.[15] Charisma can be considered to be an analogous advantage. Hence it is possible to redefine it in the context of inequality in power distribution. Charisma then refers to a particular benefit a leader can count on in power competitions: a legitimacy that supplements, outweighs or supersedes plain quantitative, democratic approval and argument-based support. Formal approval is essentially rational, as it is based on formal rules. The additional charisma-based support is essentially emotional, affective or psychological in nature. And here again an analogy can be made with nationalism: whether one likes it or not, emotions are part of political behaviour.[16]

By shifting the emphasis in the study of charisma to the interaction with the followers, it becomes possible to deal with these emotions. Indeed, charisma only becomes relevant when it is acknowledged and 'activated' in the interaction between a leader and the led. There must be a reason why a sufficiently large group of followers consider those qualities to be exceptional and why they legitimize in their view a concentration of power in the hands of the charismatic individual. In a premodern context the relationship which engendered charismatic legitimacy was easy to explain: because of religious duty one had to accept and obey the appointed leader whose charisma was confirmed in a public crowning ritual. In a secular context, religious duty is replaced sometimes by dictatorial coercion but mostly by attraction or seduction.

A research strategy that deals with the central issue of the charismatic relationship between a leader and his followers can focus on the way the leader is perceived, as Weber already implied. In this perspective perception reflects a framing of, in a broad sense, needs and sensibilities. This is not an entirely novel idea in this context, as it has been suggested for instance that charisma tends to become more important in times of crisis and of dramatic political change in general. In such times trust in rational democratic deliberation dwindles because it is considered to lack the efficiency, dexterity, firmness or sense of urgency that are felt to be needed in times of rapid change. Or there is no need felt for deliberation because of the consensus on what is to come about: change. This feeling engenders a call for an exceptional leader to clean up the mess, to speed matters up and to voice the common goal. Whether these assumptions and perceptions are accurate or not, again this indicates that charisma is not abstract and objective, but contingent and subjective.

At its core charisma reflects the need for a firm leader and if a suitable one presents him- or herself, he or she will be recognized as such, although in this case suitability still has to be elaborated and explained. If there is no need for a charismatic leader, because no radical change is wished for, no individual will be perceived or recognized as such, however many characteristics of this kind of leadership an individual might hold. The charismatic leader is the right person at the right place at the right time.

This also means that the followers are not mere passive objects of the charismatic effect: their acknowledgement of someone as charismatic implies some kind of approval, an alternative legitimacy. Maybe this conclusion might abate the democratic uneasiness of some scholars of the phenomenon. Even the deification of Mao Zedong after his death, as described by Arif Dirlik, illustrates the agency of the followers, as it shows to what extent followers can act autonomously by remodelling a charismatic leader, so that he can remain the 'embodiment', even posthumous, of their needs, as the symbol into which they can project their hopes and aspirations or even their melancholy, regrets and frustrations.

What is then a suitable charismatic leader? Many contributors to this volume point out that the ones they studied were excellent orators (Pasionaria, Malatesta, Domela Nieuwenhuis, D.F. Malan and others) and that they owed of lot of their charismatic attraction to this particular and unevenly distributed skill. But to describe charismatic leaders as men (or women) of the spoken word (as Te Velde puts it, in his contribution to this volume) is probably too narrow an interpretation, as it only refers to an 'accidental' talent of an individual. It does not explain why it is an advantage.

What matters here is not oratorical talent as such – apparently Mao was not even a gifted speaker in the conventional sense. The issue at hand is communication, the ability to create a connection with a following. This bond establishes the interaction through which symbolic meaning can be attributed and shared values articulated. Through this connection, e.g. by speaking the language of their followers, Dolores Ibárruri, Domela Nieuwenhuis, Gandhi or Mao could be legitimized as alternative leaders. By using what might be called a shared political vernacular, they could establish a symbiotic relation with their followers. It enabled them to be perceived as being close to the common people, as rejecting traditional hierarchy and, by voicing the needs of their followers, as speaking the truth. Some of them emphasized their closeness to their following by convincing it that they were genuine and virtuous, prepared to make sacrifices for the common cause and not after personal material gains.

Here an interesting paradox must be noted. As most charismatic leaders embody and advocate radical or even revolutionary change, they represent a 'counterculture' within the existing political context. Nevertheless, political continuity remains important as well. Such leaders are more easily accepted or acknowledged if they show formal traits of traditional leadership: Mao as the new emperor, Stalin as the new czar, etc. It makes it easy to recognize them as leaders. This point is illustrated very well by D.F. Malan. The political success of this 'unsmiling man' might seem puzzling, but there was an excellent reason why his Afrikaner following and voters considered him to be a fit leader. He was very clearly the embodiment of the traditional authority figure in the community he wanted to represent and lead: the man of the pulpit, the *dominee*. And such a leader was not expected to be a smiling man at all, on the contrary. Malan did not even have to imitate the language, the skills or the ways of that traditional leader, as he himself was a minister in the Dutch Reformed Church. He only had to extend or to export his undisputed religious authority to the political arena.

This persistence of political tradition – which, if one wishes to do so, might also be defined as the inertia in the framing of political thinking – sheds an interesting light on Henk te Velde's remark about the relationship between charisma and democracy. And again one might go further: it illustrates how charisma offers an outstanding focus for the study of mass political behaviour, as charisma reveals how, why and in which conditions large groups can be mobilized and how political power is accumulated and legitimized.[17]

Notes

1. R.C. Van Caenegem.1990. *Legal History: A European Perspective*, London: Hambledon, 189.
2. The dichotomous concept of rulership, distinguishing between the office and the person of the sovereign, is explored in: E.H. Kantorowicz. 1957. *The King's Two Bodies: A Study in Mediaeval Political Theology*, Princeton: Princeton University Press. The 'miraculous' healing powers of medieval kings are studied in: M. Bloch. 1924. *Les rois thaumaturges: étude sur le caractère surnaturel attribué à la puissance royale particulièrement en France et en Angleterre*, Strasbourg: Publications de la Faculté des lettres de l'Université de Strasbourg.
3. M. Weber. 1922. *Wirtschaft und Gesellschaft. Grundriss der verstehende Soziologie*, Tübingen: J.C.B. Mohr.
4. T. Poguntke and P. Webb (eds). 2005. *The Presidentialization of Politics: A Comparative Study of Modern Democracies*, Oxford: Oxford University Press.
5. F. Furet. 1995. *Le passé d'une illusion. Essai sur l'idée communiste au XXe siècle*, Paris: Robert Laffont/Callman-Lévy, 505. Some authors gave it a try by pointing to Stalin's systematic use of terror (S. Courtois et al. 1997. *Le livre noir du communisme. Crimes, terreur, répression*, Paris: Robert Laffont, 277), but of course this only indicates a method by which Stalin ruled, without explaining why he was able to do so to the extent he did.
6. The context is more complex as far as Weber was concerned: he saw charismatic leadership as a solution for the instability of the German government. S. Eliaeson. 2000. 'Constitutional Caesarism: Weber's Politics in Their German Context', in S. Turner (ed.), *The Cambridge Companion to Weber*, Cambridge: Cambridge University Press, 134–36.
7. S. Bellow. 1975. *Humboldt's Gift*, New York: Viking Press, 29.
8. R.C. Van Caenegem. 1978. *Over koningen en bureaucraten. Oorsprong en ontwikkeling van de hedendaagse staatsinstellingen*, Amsterdam and Brussels: Elsevier, 167–68.
9. E.J. Hobsbawm. 1992. *Nations and Nationalism since 1780: Programme, Myth, Reality*, 2nd ed., Cambridge: Cambridge University Press, 5–13.
10. B. Anderson. 1991. *Imagined Communities: Reflections on the Origin and Spread of Nationalism*, 2nd ed., London: Verso.
11. B. Crick. 2000. *In Defence of Politics*, 5th ed., London: Continuum, 77.
12. E.G.M. Pigenet. 1992. *Au coeur de L'activisme communiste des années de Guerre Froide: la manifestation Ridgway*, Paris: L'Harmattan, 157.
13. G. Aly. 2005. *Hitlers Volksstaat. Raub, Rassenkrieg und nationaler Sozialismus*, Frankfurt: Fisher.
14. E.H. Kossmann. 1976. 'The Singularity of Absolutism', in R. Hatton (ed.), *Louis XIV and Absolutism*, London: Macmillan, 9.
15. J.V. Femia. 2001. *Against the Masses: Varieties of Anti-democratic Thought since the French Revolution*, Oxford: Oxford University Press, 67–109.
16. R.C. Luskin. 2002. 'Political Psychology, Political Behavior, and Politics: Questions of Aggregation, Causal Distance, and Taste', in J.H. Kuklinski (ed.), *Thinking about Political Psychology*, Cambridge: Cambridge University Press, 243.
17. I would like to thank Dr Geert Van den Bossche for her comments on an earlier version of this chapter.

CHAPTER 9

INCENDIARY PERSONALITIES

Uncommon Comments on Charisma in Social Movements

Thomas Welskopp

For historians and social scientists, charisma is a difficult business. As the contributions to this volume have amply demonstrated, the concept – substantially unchanged since Max Weber imported the religious term into political sociology – remains elusive and is at the same time nevertheless acknowledged as indispensable for the historical analysis of personalized leadership.[1] Its elusiveness mirrors not only a conceptual problem, as Marc Reynebeau argues in his chapter, but more fundamentally an empirical one. It is by definition almost impossible for the historian to observe charismatic interaction *in actu*, that is, as an ongoing practice generating – and responding to – charismatic effects. Charismatic authority does not follow predictable rules; it endows a bond between the charismatic figure and his followers which is purely emotional. Although nearly everybody has experienced the intense sentiment commonly called 'love', nobody would be able to communicate exhaustively this intensity by giving reasons or constructing phenomenological taxonomies. This lies at the very heart of the observation, mentioned by virtually all of the contributors to this volume, that we find charismatic capabilities and effects frequently described in religious and/or metaphorical terms. It seems impossible even for contemporaries to communicate the working of deep emotional ties such as these to those outside of the charismatic relation who do not share the communal sentiment. The most appropriate approach to this problem, therefore, might be a revisiting of the concept of 'thick description' as laid out by Clifford Geertz and exemplified in his famous analysis of Balinese cockfights. The intensity with which the participants (with the exception, probably, of the birds) are drawn into this form of 'deep play' resembles many of the metaphorical accounts that we have on charismatic relations.[2]

Saying this should make clear that my point of departure in coming to terms with the inflationary use of the term would be to treat 'charisma' as a phenomenon first of all rooted in the micro-level of social interaction. Charisma works as an emotional bond among an inside constituency of social actors. Charisma, therefore, has to be enacted, and this, in turn, implies copresence, at least on the level of a basic definition, consideration of the effects of the audiovisual media notwithstanding. This means insisting on the personal nature of charisma in the first place and questioning the distinction Juan Avilés has suggested between 'personal' and 'institutional' charisma. I think that the working of charisma in larger institutional settings has to be explained as a phenomenon in itself rather than treated as a given. It is striking that much of the terminological uneasiness encountered in these chapters stems from the fact that most contributors have fashioned their case studies as analyses on the macro-level of national political organizations such as parties or political regimes. This might be misleading, however, since charismatic authority in face-to-face relations cannot readily be equated with what in Mao Zedong's case might arguably be called charismatic rule. Arif Dirlik's case study shows that charismatic narratives can be instrumental in solving problems of legitimization in autocratic regimes with personalized leadership. This implies that the charismatic bond between leader and people may be the mere fictional product of leadership circles or party or state organizations, disseminated by means of controlled mass media. Charisma, then, is reduced to a meaningless category used to discipline the public discourse, a means of enforcing subordination, or it is – I believe frequently – projected backwards into some charismatic episode with only historical meaning for the present.[3]

I do not doubt the validity of Arif Dirlik's presentation of Mao Zedong as a charismatic leader of changing sorts over the course of fifty years – a time span normally much too long to sustain 'ordinary' charismatic rule. This is true even if Mao's charisma was officially exploited only after 1950. The appropriation of the Mao cult during the Cultural Revolution by the younger generation as a weapon against the established party bureaucracy in particular points in that direction. This seems to have been a case of charismatic rule built around authentic personal charismatic authority. Yet two questions remain – and that they arise in the first place might demonstrate the usefulness of the narrow definition of charisma: What accounted for the charismatic authority of Mao, whom insiders of his charismatic following describe as an ordinary personality without exceptional physical traits and lacking oratory brilliance? And how was this charismatic authority magnified and transformed into charismatic rule? It is a long way from the description of charismatic authority to giving an adequate account of these magnifying mechanisms which must be considered as institutional effects rather than personal capabilities. Richard Nixon and Henry Kissinger seemed impressed by Mao just because of the discrepancy between the power radiating from Mao's surroundings and his unassuming personal appearance – a clear indication that the institutional mechanisms of charismatic rule worked, at least to the extent that they mesmerized outsiders from foreign nations and remote cultures.

What appears as a contradiction in contemporary characterizations of Mao's personality, therefore, might rather point toward the distinction between charismatic authority and charismatic rule (and its derivatives) as introduced above. Arif Dirlik does not employ any historical argument when discussing Mao's charismatic qualities. I would assume that his personal myth was rooted in the revolutionary period and the experience of the 'Long March'. The dust-covered, haggard-looking Mao riding on a donkey, as depicted on grainy photographs from the 1930s and early 1940s, may have become the visual cornerstone of his stylization as a man with great willingness to make sacrifices on behalf of the people and with unrelenting determination. Mao's military leadership and his tactical flexibility, by which he fended off defeat against numerically superior Guomindang forces, may have earned him a heroic nimbus among his fellow officers and troops – and therefore have endowed him with charismatic authority. Rumours of the enigmatic struggle of the People's Liberation Army may have spread this reputation throughout the countryside, where they helped recruit his followers from among the vast rural population. If this is correct – and I can only hypothesize from commonsensical knowledge – this would be a classic case of charismatic authority acquired by personal example, as is often the case in military environments.

This charismatic episode became history with the establishment of the communist regime in Beijing. Yet its symbolic content would later on inform the mechanisms by which the regime – and later the young rebels of the Cultural Revolution – would transform and magnify past performance into timeless personal qualities as the legitimating basis of charismatic rule. Here it is telling that contemporary observers can agree that Mao radiated determination, his rustic down-to-earthness, and a quantum of peasant's cunning. His plain uniform is symbol enough of the medial projection that the leader Mao, a man of the ordinary people, later became in his changing regimes of charismatic rule.

I will return to the fabrication of charismatic rule later. The narrow definition of charisma as a phenomenon of face-to-face interaction redirects the focus onto the question of what outstanding personal qualities or capabilities constitute charismatic authority. Weber's reference to the community of followers who would exclusively decide what they would recognize as charismatic or not is, as Marc Reynebeau correctly argues, tautological, but only if considered on this most abstract level. If read as an appeal to take the context seriously, it shows once again the usefulness of the narrow concept applied here. Charisma is an emotional bond among copresent actors and, therefore, differs from context to context in idiosyncratic ways. Consequently, what counts as charismatic in one case – Charles de Gaulle's towering frame – may well appear as counterintuitive in another – Napoleon Bonaparte's shortness. Yet I would argue that the ascription of charismatic qualities does not follow random patterns. We can obviously distinguish between charismatic and decidedly uncharismatic figures in personal encounters or media representations. We can probably agree on the impression that the uncharismatic people by far outnumber the charismatic. We can probably also identify some uncontroversial attributes of uncharismatic characters: dull, boring, servile, introverted, shy, risk-averse, phlegmatic, uninspiring, and so on.

It is not too difficult, at this point, to acknowledge that charismatic personalities usually share one or more of the antinomies of these adjectives. The metaphorical language applied to describe charismatic characters frequently rings with terms like 'radiating', 'aureatic' and 'magnetizing'.[4] Accounts of the personal impressions of prominent speakers in early German social democracy centre on a mysterious intensity these orators would emanate and condense to a suspense-packed, spellbinding atmosphere that culminated either in tense silence or in loud outbursts of cheers.[5] Contemporary observers often refer to the fact that a person described as charismatic had a firm gaze, an imposing figure, determined gestures and expressions, a dynamic bodily appearance, and, in virtually all cases, an impressive voice which might be thundering but also 'splendid, metallic, coarse, harmonious', as in the case of Juan Avilés' Pasionaria. Since charisma is a phenomenon of face-to-face communication, the role of the voice must not be underestimated. Speakers may be characterized as having an insistent, hoarse, hurried, passionate or – on the contrary – a calm, well-set, reflective way of talking; in any case there will be mention of its stirring, carrying and mobilizing effects.[6]

Charismatic personalities often leave the impression that they operate in another key, more highly tuned, excessively focused, to the utmost degree dedicated to the collective moment. Recent medical research attributes these features to symptoms that people with attention deficit disorder display. While they have problems sustaining a certain degree of concentration over a prolonged stretch of time, they are able to mobilize unusual degrees of energy at specific moments which observers might then experience as charismatic. Patients suffering from this disorder appear audacious to the point of recklessness when involved in collective situations where leadership is needed. They are usually emotionally insecure and, therefore, go out of their way to win a group's approval – and personal recognition. Interestingly enough, attention deficit disorder is diagnosed more frequently in times of crisis or in societies with a high proportion of recent immigrants – as if traits that are considered pathological under 'normal' circumstances become functional in critical contexts or as if it needed this quantum of extra energy which such personalities are able to mobilize to make the extreme and momentous decision to leave home and migrate.

I am conscious of the very hypothetical nature of my considerations, but the convergence of accounts of charismatic appearances around terms like 'intensive', 'radiating', 'mesmerizing', or 'spellbinding' is startling. Descriptions of German social democrats in the 1860s and early 1870s frequently characterize prominent figures as 'red-haired' and 'dark-eyed' even if police protocols register them as brunette and of pale complexion. By no means rare are contemporary reminiscences of these people as 'male beauties', even if we know from photographs of this time that beauty in some of these cases lay very much in the eye of the beholder. Yet my point here is that charismatic authority has a strong aesthetic component. Oratorical charisma seems, on the one hand, the most common form of charisma as such, especially in contexts where public speeches are central for community building or for collective mobilizing. Several contributors to this volume mention this fact, wondering how the alleged rationality of parliamentary reasoning might relate to the presumed emotional and rousing – and therefore irrational and manipulative – nature of charismatic speaking. Yet the content, modus and effect of rhetoric and eloquence may vary from context to context. The early social democrats would consider their oratorical culture as fully rational, more rational indeed than what was going on at the bourgeois-dominated Reichstag in Berlin. August Bebel, a young wood-turner at that time, played eloquently on the note of a 'pathos of rationality', and it was exactly this habitual gesture of respectability which caught his audiences.

We have to distinguish, therefore, between the charismatic effect of a speech and its content or truthfulness. All depend on the particular context, but it is by no means the case that all charismatic rhetoric is irrational or manipulative. It is rather the aesthetic component that makes charismatic oratory stand out among the bulk of dull and boring speeches. Robert Michels put it like this:

> The prestige acquired by the orator in the minds of the crowd is almost unlimited. What the masses appreciate above all are oratorical gifts as such, beauty

and strength of voice, suppleness of mind, badinage; whilst the content of the speech is of quite secondary importance. A spouter who, as if bitten by a tarantula, rushes hither and thither to speak to the people, is apt to be regarded as a zealous and active comrade, whereas one who, speaking little but working much, does valuable service for the party, is regarded with disdain, and considered but an incomplete socialist.[7]

It is true, however, that charisma is often tied to a specifically oratorical talent and that aspiring social movements – such as the labour movement in Europe in the nineteenth century – have provided those talents with contexts in which they could flourish and rise to leadership positions. In some of the contributions to the present volume a certain uneasiness resonates when dealing with charisma in connection with the labour movement. This may be due to some normative reservation against the depiction of the labour movement as just another social movement, including all the dynamics, improvised trials-and-error, and the organizational skinnings such movements regularly undergo. Charisma is, consequently, picked up rather gingerly, as something marginal to or exogenous of a seemingly well organized, disciplined, sober and rational party machine. Yet this self-image has proven a myth almost everywhere. And Marxist theory is – despite its aspirations to be a valid theory of society – an ideological construct, and as such it indeed is a matter of internal discourse within theatres of rhetorical exchange, the stages of charismatic eloquence.

Therefore, charisma and democracy only clash on a categorical level if the phenomenon of charisma is reduced to singular outstanding figures like Mao Zedong or the frequently cited Ferdinand Lassalle. The narrow definition of charisma, however, allows us to acknowledge that the phenomenon is usually far more widespread in social movements and, yes, that social movements are more often than not to a high degree coalitions of charismatic communities. Early social democracy in Germany again serves as an exemplary case in point. The oratorical gifts which served as the most highly esteemed 'symbolic capital' for a rise within the movement were quite widely distributed; even latter-day celebrities like August Bebel had risen from the anonymous rank and file thanks to their noteworthy eloquence and their courage and ability to stand up and speak in public. The German landscape of the 1860s and early 1870s was dotted with local workers' associations which established a culture of club life and mass meetings where dozens of rhetorical hopefuls from the ranks of journeymen, small master artisans and petty urban tradesmen – along with bourgeois intellectuals like Lassalle or outcasts of even noble descent – trained, thrived and yearned for public recognition as manly citizens claiming full respectability. Charismatic orators in early social democracy not only fought for the ideological goal of radical democracy – their charismatic performances should be addressed as a 'democratic' phenomenon in themselves. Take the civil rights movement in the United States of the 1950s and 1960s as a further case in point, where dozens of black pastors and reverends emerged as potent community leaders transgressing the boundaries between contemplative religiosity and political mobilization. As it happened, one of the local heroes who thus made a name for himself was a man by the name of Martin Luther King. Yet he was by no means a lonesome, singular shooting star – an isolated figure.

In this context, it is advisable to jettison the idea that the relation between a charismatic personality and his followers must by definition always be unilateral, like the one between an emitter and its passive recipients. If this position is taken, then charismatic authority does indeed tend to appear exclusively as charismatic rule in its more despotic and manipulative forms. Yet this is by no means a necessity that rests in the very nature of charismatic authority. Charismatic characters and their community of followers are bound up in a symbiosis, a relation of mutual dependency. As the followers can only react to a performance which strikes them as emotionally truly deep ('authentic') and incendiary, charismatic personalities, in turn, vitally depend on positive emotional feedback to their acts and words. Positive recognition fuels the charismatic personalities' performance; for them, it is as inebriating as a habit-forming drug. Charismatic characters long for their audiences' and followings' approval and acclaim. Only when recognized as such are they able to bring to bear their extraordinary talents and capabilities; they then even dare to embark on endeavours – for instance, exemplary military bravery – which they would never have dreamt of outside a charismatic context. Recent biographies have stressed in this respect that, whereas it is not too difficult to decode the charismatic effects of Adolf Hitler's public appearances, it seems virtually impossible to penetrate his personality as an individual. He seems to have been a bland, shallow character, functioning as a charismatic leader only when he felt like the projection site of his followers' hopes and hatred.

The social democratic example suggests, furthermore, that the approval of charismatic authority does not have to be purely irrational, uncritical or infatuated. The mass gatherings of that time more often attracted critical audiences who followed the speech duels like literary critics, many of the listeners would-be oratorical stars in themselves. Numerous protocols of mass meetings read like battle reports – or sportscasts of thrilling football matches, with the attendees highly entertained, like home supporters, intensively drawn into the rhetorical barrage and critically appreciative, like the true fan who is always an expert, and a freak, as well. There was nothing religious about these events. Lassalle's few speeches were popular, this is true, but listeners like the aspiring August Bebel could not help but remark dryly that Lassalle did not speak freely and that he tended to lisp.[8] Academics of long standing and high reputation are often said to be charismatic characters; their disciples – themselves aspiring scholars – will direct their admiration (and imitation) more toward the academic oeuvre and the ability to fascinate by lecturing than toward the individual character, as a loving person would do. There are exceptions to this, of course; read, for instance, the novels by David Lodge. Finally, charisma is commonly distributed broadly throughout rising social movements. This may reflect the fact that charismatic effects derive their impact from inspiring examples of leadership rather than from passive idolization. To use Max Weber's words if not his thinking in this respect: charisma is a way to mobilise solidarity in face of conflict.

This is a crucial point, since in their critical initial stages social movements are all about resource mobilization. Older social movement research understood this term as a rational project often undertaken by specialized organizations within the movement. In order to confront even older views, which saw in social movements mainly irrational mass psychology at work, resource mobilization theorists cast their explanatory mechanisms in the vocabulary of rational choice.[9] Yet there was no doubt that, however planned and rationalistic the respective schemes and techniques were, they aimed at recruiting new followers and at binding them to the movement by creating emotional ties. Niklas Luhmann aptly remarked that the overarching, almost exclusive function of all institutions involved in social movements is to mobilize fellow campaigners and to keep them on board.[10] The goal of all social movements must be to mobilize a mass following which can rightfully claim to represent a considerable part of the people – if not the people as a whole. To achieve this goal, Luhmann says, institutions in social movements cannot rely on the mechanisms formal organizations employ to reproduce themselves: formal membership, contractual obligations, disciplinary rules, and pay. Social movements are forced to endow emotional bonds instead. Identification thus is stronger in social movements than in formal organizations because it is intrinsically rooted in emotional commitment. In turn, it is less stable and more difficult to sustain over a prolonged time.

It is not difficult to see at this point where charisma fits in. Actually, it is charisma which accounts for most of the emotional bonds tying young social movements together. And this is true regardless of whether a social movement is stirred up by a group of individuals, by informal leaders of pre-movement communities or milieus, or by formal organizations – as we shall see. In contrast to formal organizations, authority in social movements cannot rely on hierarchy and bureaucracies. It is, therefore, to an overwhelming degree *charismatic* authority. The charismatic relation between leaders and followers in social movements is not of the emitter and passive audience type mentioned above. Social movements have to mobilize their constituency, to make sympathizers into fellow campaigners and into fellow combatants, especially if this means to instil into them the willingness to face grave dangers on behalf of a blurry goal in some distant future. In these contexts, therefore, charismatic authority usually bears an 'empowering' character. To promote risky commitment, the emotional ties must be consuming and directly rewarding for the would-be participants. Charismatic personalities in such a context do not only have to arouse a public to enthusiastic support by giving incendiary speeches. They also have to lead the way by outstanding, exemplary leadership, by setting examples as inspiring role models in order to 'empower' would-be followers to act as a collective force.

Within early German social democracy August Bebel and others of his age (almost all activists were in their twenties in the late 1860) personified this type of charismatic leader to a much larger extent than the self-styled 'lonesome genius', Ferdinand Lassalle, who eschewed frequent mass meetings and communication beyond memorized speeches and who did not live long enough to head a true mass movement that was later to become German social democracy. This means that charisma in social movements is likely to be a 'bottom-up' phenomenon. Charismatic leaders rise by surging ahead of the rest of their communities and familiar social milieus. They gain leadership status as 'the best of our men', 'the best of us'. Their steadfastness, their courageous and audacious deeds, their oratorical energy win recognition among their companions, many of whom yearn to be just like their leaders. These mechanisms are especially visible in German social democracy, because, although members and leaders came from the same artisanal-petty commercial backgrounds, leaders rose not so much as personifications of their ancestral milieu but by means of stardom in the newly established institutional milieu of workers' clubs and associational gatherings which leaders and followers all entered as *homines novi*.

The contributions to this volume, in contrast, present us with a range of charismatic personalities whose charismatic authority was based on either oratorical eloquence or the personification of 'milieu icons' or both. They did not create a new sphere with an innovative charismatic repertoire as the social democrats did – with the notable exception of Mahatma Gandhi, who succeeded, as Dilip Simeon has shown in his chapter, in creating a new spectrum of ideas and practices which transformed virtuous behaviour formerly despised as effeminate into manifestations of a new – and very virile – type of manliness. In some respects, Gandhi's example comes closest to the charismatic world of early German social democracy. The chapter on D.F. Malan makes a paradigmatic case for those social movements which mobilize a probably age-old community structure with familiar forms of communication by means of charismatic authority. Here, personalities best described as milieu brokers use their charismatic gifts – like the 'deep vibrant voice' of D.F. Malan – to spark rather contemplative communities into political action. The charismatic effect at work here is the 'empowerment' mentioned above; the form of resource mobilization conforms to what Doug McAdam, Sidney Tarrow and Charles Tilly have defined as 'social appropriation' – the utilization of older, pre-existing patterns of communal sociability, life-world and organizations as the basis for innovative forms of mobilization.[11] The U.S. civil rights movement which turned the rather introspective black communities of Southern evangelical churches into a political force, with pastors becoming political leaders and black students, often trained in universities of the North, the 'front officers' of nonviolent resistance, can serve as a formidable example of 'social appropriation'.

This case of 'social appropriation' should sensitize us to the problem of religion as mentioned in a number of the chapters in this book. There is again an undercurrent of uneasiness when it comes to charisma, especially since charismatic personalities are frequently characterized in religious terms and charismatic effects appear in an almost revivalist wording.[12] Some writers link this language to ideas of 'political religion', which again highlights – rather unconvincingly, from my point of view – the irrational, manipulative sides of politics. If charisma is only an instrument for dispersing 'political religion', it appears as a rather dubious concept when it comes to analysing social movements in general, and the labour movement in particular. Jan Willem Stutje's chapter on Ferdinand Domela Nieuwenhuis – which also alerts us to the distinction between charismatic authority and charismatic rule, a transformation that Nieuwenhuis failed to initiate or relinquish – shows that social movements often profit from expert personnel trained for generating charismatic effects in completely different contexts. In the same way that the black reverends rose to political leadership in the civil rights movement as seasoned orators with voices steeled on the pulpit and in command of the metaphorically rich, rhythmic and redundant rhetoric the black evangelical churches are especially known for, Domela Nieuwenhuis, a former Lutheran vicar, obviously capitalized on his profession and probably catered to a following that longed for more emotional commitment than the sober Lutheran rituals in their community church would provide. Perhaps his rhetoric reached just the level of incendiary intensity that was necessary to draw his listeners onto political terrain and into the Social Democratic Workers Party.

If charismatic personalities are called 'redeemers' (Domela) or 'martyrs' (Pasionaria) or if they see themselves on a (holy) 'mission' like D.F. Malan, this does not necessarily mean that religion in a true, transcendental sense of the word is involved. Charismatic leaders are not by definition 'saints' of 'political religions'. The first explanation of the frequent references to religion in descriptions of charisma may just be of a linguistic nature, since, as we have seen in the introduction to this chapter, there is no analytical access to the actual working of specific charismatic effects, so that observers, in their quest to communicate the phenomenon, are almost thrown back onto a metaphorical vocabulary designed to characterize the extraordinary – the 'supernatural'. There are probably no alternative words powerful enough to hint at the compelling nature of charisma for those inside the community.

In a second attempt to explain the frequent emergence of religious language in the context of charisma I have linked this phenomenon to specific forms of 'social appropriation'. Here, religious gatherings, religious practices and especially a ritualistic rhetoric serve as resources of social movements. Regardless of whether they lose their strict religious appearance, function and content in the process, these features provide the movement's targeted constituency with accustomed patterns of socializing and communication, with customary meeting places and familiar rituals, and the charismatic leaders can capitalize on a well established social infrastructure and rhetorical culture to which the audiences are, furthermore, habitually sensitized. Even if the religious community life continues side by side with the movement, the translation of social forms into the political realm transforms these into innovative practices of contentious politics, and this is a completely different matter from a 'political religion'.[13]

American politics are, as is well known, impregnated by religious if not outright evangelical rhetoric. As James Morone has cunningly observed, social movements in the United States – from Left to Right – always contain a revivalist appeal within themselves.[14] This is true for social movements with a direct link to a church basis – as we will see below. Yet it is also true for rationalist or hedonist movements like those of the students of 1968 or the hippies (whose backlash into esoteric religions was, in this way, telling) which openly opposed the customary forms of religion as part of the 'establishment' and fought against church influence. Even Barack Obama's recourse to 'town hall meetings' where he cultivates his stirring rhetoric in orchestrated face-to-face situations resonates with echoes of a religious past without calling for a 'political religion'. Yet his revisiting of this strategy of mobilization again points to the problems one faces when trying to transform charismatic authority into charismatic rule. A charismatic candidate without doubt, Obama has certainly failed to be a charismatic president throughout his first term, and he still has to prove that he can be a charismatic candidate again in the run-up to the next general elections.

There have been instances in American history, however, when a decidedly and explicitly religious charisma did become the fuel of social movements of some sort. Emile Durkheim has termed the highly emotional style of evangelical church services 'effervescent', an uncontrollable 'bubbling up' of emotions on the part of the churchgoers resulting in the overwhelming climax of the convened individuals' 'rebirth'.[15] The climactic moment of 'rebirth' is experienced as an immediate connection with the touch of God, a sign of God's grace for the individual. It is, at the same time, the manifestation of social integration into the community, whose members will enthusiastically approve of the words and gestures of the 'reborn', which they take as signs of the expected catharsis and thereby bestow social recognition upon the respective person, the emotional gratification which brought the individual here in the first place. If the individual shows the signs of a successful 'rebirth', the whole community feels rewarded with God's grace and takes off into a stage of collective euphoria. 'Effervescence' appears as a form of collective, self-inflicted charisma. Although the alleged spontaneity of the event is an integral part of its claim to divine intervention, 'effervescent' meetings are carefully staged procedures. Everybody attending nurtures fixed expectations as to how the divine spark shall strike the would-be 'reborn' person and how he or she has to behave to appear plausibly struck. 'Effervescent' charisma thus works infallibly, like a self-fulfilling prophecy.

An imposing minister with just the right thundering eloquence helps to catalyse the process, however, so that the charismatic effect, albeit experienced as such, is by no means totally self-inflicted. In truth, 'effervescence' is to a considerable extent the product of conventional charismatic authority, yet within a special context which shapes the expectations of the community members and endows a bond between them which under certain circumstances inspires a stunning willingness to make sacrifices. Evangelical church life of this form can be completely detached from the world and, therefore, be apolitical. Yet in times of crisis it bears a volatile political potential.

This was the case when the Anti-Saloon League in the United States started its crusade for a national ban on alcohol in the 1890s, and the 'second' Ku Klux Klan emerged as both an ally and a rival early in the 1920s. The Anti-Saloon League won over local church communities to hold services against alcohol and saloons and to invite the league's speakers. Professional speakers would then use their charismatic authority to create 'effervescent' moments of a superior quality, adding an experience of 'empowerment' for the community members. This was the decisive step from contemplative church life into the arena of politics. The 'empowerment' the league's speakers provided was limited to the act of pledging donations by the community members. Yet still, for them it was a militant act in the fight against 'Demon Rum' and everything that he stood for.

The enormous amounts of money the league raised by means of this technique served two purposes. First, money would be reinvested in the communities and in the development of ever more attractive event programmes. Many poorer churches, especially in the South, gained a chapel and a professional minister only with league money. League money sponsored professional speakers who toured the countryside and provided the attendees of the swelling mass meetings with 'effervescent' experiences of ever increasing intensity. Since donations kept pace with this rise, the communities actually paid for their memorable events by themselves – a commercial charisma machine with charismatic orators and ministers as functionaries who calculably evoked 'effervescent' moments in audiences longing for this experience.

Second, the bulk of the money went into buying politicians in order to bring them to vote for the Anti-Saloon League's single issue: prohibition. The league proved to be the most successful and powerful lobby organization in the United States of the early twentieth century. It pushed through National Prohibition in 1917 (in effect from 1920) and controlled both parties in both houses of congress for most of the 1920s. I will not detail this side of the organization's operations. Suffice it to say here that its political clout and its money-raising activities at the basis of the church communities were almost unrelated. The Anti-Saloon League (and to a large degree the 'second' Ku Klux Klan as well) were social movements only insofar as resource mobilization by means of fabricating charisma on a commercial basis was involved. The league's political action, in contrast, was a matter of elitist, cynical string-pullers in Washington, D.C., who were totally detached from their churchy following.[16]

It is debatable both whether one can call commercially orchestrated social movements 'social movements' at all and whether the commercial evocation of charisma in 'effervescent' environments makes the Anti-Saloon League or the 'second' Ku Klux Klan 'charismatic organizations'. Yet the broader question of the relationships between charisma and organizations (or more specifically, bureaucracies) remains open. Within social movements organizations can be especially designed and employed to magnify and disseminate charismatic authority. This has become a major task for campaign staff dealing with the mass media or systematically utilizing audiovisual media for this purpose. Charisma does not work through the written word. It must remain a focus of further research, therefore, when and to what extent the diffusion of audiovisual media has contributed to the emergence of new charismatic styles and to the vast improvement in the reach of charismatic rule.

In early German social democracy the party organization usually did not fulfil the above-mentioned function. It must rather be seen as a sociocultural infrastructure, a newly established discursive culture in which charismatic up-and-coming talents could flourish. Of course, Ferdinand Lassalle designed the Allgemeine Deutsche Arbeiterverein (General Association of German Workers) as an organization for charismatic rule, but he failed, and the organization underwent many changes after his demise. Club life and mass meetings rather followed the pattern of mainstream social democracy which I have introduced as 'democratic charisma'. Although the social democrats depended on widespread charismatic authority (a resource which the social democrats of today dearly lack), they never designed their organizational hierarchy to fit a system of charismatic rule.

Again it depends on the context, then, whether organizations oriented towards charisma as a political tool promote charismatic rule or only veil a despotic regime with a made-up charismatic narrative. In the first case, we would have to look for charismatic authority at the centre of all organizational activity, which should in such cases focus on magnifying and disseminating this authority, transforming it into an institutional effect where copresence is no longer of first priority. This can actually only happen where audiovisual media are open to the public at large. In the second case, we should scrutinize the charismatic narratives and find out whether they develop 'traction' or not. We should sensitize ourselves to narratives that place the charismatic capabilities or performances in a distant past which has long been detached from the alleged bearer of charismatic authority. In these cases, history rather than the vaunted personality is the true locus of charisma.

I want to close with a paradox. Whereas the inflationary use of the concept of charisma often indeed blurs the phenomenon – in Hans-Ulrich Wehler's monumental *Gesellschaftsgeschichte*, for instance, charisma is a mere residual of structural explanation – it may be far more widespread as a phenomenon than widely perceived. I think that charisma lies at the very heart of social movements or, as McAdam, Tarrow and Tilly would have it: 'contentious politics'.[17] Charisma is probably an essential ingredient in all politics. It is not reserved for singular outstanding personalities but may be distributed quite 'democratically'. The widespread identification of charismatic authority with charismatic rule and of charismatic rule with one-person-leadership systems is responsible for the confusion of charismatic rule and outright despotism. These may fuse, depending on the context, but, as Mao Zedong's case has demonstrated, this is no necessity, and the constellations can change over time.

Charisma, furthermore, has an 'empowering' quality and cannot be reduced, therefore, to the relation between an entertainer and a passive – if appreciative – audience. This means that we can expect to encounter charismatic phenomena primarily in the context of social movements and other forms of 'contentious politics' whose priority it is to mobilize a mass constituency of fellow combatants. We do not have much more than the metaphorical or religiously worded accounts to identify charismatic authority and charismatic effects at work. Yet even the use of audiovisual media as sources – which is only possible since the early twentieth century – will be of limited help. We as historians remain outsiders. The context matters most. A Hitler speech on film watched today leaves us shrugging with regard to its charismatic effects (Charlie Chaplin's parody of 1940 points to the rather comical aspects of his rhetorical style but does not grasp the actual effects on Germans). Leni Riefenstahl's *Triumph of the Will* bores us with endless takes of marching bodies and columns so that the actual charismatic effect – the juxtaposition of the lonesome 'Führer' and the German people as a belligerent, disciplined collective on a vast scale – threatens to get lost even as we are watching. We should, therefore, take the metaphorical descriptions seriously. At least they can tell us that something is going on here which might resemble charisma. We should then explore the context. And finally we should try to see – for ourselves – what the contemporaries could only express in a cumbersome way, by stacking layer after layer of close description on one another, until a picture of charisma – not abstract, but charisma in a specific time and place and context – emerges.

Notes

1. J. Potts. 2009. *A History of Charisma*, Basingstoke and New York: Palgrave Macmillan, provides the most recent conceptual history of the term, but remains at a loss when it comes to dealing with the sociological phenomenon itself.
2. C. Geertz. 1995. '"Deep Play": Bemerkungen zum balinesischen Hahnenkampf', in idem (ed.), *Dichte Beschreibung. Beiträge zum Verstehen kultureller Systeme*, 4th ed., Frankfurt: Suhrkamp, 202–60.
3. North Korea would be an interesting test case. Another illustrative case is the late German Democratic Republic (GDR), with a regime that orchestrated a modest personal cult with rather uncharismatic figures. Ironically, this fiction of charismatic rule backfired when a truly charismatic leader entered the stage. The photographs showing Erich Honecker and Mikhail Gorbachev side by side on the tribune watching the parade for the fortieth anniversary of the GDR have become an historical icon that symbolizes the crucial difference. Ordinary East Germans could then subversively play on the instrument of the personal cult when chanting 'Gorbi, Gorbi!' and thereby decertify their own regime and its leaders.
4. Potts, *A History of Charisma*, 215f.

5. T. Welskopp. 2000. *Das Banner der Brüderlichkeit. Die deutsche Sozialdemokratie vom Vormärz bis zum Sozialistengesetz*, Bonn: J.H.W. Dietz Nachf., 384ff.
6. The connection between oratorical skills and charisma is noted by Potts, *A History of Charisma*, esp. 218f., but is not explored systematically.
7. R. Michels. 1959 (1910). *Political Parties: A Sociological Study of the Oligarchical Tendencies of Modern Democracy*, trans. E. Paul and C. Paul, New York: Dover Publications, 71.
8. A. Bebel. 1986. *Aus meinem Leben*, Berlin and Bonn: J.H.W. Dietz Nachf., 62f.
9. J.D. McCarthy and N.Z. Mayer. 2001. 'The Enduring Vitality of the Resource Mobilization Theory of Social Movements', in J.H. Turner (ed.), *Handbook of Sociological Theory*, New York: Springer, 533–65.
10. N. Luhmann. 1998. *Die Gesellschaft der Gesellschaft*, Frankfurt: Suhrkamp, 850; cf. T. Kern. 2008. *Soziale Bewegungen. Ursachen, Wirkungen, Mechanismen*, Wiesbaden: VS Verlag, 134.
11. D. McAdam, S. Tarrow and C. Tilly. 2001. *Dynamics of Contention*, Cambridge and New York: Cambridge University Press, 47f.
12. Although Max Weber is said to have secularized the term, I think that the religious connotations of charisma have never been lost completely. Cf. Potts, *A History of Charisma*, 108ff.
13. Potts, *A History of Charisma*, 218f.
14. J.A. Morone. 2003. *Hellfire Nation: The Politics of Sin in American History*, New Haven and London: Yale University Press.
15. E. Durkheim. 1981. *Die elementaren Formen des religiösen Lebens*, Frankfurt: Suhrkamp, 289, 301.
16. T. Welskopp. 2010. '*Anti-Saloon League* und *Ku Klux Klan*: die Stunde der "charismatischen Verbände"', in idem, *Amerikas große Ernüchterung. Die Vereinigten Staaten in der Zeit der Prohibition, 1919–1933*, Paderborn: Ferdinand Schöningh, 399–427.
17. McAdam, Tarrow and Tilly, *Dynamics of Contention*, 92.

BIBLIOGRAPHY

Afrikaanse Taal- en Kultuurvereniging. 1940. *Gedenkboek van die Ossewaens op die Pad van Suid-Afrika, Eeufees: 1838–1939*, Cape Town: Nasionale Pers Beperk.

Allen, K. 2004. *Max Weber, a Critical Introduction*, London: Pluto Press.

Altena, B. (ed.). 1979. *'En al beschouwen alle broeders mij als den verloren broeder', de familiecorrespondentie van en over Ferdinand Domela Nieuwenhuis, 1846–1923*, Amsterdam: Stichting Beheer IISG.

Altena, B. 1989. 'Domela's beeld van de Jezusfiguur', *De AS, anarchistisch tijdschrift* 17(87), 1–6.

Aly, G. 2005. *Hitlers Volksstaat. Raub, Rassenkrieg und nationaler Sozialismus*, Frankfurt: Fisher.

Anderson, B. 1991. *Imagined Communities: Reflections on the Origin and Spread of Nationalism*, 2nd ed., London: Verso.

Andreas, J. 2007. 'The Structure of Charismatic Mobilization: A Case Study of Rebellion during the Cultural Revolution', *American Sociological Review* 72(3), 434–58.

Apter, D.E. and T. Saich. 1994. *Revolutionary Discourse in Mao's Republic*, Cambridge, MA: Harvard University Press.

Arendt, H. 1994. 'At Table with Hitler', in H. Arendt, *Essays in Understanding 1930–1954*, ed. J. Kohn, New York: Harcourt, Brace, 291–93.

Aruffo, A. 2005. *Breve storia degli anarchici italiani 1870–1970*, Rome: Datanews.

Avrich, P. 1991. *Sacco and Vanzetti: The Anarchist Background*, Princeton, NJ: Princeton University Press.

Ay, K.-L. 1999. 'Max Weber: A German Intellectual and the Question of War Guilt after the Great War', in S. Whimster (ed.), *Max Weber and the Culture of Anarchy*, Basingstoke: Macmillan, 110–28.

Baehr, P.R. 2008. *Caesarism, Charisma and Fate: Historical Sources and Modern Resonances in the Work of Max Weber*, New Brunswick, NJ: Transaction Publishers.

Banerjee, M. 2000. *The Pathan Unarmed: Opposition and Memory in the North West Frontier*, Karachi and New Delhi: Oxford University Press.

Barker, C., A. Johnson and M. Lavalette (eds). 2001. *Leadership and Social Movements*, Manchester and New York: Manchester University Press.

Bebel, A. 1986. *Aus meinem Leben*, Berlin and Bonn: J.H.W. Dietz Nachf.

Becker, M. 2006. 'Charisma tussen analyse en overgave, een inleiding', in M. Becker (ed.), *Charisma: de fascinatie van leiders*, Nijmegen: Damon Budel, 7–18.

Beetham, D. 1977. 'From Socialism to Fascism: The Relation between Theory and Practice in the Work of Robert Michels', *Political Studies* 25(1), 3–24, and 25(2), 161–81.

Beetham, D. 1985. *Max Weber and the Theory of Modern Bourgeois Politics*, Cambridge: Polity.

Bell, R. 1986. 'Charisma and Illegitimate Authority', in R. Glassmann and R. Swatos (eds), *Charisma: History and Social Structure*, New York: Greenwood Press, 57–70.

Bellow, S. 1975. *Humboldt's Gift*, New York: Viking Press.

Bendix, R. 1960. *Max Weber: An Intellectual Portrait*, Garden City, NY: Doubleday and Co.

Bendix, R. and G. Roth. 1971. *Scholarship and Partisanship: Essays on Max Weber*, Berkeley: University of California Press.

Berti, G. 2003. *Errico Malatesta e il movimento anarchico Italiano e Internationale*, Milan: Francoangeli.

Bhattacharya, S. (ed.). 2008. *The Mahatma and the Poet: Letters and Debates between Gandhi and Tagore 1915–1941*, New Delhi: National Book Trust India.

Biagini, E. 1992. *Liberty, Retrenchment and Reform: Popular Liberalism in the Age of Gladstone, 1860–1880*, Cambridge: Cambridge University Press.

Bloch, E. 1960. *Thomas Münzer als Theologe der Revolution*, Berlin: Aufbau.

Bloch, E. 1967. *Naturrecht und menschliche Würde*, Frankfurt am Main: Suhrkamp.

Bloch, M. 1924. *Les rois thaumaturges: étude sur le caractère surnaturel attribué à la puissance royale particulièrement en France et en Angleterre*, Strasbourg: Publications de la Faculté des lettres de l'Université de Strasbourg.

Bloemgarten, S. 1981. 'De Tweede Internationale en de geboorte van de SDAP (1889–1896)', *Tijdschrift voor Sociale Geschiedenis* 7(22), 101–41.

Bokkel, J.G.A. ten. 2003. *Gidsen en genieën. De Dageraad en het vrije denken in Nederland 1855–1898*, Haarlem: FAMA.

Bologh, R. 1995. *Love or Greatness: Max Weber and Masculine Thinking – A Feminist Enquiry*, London: Unwin Hyman.

Bondurant, J.V. 1965 (1958). *Conquest of Violence: The Gandhian Philosophy of Conflict*, Berkeley: University of California Press.

Booyens, B. 1969. *Die lewe van D.F. Malan: die eerste veertig jaar*, Cape Town: Tafelberg Uitgewers.

Bos, D. 2001. *Waarachtige volksvrienden. De vroege socialistische beweging in Amsterdam 1848–1894*, Amsterdam: Bert Bakker.

Brits, J.P. 1993. 'Apartheid en die politieke grondverskuiwing van 1948', *Historia* 38(1), 64–81.

Brunello, P. and P. Di Paola (eds). 2003. *Errico Malatesta. Autobiografia mai scritta: Ricordi (1853–1932)*, Caserta: Spartaco.

Bymholt, S. 1976 (1894). *Geschiedenis der arbeidersbeweging in Nederland*, Amsterdam: Van Gennep.

Canovan, M. 1981. *Populism*, New York: Harcourt Brace Jovanovich.

Canovan, M. 1999. 'Trust the People! Populism and the Two Faces of Democracy', *Political Studies* 47, 2–16.

Canovan, M. 2004. 'Hannah Arendt on Totalitarianism and Dictatorship', in P. Baehr and M. Richter (eds), *Dictatorship in History and Theory*, Cambridge: Cambridge University Press, 241–63.

Carr, K. 1992. *The Banalization of Nihilism: Twentieth Century Responses to Meaninglessness*, Albany, NY: SUNY Press.

Carrillo, S. 1993. *Memorias*, Barcelona: Planeta.

Chalcraft, D. 1993. 'Weber, Wagner and Thoughts of Death', *Sociology* 27(3), 433–39.

Chan, A. 1985. *Children of Mao: Personality Development and Political Activism in the Red Guard Generation*, Seattle, WA: University of Washington Press.

Cilliers, G.G. 1955. 'Doktor Gawie Vertel...', *Die Stellenbosse Student: D.F. Malan uitgawe*, 22–23.

Claudín, F. 1983. *Santiago Carrillo: crónica de un secretario general*, Barcelona: Planeta.

Clercq, D. de. 1916. 'Domela Nieuwenhuis en het vegetarisme', in *Gedenkboek ter gelegenheid van den 70sten verjaardag van F. Domela Nieuwenhuis, 31 december 1916*, Amsterdam, 142–44.

Conway, M. 2002. 'Democracy in Postwar Western Europe: The Triumph of a Political Model', *European History Quarterly* 32, 59–84.

Conway, M. 2004. 'The Rise and Fall of Western Europe's Democratic Age, 1945–1973', *Contemporary European History* 13, 67–88.

Courtois, S., et al. 1997. *Le livre noir du communisme. Crimes, terreur, répression*, Paris: Robert Laffont.

Crick, B. 2000. *In Defence of Politics*, 5th ed., London: Continuum.

Dalton, D. 1970. 'Gandhi during Partition: A Case Study in the Nature of Satyagraha', in C.H. Philips and M.D. Wainwright (eds), *The Partition of India: Policies and Perspectives 1935–1947*, London: George Allen and Unwin, 222–44.

Davenport, T.R.H. 1966. *The Afrikaner Bond*, Cape Town: Oxford University Press.

Davenport, T.R.H. and C. Saunders. 2000. *South Africa: A Modern History*, London: Macmillan.

Deng L.Q. (ed.). 2004. *Zhongwai Mingren Pingshuo Mao Zedong* (Famous Chinese and Non-Chinese on Mao Zedong), Beijing: Zhongyang minzu chuban she.

Dieteren, F. and I. Peeterman. 1984. *Vrije Vrouwen of Werkmansvrouwen? Vrouwen in de Sociaal-Democratische Bond (1879–1894)*, Utrecht: Fischluc.

Di Lembo, L. 2001. *Guerra di classe e lotta umana. L'Anarchismo in Italia dal biennio rosso alla guerra di Spagna (1919–1939)*, Pisa: BFS.

Di Paola, P. 2007. 'The Spies who Came in from the Heat: The International Surveillance of the Anarchists in London', *European History Quarterly* 37(3), 189–215.

Dirlik, A. 2003. 'The Politics of the Cultural Revolution in Historical Perspective', in K.Y. Law (ed.), *The Chinese Cultural Revolution Reconsidered: Beyond Purge and Holocaust*, Basingstoke and New York: Palgrave, 158–83.

Dittmer, L. 1987. *China's Continuous Revolution: The Post-Liberation Years, 1949–1981*, Berkeley: University of California Press.

Domela Nieuwenhuis, F. 1890. 'Die sozialistische Bewegung in Holland', *Die Neue Zeit* 9(2), 51–57.

Dongen, B. van. 1992. *Revolutie of Integratie. De Sociaal Democratische Arbeiders Partij in Nederland (SDAP) tijdens de Eerste Wereldoorlog*, Amsterdam: Stichting Beheer IISG.

Downton, J.V. 1973. *Rebel Leadership: Commitment and Charisma in the Revolutionary Process*, New York: The Free Press.

Durkheim, E. 1981. *Die elementaren Formen des religiösen Lebens*, Frankfurt: Suhrkamp.

Dutton, M.R. 2005. *Policing Chinese Politics: A History*, Durham, NC: Duke University Press.

Eatwell, R. 2002. 'The Rebirth of Right-wing Charisma? The Cases of Jean-Marie Le Pen and Vladimir Zhirinovsky', *Totalitarian Movements and Political Religions* 3, 1–23.

Eatwell, R. 2006. 'The Concept and Theory of Charismatic Leadership', *Totalitarian Movements and Political Religions* 7(2), 141–56.

Eatwell, R. 2007. 'The Concept and Theory of Charismatic Leadership', in A.C. Pinto, R. Eatwell and S.U. Larsen (eds), *Charisma and Fascism in Interwar Europe*, London: Routledge, 3–18.

Eliaeson, S. 2000. 'Constitutional Caesarism: Weber's Politics in Their German Context', in S. Turner (ed.), *The Cambridge Companion to Weber*, Cambridge: Cambridge University Press, 131–48.

Ellemers, J.E. 2002. 'Pim Fortuyn: een zuiver geval van charismatisch gezag', *Facta. Sociaalwetenschappelijk magazine*, November, 2–5.

Ellis, R.J. 1991. 'Explaining the Occurrence of Charismatic Leadership in Organizations', *Journal of Theoretical Politics* 3(3), 305–19.

Fabbri, L. 1951. *Malatesta, l'uomo e il pensiero*, Naples: Edizioni RL.

Faber, H. 1970. *Ontkerkelijking en buitenkerkelijkheid in Nederland, tot 1960*, Assen: Van Gorcum.

Falasca-Zamponi, S. 1997. *Fascist Spectacle: The Aesthetics of Power in Mussolini's Italy*, Berkeley: University of California Press.

Falcón, I. 1996. *Asalto a los cielos: mi vida junto a Pasionaria*, Madrid: Temas de Hoy.

Fedele, S. 1996. *Una breve illusione. Gli anarchici italiani e la Russia Sovietica 1917–1939*, Milan: FrancoAngeli.

Femia, J.V. 2001. *Against the Masses: Varieties of Anti-democratic Thought since the French Revolution*, Oxford: Oxford University Press.

Finzi, P. 1990. *La nota persona. Errico Malatesta in Italia. Dicembre 1919–Luglio 1920*, Ragusa: La Fiaccola.

Fiorina, M.P. and K.A. Shepsle. 1989. 'Formal Theories of Leadership: Agents, Agenda Setters and Entrepreneur', in B.D. Jones (ed.), *Leadership and Politics*, Kansas: University of Kansas Press, 17–40.

Fogg, B.J. 1997. 'Charismatic Computers: Creating More Likable and Persuasive Interactive Technologies by Leveraging Principles from Social Psychology', retrieved from http://virtual.inesc.pt/rct/show.php?id=73.

Fortuyn, P. 1995. *De verweesde samenleving: een religieus-sociologisch traktaat*, Utrecht: Bruna.

Fortuyn, P. 2002. *De puinhopen van acht jaar Paars*, Rotterdam: Speakers Academy Uitgeverij.

Friedland, W.H. 1964. 'For a Sociological Concept of Charisma', *Social Forces* 43(1), 16–26.

Frieswijk, J. 1992. 'The Labour Movement in Friesland, 1880–1918', *Tijdschrift voor Sociale Geschiedenis* 18(2/3), 370–89.

Furet, F. 1995. *Le passé d'une illusion. Essai sur l'idée communiste au XXe siècle*, Paris: Robert Laffont/Callman-Lévy.

Gage, B. 2009. *The Day Wall Street Exploded: A Story of America in its First Age of Terror*, Oxford: Oxford University Press.

Gandhi, M. 1999. *The Collected Works of Mahatma Gandhi*, New Delhi: Publications Division Government of India.

Gandhi, M.K. 2003 (1909). *Hind Swaraj, or Indian Home Rule*, Ahmedabad: Navjivan Publishing House.

Gandhi, R. 2004. *Ghaffar Khan: Nonviolent Badshah of the Pakhtuns*, New Delhi: Penguin-Viking.

Gandhi, R. 2006. *Mohandas: A True Story of a Man, His People, and an Empire*, New Delhi: Penguin-Viking.

Gao, M.B. 1999. *Gao Village: A Portrait of Rural Life in Modern China*, Hong Kong: Hong Kong University Press.

Gao, M.B. 2008. *The Battle for China's Past: Mao and the Cultural Revolution*, London: Pluto Press.

Geertz, C. 1995. '"Deep Play": Bemerkungen zum balinesischen Hahnenkampf', in idem (ed.), *Dichte Beschreibung. Beiträge zum Verstehen kultureller Systeme*, 4th ed., Frankfurt: Suhrkamp, 202–60.

Gentile, E. 1989. *Storia del Partito Fascista 1919–1922. Movimento e milizia*, Bari: Laterza.

Gentile, E. 2005. 'Political Religion: A Concept and Its Critics – a Critical Survey', *Totalitarian Movements and Political Religions* 6(1), 19–32.

Gentile, E. 2006. *Politics as Religion*, Princeton, NJ: Princeton University Press.

Gerth, H.H. and C. Wright Mills (eds and trans.). 1947. *From Max Weber: Essays in Sociology*, London: Kegan Paul.

Giele, J. 1976. 'Arbeidersbestaan, levenshouding en maatschappijbeeld van de arbeidende klasse in Nederland in het midden van de negentiende eeuw', in J. Giele et al. (eds), *Jaarboek voor de Geschiedenis van Socialisme en Arbeidersbeweging in Nederland*, Nijmegen: SUN, 21–92.

Giliomee, H. 2003. 'The Making of the Apartheid Plan, 1929–1948', *Journal of Southern African Studies* 29(2), 373–92.

Giliomee, H. 2003. 'The Weakness of Some: The Dutch Reformed Church and White Supremacy', *Scriptura* 83, 212–44.

Giliomee, H. 2004. *The Afrikaners: Biography of a People*, Cape Town: Tafelberg.

Gill, G. 1980. 'The Soviet Leader Cult: Reflections on the Structure of Leadership in the Soviet Union', *British Journal of Political Science* 10(2), 171.

Giulietti, F. 2004. *Il Movimento anarchico italiano nella lotta contro il fascismo*, Manduria, Bari and Rome: Lacaita.

Giulietti, F. 2007. 'Anarchici contro comunisti. Movimento anarchico italiano e i bolscevichi', *Italia Contemporanea* 247, 165–93.

Gramsci, A. 1975. *Quarderni del Carcere*, 4 vols, ed. V. Gerratana, Turin: Einaudi.

Greenfeld, L. 1983. 'Reflections on Two Charismas', *The British Journal of Sociology* 36(1), 117–32.

Grundlingh, A. and S. Swart. 2009. *Radelose rebellie? Dinamika van die 1914–1915 Afrikaner-rebellie*, Pretoria: Protea Boekhuis.

Haan, I. de. 2000. 'From Moses to Maggie: Popular Political Wisdom and the Republican Tradition in Political Thought', *The Public* 2, 33–44.

Han, D.P. 2000. *The Unknown Cultural Revolution: Educational Reforms and Their Impact on China's Rural Development*, New York: Garland Publishers.

Hancock, W.K. 1962. *Smuts: The Sanguine Years, 1870–1919*, Cambridge: Cambridge University Press.

Hartmans, R. 1994. 'Pieter Jelles Troelstra: advocaat en agitator', in *Van Troelstra tot Den Uyl, Het Jaarboek voor het Democratisch Socialisme* 15, 19–59.

Havers, W. and S.W. Coltof. 1916. 'Ferdinand Domela Nieuwenhuis', in *Gedenkboek ter gelegenheid van den 70sten verjaardag van F. Domela Nieuwenhuis, 31 december 1916*, Amsterdam, 155–83.

Hennis, W. 1988. *Max Weber: Essays in Reconstruction*, London: Allen & Unwin.

Hinton, W. 1972. *Hundred Day War: The Cultural Revolution at Tsinghua University*, New York: Monthly Review Press.

Hirschman, A. 1977. *The Passions and the Interests: Political Arguments for Capitalism before Its Triumph*, Princeton, NJ: Princeton University Press.

Hobsbawm, E.J. 1959. *Primitive Rebels: Archaic Forms of Social Movement in the 19th and 20th Centuries*, Manchester: Manchester University Press.

Hobsbawm, E.J. 1965. *Primitive Rebels: Archaic Forms of Social Movement in the 19th and 20th Centuries*, New York: W.W. Norton.

Hobsbawm, E.J. 1986. 'Weber und Marx. Ein Kommentar', in J. Kocka (ed.), *Max Weber, der Historiker*, Göttingen: Vandenhoeck & Ruprecht, 84–90.

Hobsbawm, E.J. 1992. *Nations and Nationalism since 1780: Programme, Myth, Reality*, 2nd ed., Cambridge: Cambridge University Press.

Hobsbawm, E.J. 1995. *The Age of Empire, 1875–1914*, New York: Pantheon Books.

Horssen, P. van and D. Rietveld. 1975. 'De Sociaal Democratische Bond. Een onderzoek naar het ontstaan van haar afdelingen en haar sociale structuur', *Tijdschrift voor Sociale Geschiedenis* 1, 5–71.

Horssen, P. van and D. Rietveld. 1977. 'De Sociaal Democratische Bond. Een onderzoek naar het ontstaan van haar afdelingen en haar sociale structuur', *Tijdschrift voor Sociale Geschiedenis* 7, 3–54.

Ibárruri, D. 1968. *En la lucha: palabras y hechos, 1936–1939*, Moscow: Progreso.

Janoska-Bendl, J. 1965. *Methodologische Aspekte des Idealtypus. Max Weber und die Soziologie der Geschichte*, Berlin: Duncker und Humblot.

Johnston, T. 1925. 'James Keir Hardie: The Founder of the Labour Party', in H. Tracey (ed.), *The Book of the Labour Party: Its History, Growth, Policy, and Leaders III*, London: Caxton, 105–18.

Jonas, H. 1996. *Mortality and Morality: A Search for the Good after Auschwitz*, Evanston, IL: Northwestern University Press.

Jong, A.A. de. 1966. *Domela Nieuwenhuis*, The Hague: Kruseman.

Kalma, J.J. 1978. *Er valt voor recht te strijden. De roerige dagen rond 1890 in Friesland*, The Hague: Boekencentrum.

Kantorowicz, E.H. 1957. *The King's Two Bodies: A Study in Mediaeval Political Theology*, Princeton, NJ: Princeton University Press.

Karádi, É. 1987. 'Ernst Bloch and Georg Lukács in Max Weber's Heidelberg', in W.J. Mommsen, and J. Osterhammel (eds), *Max Weber and His Contemporaries*, London: Allen & Unwin, 499–514.

Kern, T. 2008. *Soziale Bewegungen. Ursachen, Wirkungen, Mechanismen*, Wiesbaden: VS Verlag.
Kissinger, H. 1979. *The White House Years*, Boston, MA: Little, Brown and Co.
Klandermans, B. 1997. *The Social Psychology of Protest*, Oxford: Blackwell.
Kleu, S.J. 1954. 'Die man agter die stroewe masker: Staaltjies oor SA se Eerste Minister by geleentheid van sy tagtigste verjaardag', *Die Burger*, 22 May.
Knottnerus, O.S. 1988. 'Het anarchisme als geseculariseerde bevindelijkheid', *Bulletin Nederlandse Arbeidersbeweging* 18, 38–53.
Koch, J. 2006. *Abraham Kuyper. Een biografie*, Amsterdam: Boom.
Kocka, J. 1966. 'Karl Marx und Max Weber. Ein methodologischer Vergleich', *Zeitschrift für die gesamten Staatswissenschaften* 122(April), 328–57.
Kocka, J. (ed.). 1986. *Max Weber, der Historiker*, Göttingen: Vandenhoeck & Ruprecht.
Korf, L. 2007. 'Podium and/or Pulpit? D.F. Malan's Role in the Politicisation of the Dutch Reformed Church, 1900–1959', *Historia* 52(2), 214–38.
Korf, L. 2008. 'Behind Every Man: D.F. Malan and the Women in His Life, 1874–1959', *South African Historical Journal* 60(3), 397–421.
Korf, L. 2010. 'D.F. Malan: A Political Biography', D.Phil Thesis. Stellenbosch: University of Stellenbosch.
Kossmann, E.H. 1976. 'The Singularity of Absolutism', in R. Hatton (ed.), *Louis XIV and Absolutism*, London: Macmillan, 3–17.
Kraus, R.C. 1981. *Class Conflict in Chinese Socialism*, New York: Columbia University Press.
Kruijt, J.P. 1933. *De Onkerkelijkheid in Nederland, haar verbreiding en oorzaken, proeve ener sociografiese verklaring*, Groningen and Batavia: P. Noordhoff.
Kruithof, B. 2006. 'Godsvrucht en goede zeden bevorderen. Het burgerlijk beschavingsoffensief van de Maatschappij tot Nut van 't Algemeen', in N. Bakker, R. Dekker and A. Janssens (eds), *Tot burgerschap en deugd. Volksopvoeding in de Negentiende Eeuw*, Hilversum: Verloren, 69–81.
Krüger, D.W. 1958. *The Age of the Generals: A Short Political History of the Union of South Africa, 1910–1948*, Johannesburg: Dagbreek Book Store.
Labrie, A. 2001. *Zuiverheid en decadentie. Over de grenzen van de burgerlijke cultuur in West-Europa, 1870–1914*, Amsterdam: Bert Bakker.
Landsberger, S. 2008. *The Mao Cult*, retrieved from http://chineseposters.net/themes/maocult.php
Lassman, P. and R. Speirs (eds). 1995. *Weber: Political Writings*, Cambridge: Cambridge University Press.
Lee, H.Y. 1978. *Politics of the Chinese Cultural Revolution: A Case Study*, Berkeley: University of California Press.
Levy, C. 1981. 'Malatesta in Exile', *Annali della Fondazione Einaudi* 15, 245–70.
Levy, C. 1987. 'Max Weber and Antonio Gramsci', in W.J. Mommsen and J. Osterhammel (eds), *Max Weber and His Contemporaries*, London: Allen & Unwin, 382–402.
Levy, C. 1989. 'Italian Anarchism, 1870–1926', in D. Goodway (ed.), *For Anarchism: History, Theory, Practice*, London: Routledge, 25–78.
Levy, C. 1993. 'Malatesta in London: The Era of Dynamite', in L. Sponza and A. Tosi (eds), *A Century of Italian Emigration to Britain 1880 to 1980s: Five Essays*, Supplement to *The Italianist* 13, 25–42.
Levy, C. 1998. 'Charisma and Social Movements: Errico Malatesta and Italian Anarchism', *Modern Italy* 3(2), 205–17.
Levy, C. 1999. *Gramsci and the Anarchists*, Oxford: Berg.
Levy, C. 1999. 'Max Weber, Anarchism and Libertarian Culture: Personality and Power Politics', in S. Whimster (ed.), *Max Weber and the Culture of Anarchy*, Basingstoke: Macmillan, 83–109.
Levy, C. 2000. 'Currents of Italian Syndicalism before 1926', *International Review of Social History* 45(2), 209–50.

Levy, C. 2001. 'The People and the Professors: Socialism and the Educated Middle Classes in Italy, 1870–1915', *Journal of Modern Italian Studies* 6(2), 195–208.

Levy, C. 2007. '"*Sovversivismo*": The Radical Political Culture of Otherness in Liberal Italy', *Journal of Political Ideologies* 12(1), 147–61.

Levy, C. 2007. 'The Anarchist Assassin in Italian History 1870s to 1930s', in S. Gundle and L. Rinaldi (eds), *Assassination and Murder in Modern Italy: Transformations in Society and Culture*, New York and London: Palgrave Macmillan, 207–32.

Levy, C. 2011. *Antonio Gramsci: Marxism, Modernity and Machiavelli*, Cambridge: Polity.

Levy, C. Forthcoming. *The Rooted Cosmopolitan: Errico Malatesta, the Life and Times of an Italian Anarchist in Exile*.

Li, Z.S. 1994. *The Private Life of Chairman Mao: The Memoirs of Mao's Personal Physician*, trans. H.C. Tai, New York: Random House.

Liang, H. and J. Shapiro. 1983. *Son of the Revolution*, New York: Vintage Books.

Lifton, R.J. 1968. *Revolutionary Immortality: Mao Tse-tung and the Chinese Cultural Revolution*, New York: Vintage Books.

Linden, M. van der. 2004. '"Normalarbeit" – das Ende einer Fiktion. Wie der Proletar verschwand und wieder zurück kehrte', *Fantômas* 6, 26–29.

Lindholm, C. 1990. *Charisma*, Cambridge, MA: Basil Blackwell.

Linse, U. 1999. 'Sexual Revolution and Anarchism: Erich Mühsam', in S. Whimster (ed.), *Max Weber and the Culture of Anarchy*, Basingstoke: Macmillan, 110–28.

Lipset, S.M. 1960. *Political Man: The Social Bases of Politics*, Garden City, NY: Anchor Books.

Loreck, J. 1978. *Wie man früher Sozialdemokrat wurde. Das Kommunikationsverhalten in der deutschen Arbeiterbewegung und die Konzeption der sozialistischen Parteipublizistik durch August Bebel*, Bonn and Bad Godesberg: Neue Gesellschaft.

Lotti, L. 1965. *La Settimana Rossa*, Florence: Le Monnier.

Löwith, K. 1923. 'Max Weber und Karl Marx', *Archiv für Sozialwissenschaft und Sozialpolitik* 67. Band, Tübingen.

Löwy, M. 1976. *Pour une sociologie des intellectuels révolutionnaires*, Paris: Presses Universitaires de France.

Löwy, M. 1993. 'Weber against Marx? The Polemic with Historical Materialism in *The Protestant Ethic*', in *On Changing the World: Essays in Political Philosophy, from Karl Marx to Walter Benjamin*, Atlantic Highlands, NJ: Humanities Press, 43–54.

Löwy, M. 1996. 'Figures of Weberian Marxism', *Theory and Society* 25(3), 431–46.

Löwy, M. 2007. 'Marx and Weber: Critics of Capitalism', *New Politics* 11(2), 1–12.

Löwy, M. and R. Sayre. 1992. *Révolte et mélancholie. Le romantisme à contre-courant de la modenité*, Paris: Editions Payot.

Luhmann, N. 1998. *Die Gesellschaft der Gesellschaft*, Frankfurt: Suhrkamp.

Luparini, A. 2001. *Anarchici di Mussolini: dalla sinistra al fascismo tra rivoluzione e revisionismo*, Montespertoli: MIR Edizioni.

Luskin, R.C. 2002 'Political Psychology, Political Behavior, and Politics: Questions of Aggregation, Causal Distance, and Taste', in J.H. Kuklinski (ed.), *Thinking about Political Psychology*, Cambridge: Cambridge University Press, 217–50.

MacLean, J. 1979. 'Arbeidsconflicten in de periode 1813–1872, gegevens uit het kabinet des Konings', *Tijdschrift voor Sociale Geschiedenis* 5(16), 292–312.

Maier, H. 2007. 'Political Religion: A Concept and Its Limitations', *Totalitarian Movements and Political Religions* 8, 5–16.

Malan, D.F. 1913. *Naar Congoland: een reisbeschrijving*, Stellenbosch: Christen Studente-vereniging.

Malan, D.F. 1954. *Apartheid: Suid-Afrika gee sy antwoord op 'n groot probleem*, Pretoria: Staatsinligtingskantoor.

Malan, D.F. 1961. *Afrikaner-Volkseenheid en my ervarings op die pad daarheen*, Cape Town: Nasionale Boekhandel Beperk.

Malan, D.F. 1964. 'Boodskap vir die Toekoms', in S.W. Pienaar (ed.), *Glo in U Volk: Dr. D.F. Malan as Redenaar, 1908–1954*, Cape Town: Tafelberg Uitgewers, 234–38.

Malan, D.F. 1964.'Dan kom ek om', in S.W. Pienaar (ed.), *Glo in U Volk: Dr. D.F. Malan as Redenaar, 1908–1954*, Cape Town: Tafelberg Uitgewers, 9–18.

Malan, D.F. 1964. 'Die Party is die Moeder', in S.W. Pienaar (ed.), *Glo in U Volk: Dr. D.F. Malan as Redenaar, 1908–1954*, Cape Town: Tafelberg Uitgewers, 37–43.

Malatesta, E. 1894. 'The Duties of the Present Hour', *Liberty*, August, 61–62.

Malatesta, E. 1975 (1935). 'Dichariazioni Autodifesa alla Assise di Milano. Un Ricordo di Ancona', *Errico Malatesta pagine di lotta quotidiana e scritti vari, 1919/1923, Scritti volume 2*, Cararra: Tipiografica Cooperativa.

Malraux, A. 1967. *Anti-memoirs*, trans. T. Kilmartin, Middlesex: Penguin Books.

Mandel, E. 1986. 'The Role of the Individual in History: The Case of World War Two', *New Left Review* 157, 61–77.

Mandela, N. 1995. *Long Walk to Freedom*, Johannesburg: Macdonald Purnell.

Mantovani, V. 1979. *Mazurka blu. La strage del Diana*, Milan: Rusconi.

Margry, P.J. 2003. 'The Murder of Pim Fortuyn and Collective Emotions: Hype, Hysteria and Holiness in the Netherlands?', *Etnofoor. Antropologisch tijdschrift* 16, 102–27.

Markovits, C. 2007. 'The Calcutta Riots of 1946', retrieved 10 April 2009 from online Encyclopedia of Mass Violence: http://www.massviolence.org/The-Calcutta-Riots-of-1946

Marsh, P.T. 1994. *Joseph Chamberlain: Entrepreneur in Politics*, New Haven, CT: Yale University Press.

Marx, C. 2008. *Oxwagon Sentinel: Radical Afrikaner Nationalism and the History of the Ossewabrandwag*, Pretoria: University of South Africa Press.

Marx, K. 2004. *Die Frühschriften*, ed. S. Landshut, 7th ed., Stuttgart: Kröner.

Marx-Engles-Werke. 1985. Vol. 35. Berlin: Dietz Verlag.

Marx, K. and F. Engels. 1953 (repr. 1985). 'Die Deutsche Ideologie', in *Marx-Engles-Werke*, vol. 3, Berlin: Dietz Verlag, 3–67.

Marx, K. and F. Engels. 1967. *Werke 35*, Berlin: Dietz Verlag.

Masini, P.C. 1974. *Storia degli anarchici dal Bakunin a Malatesta (1862–1892)*, Milan: Rizzoli.

Masini, P.C. 1981. *Storia degli anarchici italiani nell'epoca degli attentati*, Milan: Rizzoli.

Matthew, H.C.G. 1995. *Gladstone 1875–1898*, Oxford: Clarendon Press.

Matthew, H.C.G. 1998. 'Gladstone, Rhetoric and Politics', in P.J. Jagger (ed.), *Gladstone*, London and Rio Grande: The Hambledon Press, 213–34.

McAdam, D., S. Tarrow and C. Tilly. 2001. *Dynamics of Contention*, Cambridge and New York: Cambridge University Press.

McCarthy, J.D. and N.Z. Mayer. 2001. 'The Enduring Vitality of the Resource Mobilization Theory of Social Movements', in J.H. Turner (ed.), *Handbook of Sociological Theory*, New York: Springer, 533–65.

Mellink, A.F. 1968. 'Een poging tot democratische coalitie-vorming: de Nederlandse kiesrechtbeweging als volkspartij (1886–1891)', *Tijdschrift voor Geschiedenis* 81(2), 174–96.

Mellink, A.F. 1970. 'Het Politiek debuut van mr. P.J. Troelstra (1891–1897)', *Tijdschrift voor Geschiedenis* 83(1), 38–59.

Mellink, A.F. 1988. 'Domela Nieuwenhuis en de voormannen van de Friese Volkspartij', in J. Frieswijk, J.J. Kalma and Y. Kuiper (eds), *Ferdinand Domela Nieuwenhuis. De apostel van de Friese arbeiders*, Drachten: Friese Pers Boekerij, 117–30.

Meyer, D.S. and S. Tarrow. 1998. 'A Movement Society: Contentious Politics for a New Century', in D.S. Meyer and S. Tarrow (eds), *The Social Movement Society: Contentious Politics for a New Century*, Lanham, MD: Rowman and Littlefield, 1–28.

Meyers, J. 1993. *Domela, een hemel op aarde*, Amsterdam: Arbeiderspers.

Michels, R. 1911/1925, reprint 1989. *Zur Soziologie des Parteiwesens in der modernen Demokratie*, Stuttgart: Kröner Verlag.

Michels, R. 1959 (1910). *Political Parties: A Sociological Study of the Oligarchical Tendencies of Modern Democracy*, trans. E. Paul and C. Paul, New York: Dover Publications.

Mitzman, A. 1973. *Sociology and Estrangement: Three Sociologists in Imperial Germany*, New York: Knopf.

Mommsen, W.J. 1974. *Max Weber und die Deutsche Politik 1890–1920*, Tübingen: Mohr.

Mommsen, W.J. 1974. *The Age of Bureaucracy: Perspectives on the Political Sociology of Max Weber*, Oxford: Basil Blackwell.

Mommsen, W.J. 1985. *Max Weber and German Politics 1890–1920*, Chicago, IL: University of Chicago Press.

Mommsen, W.J. 1986. 'Max Webers Begriff der Universalgeschichte', in J. Kocka (ed.), *Max Weber, der Historiker*, Göttingen: Vandenhoeck & Ruprecht, 51–73.

Mommsen, W.J. 1987. 'Max Weber and German Social Democracy', in C. Levy (ed.), *Socialism and the Intelligentsia 1880–1914*, London and New York: Routledge & Kegan Paul, 90–106.

Mommsen, W.J. 1987. 'Robert Michels and Max Weber: Moral Conviction versus the Politics of Responsibility', in W.J. Mommsen and J. Osterhammel (eds), *Max Weber and His Contemporaries*, London: Allen & Unwin, 121–38.

Moodie, T.D. 1980. *The Rise of Afrikanerdom: Power, Apartheid and the Afrikaner Civil Religion*, Berkeley: University of California Press.

Morán, G. 1986. *Miseria y grandeza del Partido Comunista de España, 1939–1985*, Barcelona: Planeta.

Morone, J.A. 2003. *Hellfire Nation: The Politics of Sin in American History*, New Haven and London: Yale University Press.

Muller, C.F.J. 1990. *Sonop in die Suide: Geboorte en Groei van die Nasionale Pers, 1915–1948*, Cape Town: Nasionale Boekhandel.

Multatuli. 1875. *Max Havelaar of de koffieveilingen der Nederlandsche Handelsmaatschappij*, Amsterdam: Nederlandsche Bibliotheek.

Multatuli. 1989. *Volledig Werk*, vol. 23, Amsterdam: Van Oorschot.

Nettlau, M. 1922. *Errico Malatesta*, New York: Il Martello.

Nieuwenhuis, J.A. 1933. *Een halve eeuw onder socialisten. Bijdrage tot de geschiedenis van het socialisme in Nederland*, Zeist: De Torentrans.

Nixon, R.M. 1978. *The Memoirs of Richard Nixon*, London: Sigwick and Jackson.

Noiret, S. 1991. *Massimalismo e crisi dello stato liberale. Nicola Bombacci (1879–1924)*, Milan: FrancoAngeli.

Nursey-Bray, P. 1995. 'Malatesta and the Anarchist Revolution', *Anarchist Studies* 3(1), 25–44.

O'Meara, D. 1983. *Volkskapitalisme: Class, Capital and Ideology in the Development of Afrikaner Nationalism, 1934–1948*, Cambridge: Cambridge University Press.

Orgel, S. and J. Goldberg (eds). 2004. *J. Milton, Paradise Lost*, Oxford: Oxford University Press.

Orwell, G. 1949. *Reflections on Gandhi*, retrieved 10 April 2009 from: http://orwell.ru/library/reviews/gandhi/english/e_gandhi

Ostrogorski, M. 1902, reprint 1922. *Democracy and the Organization of Political Parties*, New York and London: MacMillan.

Owen, D. 1994. *Maturity and Modernity: Nietzsche, Weber, Foucault and the Ambivalence of Reason*, London and New York: Routledge.

Parekh, B. 1989. *Colonialism, Tradition and Reform: An Analysis of Gandhi's Political Discourse*, New Delhi: Sage Publications.

Parsons, T. 1929. 'Capitalism in Recent German Literature', *Journal of Political Economy* 37, 31–51.

Pernicone, N. 1992. *Italian Anarchism 1864–1892*, Princeton, NJ: Princeton University Press.

Pernicone, N. 1993. 'Luigi Galleani and Italian Anarchist Terrorism in the United States', *Studi Emigrazione* 30, 469–88.

Pernicone, N. 2005. *Carlo Tresca: Portrait of a Rebel*, New York: Palgrave Macmillan.

Petracchi, C. 1990. *Il mito della rivoluzione sovietica in Italia, 1917–1920, Storia contemporanea* 13, 1107–30.

Pigenet, M. 1992. *Au coeur de l'activisme communiste des années de Guerre Froide: la manifestation Ridgway*, Paris: L'Harmattan.

Pivato, S. 2005. *Bella ciao. Canto e politica nella storia d'Italia*, Rome and Bari: Laterza.

Poguntke, T. and P. Webb (eds). 2005. *The Presidentialization of Politics: A Comparative Study of Modern Democracies*, Oxford: Oxford University Press.

Posel, D. 1987. 'The Meaning of Apartheid before 1948: Conflicting Interests and Forces within the Afrikaner Nationalist Alliance', *Journal of Southern African Studies* 14(1), 123–39.

Potts, J. 2009. *A History of Charisma*, Basingstoke and New York: Palgrave Macmillan.

Prazniak, R. 1999. *Of Camel Kings and Other Things: Rural Rebels against Modernity in Late Imperial China*, Lanham, MD: Rowman & Littlefield.

Radkau, J. 2005. *Max Weber: die Leidenschaft des Denkens*, Munich: Carl Hanser.

Radkau, J. 2009. *Max Weber, a Biography*, Cambridge: Polity.

Radosh, R., M. Habeck and G. Sevostianov (eds). 2001. *Spain Betrayed: The Soviet Union in the Spanish Civil War*, New Haven, CT: Yale University Press.

Ralhan, O.P. and S.K. Sharma. 1994. *Documents on Punjab*, vol. 6, part 1, *Sikh Politics (1919–1926)*, New Delhi: Anmol Publications.

Ralhan, O.P. and S.K. Sharma. 1994. *Documents on Punjab*, vol. 7, *Sikh Politics (Guru-ka-Bagh Morcha)*, New Delhi: Anmol Publications.

Rao, R. 2007 (1970). *Kanthapura*, Delhi: Orient Paperbacks.

Ratnam, K.J. 1964. 'Charisma and Political Leadership', *Political Studies* 12(3), 341–54.

Rauschning, H. 1938. *Die Revolution des Nihilismus. Kulisse und Wirklichkeit im Dritten Reich*, Zürich and New York: Europa Verlag.

Riall, L. 2007. *Garibaldi: Invention of a Hero*, New Haven, CT: Yale University Press.

Richards, V. 1965. *Malatesta: Life and Ideas*, London: Freedom Press.

Ridolfi, M. 1992. *Il PSI e la nascita del partito di massa, 1892–1992*, Bari: Laterza.

Rijn, J. van. 2010. *De eeuw van het debat. De ontwikkeling van het publieke debat in Nederland en Engeland, 1800–1920*, Amsterdam: Wereldbibliotheek.

Ringer, F.K. 2004. *Max Weber, an Intellectual Biography*, Chicago, IL: Chicago University Press.

Rocker, R. 1937. *Nationalism and Culture* [Original title: *Die Entscheidung des Abendlandes*], New York: Covici Friede.

Roland Holst, H. 1919. 'F. Domela Nieuwenhuis' Uitvaart', *De Nieuwe Tijd* 24, 747.

Romein, J. and A. Romein. 1938–1940, reprint 1977. *Erflaters van onze beschaving*, Amsterdam: Querido.

Rooy, P. de. 1971. *Een revolutie die voorbij ging: Domela Nieuwenhuis en het Palingoproer*, Bussum: van Dishoeck.

Rosdolsky, R. 1977. 'Die Rolle des Zufalls und der Groszen Männer in der Geschichte', *Kritik* 5(14), 67–96.

Rosen, S. 1969. *Nihilism: A Philosophical Essay*, New Haven, CT, and London: Yale University Press.

Rosen, S. 1989. *The Ancients and the Moderns: Rethinking Modernity*, New Haven, CT, and London: Yale University Press.

Ross, R. 1999. *A Concise History of South Africa*, Cambridge: Cambridge University Press.

Roth, G. 1971. 'The Historical Relationship to Marxism', in R. Bendix and G. Roth, *Scholarship and Partisanship: Essays on Max Weber*, Berkeley: University of California Press, 227–52.

Roth, G. 1979. 'Charisma and Counterculture', in G. Roth and W. Schluchter (eds), *Max Weber's Vision of History*, Berkeley: University of California Press, 119–36.

Roth, G. 1987. *Politische Herrschaft und Persönliche Freiheit. Heidelberger Max Weber-Vorlesungen 1983*, Frankfurt am Main: Suhrkamp.

Roth, G. 1988–89. 'Weber's Political Failure', *Telos* 78, 136–49.

Rothermund, D. 1991. *Mahatma Gandhi: An Essay in Political Biography*, Delhi: Manohar Publications.

Rothman, M.E. 1972. *My Beskeie Deel: 'n Outobiografiese Vertelling*, Cape Town: Tafelberg.

Salaris, C. 2002. *Alla festa della rivoluzione. Artisti e libertari con D' Annunzio a Fiume*, Bologna: Il Mulino.

Salotti, G. 1982. *Giuseppe Giulietti*, Rome: Bonacci.

Sánchez Montero, S. 1997. *Camino de libertad: memorias*, Madrid: Temas de Hoy.

Sanders, B. and G. de Groot. 1988. 'Without Hope of Improvement: Casual Labourers and Bourgeois Reformers in Amsterdam, 1850–1920', in L. Heerma van Voss and F. van Holthoorn (eds), *Working Class and Popular Culture*, Amsterdam: Stichting Beheer IISG, 227–43.

Sankrityayan, R. 1957. *Veer Chandra Singh Garhwali*, Allahabad: Kitab Mahal.

Saunders, C. and N. Southey. 2001. *Dictionary of South African History*, Cape Town: David Phillip.

Sayer, D. 1991. *Capitalism and Modernism: An Excursus on Marx and Weber*, London: Routledge.

Schluchter, W. 1996. *Paradoxes of Modernity: Culture and Conduct in the Theory of Max Weber*, Stanford, CA: Stanford University Press.

Scholtz, J.J.J. 1947. 'Die Dr. Malan wat die meeste lede van die publiek nie ken nie: Hy is lief vir diere, tuinmaak … en roomys', *Die Burger*, 24 May.

Schorschke, C. 1980. *Fin de Siècle Vienna: Politics and Culture*, New York: Knopf.

Schroeder, R. 1991. '"Personality" and "Inner Distance": The Conceptions of the Individual in Max Weber's Sociology', *History of Human Sciences* 4(1), 61–78.

Schwentker, W. 1987. 'Passion as a Model of Life: Max Weber, the Otto Gross Circle and Eroticism', in W.J. Mommsen and J. Osterhammel (eds), *Max Weber and His Contemporaries*, London: Allen & Unwin, 483–98.

Semprún, J. 1977. *Autobiografia de Federico Sánchez*, Barcelona: Planeta.

Shannon, R. 1963. *Gladstone and the Bulgarian Agitation 1876*, London: Thomas Nelson.

Shils, E. 1965. 'Charisma, Order, and Status', *American Sociological Review* 30(2), 199–213.

Siao-yu. 1973. *Mao Tse-tung and I Were Beggars: the True Adventures of Young Mao and His Friend on a `Begging Trip' through Central China*, New York: Collier Books.

Smith, P. 2000. 'Culture and Charisma: Outline of a Theory', *Acta Sociologica* 43, 101–11.

Snow, E. 1944. *Red Star over China*, 2nd ed., New York: Grove Press.

Snow, E. 1971. *Red China Today: On the Other Side of the River*, New York: Vintage Books.

Snyman, J.H. 1979. *Die Afrikaner in Kaapland, 1899–1902*, Pretoria: Argief Jaarboek vir Suid-Afrikaanse Geskiedenis.

Spencer, M. 1973. 'What Is Charisma?', *The British Journal of Sociology* 24(3), 341–54.

Spinrad, W. 1991. 'Charisma: A Blighted Concept and an Alternative Formula', *Political Science Quarterly* 106(2), 295–311.

Stutje, J.W. 2008. 'Ferdinand Domela Nieuwenhuis (1846–1919). Revolte en melancholie: romantiek in Domela's kritiek op de moderniteit', *Tijdschrift voor Sociale en Economische Geschiedenis* 5(2), 3–28.

Taggart, P. 1996. *The New Populism and the New Politics: New Protest Parties in Sweden in a Comparative Perspective*, London: Macmillan.

Taggart, P. 2000. *Populism*, Buckingham and Philadelphia: Open University Press.

Tagträume vom aufrechten Gang, Sechs Interviews mit Ernst Bloch. 1977. Republished and introduced by A. Münster, Frankfurt am Main: Suhrkamp.

Tenbruck, F.H. 1988. 'Max Weber und Eduard Meyer,' in W.J. Mommsen and W. Schwentker (eds), *Max Weber und Seine Zeitgenossen*, Göttingen: Vandenhoeck & Ruprecht, 337–80.

Tendulkar, D.G. 1961. *Mahatma: Life of Mohandas Karamchand Gandhi*, New Delhi: Government of India, Ministry of Information and Broadcasting, Publications Division.

Thirion, P.G. 1993. 'Die Nederduitse Gereformeerde Kerk van Riebeek-Wes, 1858–1948: 'n Ondersoek na Standpunte wat Ingeneem is en Invloede wat Uitgeoefen is', D.Theol. Thesis. Stellenbosch: University of Stellenbosch.

Thom, H.B. 1988. *Dr. D.F. Malan en Koalisie*, Cape Town: Tafelberg Uitgewers.

Tilly, C. 2004. *Social Movements, 1768–2004*, Boulder, CO, and London: Paradigm Publishers.

Toth, M.A. 1981. *The Theory of the Two Charismas*, Washington D.C.: University Press of America.

Troelstra, P.J. 1898. *Van leed en strijd. Verspreide stukken (1892–1898)*, Amsterdam: Poutsma.

Troelstra, P.J. 1927. *Gedenkschriften I, Wording*, Amsterdam: Querido.

Troelstra, P.J. 1931. *Gedenkschriften IV, Storm*, Amsterdam: Querido.

Tuccari, F. 1993. *I dilemmi della democrazia moderna. Max Weber e Robert Michels*, Bari: Laterza.

Tucker, R.C. 1979. 'The Rise of Stalin's Personality Cult', *The American Historical Review* 84(2), 347–66.

Urban, G. (ed.) 1971. *The Miracles of Chairman Mao: A Compendium of Devotional Literature, 1966–1970*, Los Angeles, CA: Nash Publishing.

Valeton, J.J.P. 1909. 'De strijd tusschen Achab en Elia: voordracht gehouden in de paedagogische vereeniging van Christelijke Onderwijzers, te Utrecht 24 April 1900', in J.J.P. Valeton, *Oud-testamentische Voordrachten IV*, Nijmegen: Firma H. ten Hoet, 1–36.

Van Caenegem, R.C. 1978. *Over koningen en bureaucraten. Oorsprong en ontwikkeling van de hedendaagse staatsinstellingen*, Amsterdam and Brussels: Elsevier.

Van Caenegem, R.C. 1990. *Legal History: A European Perspective*, London: Hambledon.

Van christen tot anarchist. Gedenkschriften van F. Domela Nieuwenhuis. 1910. Amsterdam: Van Holkema & Warendorf.

Van der Watt, P.B. 1980. *Die Nederduitse Gereformeerde Kerk*, Pretoria: N.G. Kerkboekhandel.

Velde, H. te. 1996. 'Ervaring en zingeving in de politiek. Het politieke charisma in de tijd van Abraham Kuyper', *Theoretische Geschiedenis* 23(4), 519–38.

Velde, H. te. 2002. 'Drees und Fortuyn. Der Stil politischer Führerschaft in den Niederlanden seit 1945', *Jahrbuch Zentrum für Niederlande-Studien*, 11–25.

Velde, H. te. 2002. *Stijlen van leiderschap. Persoon en politiek van Thorbecke tot Den Uyl*, Amsterdam: Wereldbibliotheek.

Velde, H. te. 2005. 'Charismatic Leadership, c. 1870–1914: A Comparative European Perspective', in R. Toye and J. Gottlieb (eds), *Making Reputations: Power, Persuasion and the Individual in Modern British Politics*, London and New York: I.B. Tauris, 42–55.

Vivarelli, R. 1991. *Storia delle origini del fascismo. L'Italia dalla grande guerra all Marcia su Roma*, 2 vols, Bologna: Il Mulino.

Vliegen, W.H. 1921. *De dageraad der volksbevrijding*, vol. 1, Amsterdam: Ontwikkeling.

Vliegen, W.H. 1930. 'Troelstra, de leider', *Het Volk*, 13 May.

Wagner, R.G. 1982. *Reenacting the Heavenly Vision: The Role of Religion in the Taiping Rebellion*, Berkeley, CA: Institute of Asian Studies.

Wang, S.G. 1995. *The Failure of Charisma: The Cultural Revolution in Wuhan*, New York: Oxford University Press.

Weber, M. 1922. *Wirtschaft und Gesellschaft. Grundriss der verstehende Soziologie*, Tübingen: J.C.B. Mohr.

Weber, M. 1947. 'Charismatic Authority', in *The Theory of Social and Economic Organization*, ed. T. Parsons, trans. A.M. Henderson and T. Parsons, New York: Oxford University Press, 358–63.

Weber, M. 1947. *The Theory of Social and Economic Organization*, ed. T. Parsons, trans. A.M. Henderson and T. Parsons, New York: Oxford University Press.

Weber, M. 1956. *Wirtschaft und Gesellschaft, Grundriss der verstehende Soziologie*, 4th ed., 2 vols, Tübingen: J.C.B. Mohr (Paul Siebeck).

Weber, M. 1968. *Max Weber on Charisma and Institution Building*, ed. S.N. Eisenstadt, Chicago, IL: University of Chicago Press.

Weber, M. 1968. 'The Prophet', in S.N. Eisenstadt (ed.), *Max Weber on Charisma and Institution Building*, Chicago, IL: University of Chicago Press, 253–67.

Weber, M. 1968. 'The Sociology of Charismatic Authority', in S.N. Eisenstadt (ed.), *Max Weber on Charisma and Institution Building*, Chicago, IL: University of Chicago Press, 18–27.

Weber, M. 1970. 'Politics as a Vocation', in H.H. Gerth and C.W. Mills (eds), *From Weber: Essays in Sociology*, London: Routledge and Kegan Paul, 77–128.

Weber, M. 1975. *Max Weber: A Biography*, New York: Wiley-Interscience.

Weber, M. 1976. *Wirtschaft und Gesellschaft. Grundrisz der verstehenden Soziologie*, republished by J. Winckelmann, 5th ed., Tübingen: Mohr.

Weber, M. 1978. *Economy and Society: An Outline of Interpretive Sociology*, 4 vols, ed. G. Roth and C. Wittich, vol. 2, Berkeley: University of California Press.

Weber, M. 1982 (1968). *Gesammelte Aufsätze zur Wissenschaftslehre*, ed. J. Winckelmann, Tübingen: J.C.B. Mohr.

Weber, M. 1983. *Economía y sociedad: esbozo de sociología comprensiva*, Mexico: FCE.

Weber, M. 2006. *Die protestantische Ethik und der Geist des Kapitalismus*, republished and introduced by D. Käsler, Munich: Beck.

Wehler, H.-U. *Deutsche Gesellschaftsgeschichte (1849–1914)*, Munich: Beck.

Weller, R.P. 1994. *Resistance, Chaos and Control in China: Taiping Rebels, Taiwanese Ghosts, and Tiananmen*, Basingstoke: Macmillan.

Welskopp, T. 2000. *Das Banner der Brüderlichkeit. Die deutsche Sozialdemokratie vom Vormärz bis zum Sozialistengesetz*, Bonn: J.H.W. Dietz Nachf.

Welskopp, T. 2010. '*Anti-Saloon League* und *Ku Klux Klan*: die Stunde der "charismatischen Verbände"', in idem, *Amerikas große Ernüchterung. Die Vereinigten Staaten in der Zeit der Prohibition, 1919–1933*, Paderborn: Ferdinand Schöningh, 399–427.

Westlind, D. 1996. *The Politics of Popular Identity: Understanding Recent Populist Movements in Sweden and the United States*, Lund: Lund University Press.

Wheeler, B.R. 2001. 'Modernist Reenchantments I: From Liberalism to Aestheticized Politics', *German Quarterly* 74(3), 223–37.

Wheeler, B.R. 2002. 'Modernist Reenchantments II: From Aestheticized Politics to the Artwork', *German Quarterly* 75(2), 113–26.

Whelehan, N. 2005. 'Luigi Galleani and Peter Kropotkin in Comparative Perspective', *Anarchist Studies* 13(2), 147–68.

Whimster, S. 2007. *Understanding Weber*, London: Routledge.

Whimster, S. and S. Lash. 1987. *Rationality and Modernity*, London: Allen & Unwin.

Whitaker, S.P. 2002. *The Anarcho-individualist Origins of Italian Fascism*, New York: Peter Lang.

White, A. 1990. *Within Nietzsche's Labyrinth*, New York: Routledge.

Wielsma, P. 1988. 'Working Class Culture: Alcohol Abuse or Abstinence', in L. Heerma van Voss and F. van Holthoorn (eds), *Working Class and Popular Culture*, Amsterdam: Stichting Beheer IISG, 121–35.

Wildavsky, A. 1984. *The Nursing Father: Moses as a Political Leader*, Alabama: University of Alabama Press.

Willner, A.R. 1968. *Charismatic Political Leadership: A Theory*, Princeton, NJ: Woodrow Wilson School of Public and International Affairs Research Monographs, no. 32.

Willner, A.R. 1984. *The Spellbinders: Charismatic Political Leadership*, New Haven, CT: Yale University Press.

Willner, A.R. and D. Willner. 1965. 'The Rise and Role of Charismatic Leaders', *The Annals of the American Academy of Political and Social Society* 358(1), 77–88.

Wolff, S. de. 1951. *En toch...! Driekwart eeuw socialisme in vogelvlucht*, Amsterdam: G.J.A. Ruys.

Wuthnow, R. 1989. *Communities of Discourse: Ideology and Social Structure in the Reformation, the Enlightenment and European Socialism*, Cambridge, MA: Harvard University Press.

Wylie, R.F. 1980. *The Emergence of Maoism: Mao Tse-tung, Chen Po-ta, and the Search for Chinese Theory, 1935–1945*, Stanford, CA: Stanford University Press.

Xing, L. 2004. *Rhetoric of the Cultural Revolution: The Impact on Chinese Thought, Culture and Communication*, Columbia: University of South Carolina Press.

Zanden, J.L. van and A. van Riel. 2000. *Nederland 1780–1914. Staat, instituties en economische ontwikkeling*, Amsterdam: Balans.

Zhang, Z.B. and Y.F. Sun. 1991. *Zhongguo: Mao Zedong re* (China: Mao Zedong Fever), Xiangtan: Beiyue wenyi chuban she.

Notes on Contributors

Juan Avilés is a Professor at the UNED in Madrid. He has researched the history of the Spanish Left and political violence. His major books are on the influence of the Russian Revolution in Spain, the Spanish Left during the Second Republic, the international aspects of the Spanish Civil War, and the lives of the anarchist intellectual Francisco Ferrer and the Communist leader Dolores Ibárruri. Currently he is preparing a study on anarchist violence in late nineteenth-century Europe.

Arif Dirlik lives in Eugene, Oregon, USA, in semi-retirement. In 2010, he served as the Liang Qichao Memorial Distinguished Visiting Professor at Tsinghua University, Beijing. He most recently held the Rajni Kothari Chair in Democracy at the Centre for the Study of Developing Societies, Delhi. His most recent book-length publication is *Culture and History in Postrevolutionary China: The Perspective of Global Modernity* (Chinese University Press, 2012). Also in print are two edited volumes, *Sociology and Anthropology in Twentieth Century China* (Chinese University Press, 2012) and *Global Capitalism and the Future of Agrarian Society* (Paradigm, 2011).

Lindie Koorts studied History at the University of Johannesburg and at the University of Stellenbosch, South Africa, where she completed the first comprehensive and critical biography of Dr D.F. Malan, the founder of apartheid. It is also the first biography of an apartheid prime minister to have been written after the fall of apartheid in 1994. She is currently a postdoctoral fellow at the University of Pretoria.

Carl Levy, Reader in European Politics at Goldsmiths, University of London, is the author or editor of six books. He is completing a biography of Errico Malatesta.

Marc Reynebeau (b. 1956) holds an M.A. in History from Ghent University. He is a senior writer with the Belgian daily *De Standaard*. He has written several books on Belgian history and on the theory of history, including *Een geschiedenis van België* ('A history of Belgium', 2003, 2009; French edition: *Histoire belge*, 2005) and *Het nut van het verleden* ('The usefulness of the past', 2006).

Dilip Simeon studied at Delhi University in the late 1960s. In 1970 he joined the Naxalite (Maoist) movement, which he left in 1972. From 1974 till 1994 he taught History in Ramjas College, and his dissertation on labour history was published in 1995. From 1984 onwards he has campaigned for communal harmony and against political violence. Dilip has been a visiting scholar at campuses in Surat, Sussex, Chicago, Leiden and Princeton. From 1998 till 2003 he worked as Research Fellow with Oxfam (India). He is now Chairperson of the Aman Trust. His first novel, *Revolution Highway*, appeared in 2010.

Jan Willem Stutje is Research Fellow at The Institute of Biography of the University of Groningen. From 2001 to 2005 he was a fellow at the International Institute of Social History and at the Free University of Brussels (VUB). He is the author of several biographies, including *Ernest Mandel, Rebel tussen droom en daad*, 2007 (*Ernest Mandel, a Rebel's Dream Deferred*, 2009; *Rebell zwischen Traum und Tat, Ernest Mandel (1923–1995)*, 2009). He is completing a biography of Ferdinand Domela Nieuwenhuis.

Henk te Velde (b. 1959) is Professor of Dutch History at Leiden University. He studied History at the University of Groningen where he was Professor of the History of Political Culture until 2005. He has written books about Dutch political history, and is currently writing on the comparative history of political culture. His interest in charisma developed when he wrote a book on the history of Dutch political leadership (*Stijlen van leiderschap. Persoon en politiek van Thorbecke tot Den Uyl*, Amsterdam: Wereldbibliotheek, 2002). See also: 'Popular Leaders in Politics, c. 1870–1914: A Comparative European Perspective', in R. Toye and J. Gottlieb (eds), *Power, Personality and Persuasion: The Impact of the Individual on British Politics since 1867* (Manchester: Taurus, 2005), 42–55.

Thomas Welskopp D.Phil. (b. 1961) is Professor for the History of Modern Societies at Bielefeld University. From 2003 to 2004 he was Fellow at the Center for Advanced Study in the Behavioral Sciences, Stanford, California; and from 2008 to 2009, Fellow of the Historisches Kolleg in Munich. Major publications are: *Arbeit und Macht im Hüttenwerk. Die deutsche und amerikanische Eisen- und Stahlindustrie von den 1860er bis zu den 1930er Jahren* (Bonn: Dietz, 1994); *Das Banner der Brüderlichkeit. Die deutsche Sozialdemokratie vom Vormärz bis zum Sozialistenge-*

setz (Bonn: Dietz, 2000); *Die Bielefelder Sozialgeschichte. Klassische Texte zu einem geschichtswissenschaftlichen Programm und seinen Kontroversen* (Co-ed, Bielefeld: Transcript, 2010); and *Amerikas große Ernüchterung. Eine Kulturgeschichte der Prohibition* (Paderborn: Ferdinand Schöningh, 2010).

INDEX

0 1341 1412871 0

CPSIA information can be obtained at www.ICGtesting.com
Printed in the USA
LVOW07*1528021013

355126LV00017B/228/P

9 780857 453297